Paul's Covenant Community: Jew and Gentile in Romans

R. David Kaylor

John Knox Press
ATLANTA

Acknowledgment is made for permission to reprint from the following sources:

To Doubleday and Co. for excerpt from James H. Charlesworth, editor, *The Old Testament Pseudepigrapha*, volume 1, copyright 1983 by Doubleday and Co.

To Fortress Press for excerpt from W.D. Davis, *Paul and Rabbinic Judaism: Some Rabbinic Elements in Pauline Theology*, fourth edition, copyright 1980 by Fortress Press.

To Fortress Press for excerpt from J. Christiaan Beker, *Paul the Apostle: The Triumph of God in Life and Thought*, copyright 1980 by Fortress Press.

To Harper & Row for excerpt from Karl Barth, *Christ and Adam*, copyright 1957 by Harper & Row, Publishers, Inc.

To Harper & Row for excerpt from C.K. Barrett, *A Commentary on the Epistle to the Romans*, copyright 1957 by Harper & Row, Publishers, Inc.

To Oxford University Press for excerpt from John G. Gager, *The Origins of Anti-Semitism: Attitudes toward Judaism in Pagan and Christian Antiquity*, copyright 1983 by Oxford University Press.

To Scholars Press for excerpt from Jacob Neusner, *Formative Judaism*, copyright 1983 by Scholars Press.

Library of Congress Cataloging-in-Publication Data

Kaylor, R. D.
    Paul's covenant community.

    Includes index.
    1. Bible. N.T. Romans—Theology.   2. Covenants
(Theology)—Biblical teaching.   I. Title.
BS2665.2.K39   1988   227'.106   88-6873
ISBN 0-8042-0220-6

©copyright John Knox Press 1988
10 9 8 7 6 5 4 3 2 1
Printed in the United States of America
John Knox Press
Atlanta, Georgia 30365

Preface

This work attempts to elucidate the most continuous expression of Paul's theology: his letter to the Romans. My thesis is that the fundamental conviction underlying all of Paul's theological expression is that in Christ God is acting to bring all humankind, Gentile and Jew, into one community of the new covenant. Although Paul seldom appeals directly to the covenant, paying attention to this underlying conviction helps to understand more clearly what he says.

I claim that covenant functions at two levels in Paul's theology: at the levels of *idea* and of *conviction*. I do not claim that Paul always consciously had this conviction in mind, or that it is an intellectual concept central to his thought, or that he sorts out Hellenistic and Jewish backgrounds depending on their theoretical or logical consistency with covenantal ideas. The validity of my claim does not rest on the frequency with which "covenant" or distinctively covenant terminology appears in Paul's letters. My main claim is that the covenant as a *conviction* rather than an *idea* functions as a persistent presence and a dominant reality in Paul's life, work, and thought.

The emphasis upon covenant both as idea and as conviction affects the treatment of Paul's theology in several significant ways:

First, it shifts the emphasis away from questions of individual sin and salvation toward a greater concern for the community of faith as the context in which one believes and lives obediently.

Second, it focuses on Paul's reiteration of "no distinction" as a key to the interpretation not only of Romans 1–3 but of the whole letter.

Third, it regards the formation of a new covenant community in which Jew and Gentile stand together in grace as central to Paul's presentation of God's saving event.

The emphasis upon community does not deny the importance of individual response to the gospel; rather it recognizes that for Paul both the possibility for response and the context for response are given within community. We neither live to ourselves nor die to ourselves. All are called to live and die as members of the one inclusive community established in Christ.

Emphasis upon community can have the effect of removing some of the abstract and remote qualities that readers often find in Paul. Seen in the context of concern for community, Paul is seen to be dealing with real issues in a real world. He brings into a social context his evangelical preaching.

Such an approach to Paul need not reduce his theology to anthropology, but it can serve to overcome the tendency to dichotomize the spiritual and the social and enable the reader to see new applications of the gospel to current social and political tensions and hostilities, even though those issues are not directly addressed in this book.

This book is a theological interpretation of Romans, not a verse-by-verse commentary. It deals with the structure, argument, and theological content of the letter, section by section, and makes clear Paul's central conviction that in Jesus Christ God's covenanting words and actions have come to their conclusive expression for both Gentile and Jew, who are bound together in one new covenant community.

My indebtedness to others is greater than I can express, but some of those who have contributed to the process by which this book came to fruition must be thanked. James L. Price's graduate seminar on Romans at Duke University (1962–63) sparked a long-time interest in Paul's letter; his generous reading of this manuscript increased my debt even further. The students in my course on Paul's theology at Davidson College during more than twenty years have both sharpened my interest and stimulated my thinking. My colleague at Davidson, Karl Plank, has through discussion and critical reading of my work opened new windows into Paul and his critics. Elizabeth Malbon of Virginia Polytechnic Institute and State University has offered invaluable encouragement and advice. St. John's Abbey and University, Collegeville, Minnesota, offered a hospitable environment at its Institute for Ecumenical and Cultural Research, where a warm association of colleagues could gather for study and mutual enrichment and where this manuscript could be completed. Patrick Henry, director of the Institute, and his predecessor, Robert Bilheimer, offered encouragement and helped provide a supportive environment for a sabbatical year. Davidson College has provided sabbatical leave and financial support. My wife and children have patiently endured the disruptions and distractions to family life which this work has entailed. To all of these I am deeply grateful.

I acknowledge my dependence upon the many scholars from whom I have learned. The notes express only a margin of that indebtedness; they have been kept to a minimum in order not to intrude. In general, notes are used only to acknowledge specific indebtedness when that is recognized or to elaborate on reasons for a particular interpretation whose justification might not be obvious.

To
my wife and children
Dot, Marilyn, Cathryn, David,
Charlie, and Marion

Contents

1

Paul's Covenant Convictions

The Apostle Paul is a towering figure in the history of Christian faith. Paul had unparalleled influence on the church of his own and succeeding times because of his dynamic faith and extensive missionary travel, founding and nurturing communities of faith in important towns and cities of the Roman empire, and writing letters of pastoral admonition and warning. He had not known Jesus personally. Indeed, he initially had been violently opposed to those who claimed that God had made the crucified Jesus to be Lord and Messiah, but a profound experience led Paul to reverse his position and to proclaim with unmatched vigor the good news that "in Christ God was reconciling the world to himself" (2 Cor. 5:19).

A Person of Conviction

The direction of Paul's work was derived from that personal experience and his interpretation of it; the dynamism of his activity derived from personal qualities which were always characteristic of him. He was a person whose central convictions controlled the whole of his life. The second half of Paul's life was dominated by the revolutionary experience in which he said God "was pleased to reveal his Son to me" (Gal. 1:16). But Paul was already a person of deep conviction when he encountered

God's Son, as is evident in his own description of his former life: "...I advanced in Judaism beyond many of my own age among my people, so extremely zealous was I for the traditions of my [ancestors]" (Gal. 1:14). The way in which Paul was driven by his deep convictions—both before and after—might cause him to be labelled a fanatic; he spoke of it as being "zealous."

In fact, there was real continuity not only in personality but also in the nature of Paul's convictions before and after that encounter. Paul's fundamental conviction throughout his life derived from his Israelite heritage and centered on the concept of covenant: God's covenant, in fulfillment of the promise to Abraham, is established anew through Jesus Christ for both Gentile and Jew. That conviction provided continuity even in Paul's radical change from persecutor of the church to Apostle of Jesus Christ.

Convictions and Covenant

Paul's interpreters have often debated the question of the center of his theology. Many have offered candidates: justification by faith, understood as being acquitted by God solely on the grounds of believing in Jesus; a mystical experience of "being one with Christ," an ecstatic or at least emotional experience of being caught up out of oneself and united with God; the expectation of the establishment of God's righteousness in the social and political world; the eschatological notion that the world will soon experience the return of Christ and the judgment of God. Some doubt that there *is* a dominating center which can be discovered in all of Paul's letters. He may finally be an eclectic and unsystematic (or even inconsistent) thinker, who constantly changes the focus of his thought as he addresses concrete problems in particular localities, as he becomes "all things to all [people]" (1 Cor. 9:22).

The quest for the center of Paul's thought is frustrated by the fact that Paul's letters which have survived do not attempt to express a systematic and self-contained theology. Attempts to find such a theology may easily distort Paul's purpose in writing letters by imposing upon them an alien concern for system or by exaggerating one aspect of his rhetoric at the expense of others. It may well be that important presuppositions underlying Paul's thought never clearly emerge as he deals with pressing problems.

Yet I believe that central to Paul's thought is an underlying convictional center which he seldom articulates: an underlying conviction concerning the covenanting words and actions by which God chooses to be bound to the people of Israel and to all humankind. I do not claim that Paul always consciously had "covenant" in his mind, or that it is an intellectual concept which is central to his thought, or that he sorts out Hellenistic and Jewish concepts according to their theoretical or logical consistency with covenantal ideas. Nor does the validity of my claim rest on the frequency with which "covenant" or distinctively covenant terminology appears in Paul's letters. Covenantal *ideas* actually are present in much of what Paul says, more than is often recognized; but the main claim made here is that the covenant as conviction rather than as concept functions as a persistent presence and a dominant reality in Paul's life, work, and thought.

"Covenant" points to a fundamental conviction which underlies many of Paul's statements: "To the Jew first..." (Rom. 1:16; 2:9,10); "God has not rejected his people ..." (Rom. 11:2). The knowledge that "I belong to God's people," imbibed with his mother's milk, would have dominated Paul's world from the beginning. To change the metaphor, covenant was one of the primary but unconsciously worn lenses through which Paul perceived himself and his world; his experiences might have removed many of Paul's lenses, but the one which he never removed was that provided by the covenant.[1] Covenant remains for him an unquestioned assumption, through which everything else was experienced.

If Paul grew up in a Pharisaic home, he would have known of his participation in the covenant community even before he could articulate a belief about it. Given Paul's own emotional makeup, as the conviction became more articulated and reflective, everything he encountered would have been processed according to that central conviction.

Paul reflects the way that conviction was ingrained within him when he says he was "circumcised on the eighth day, of the people of Israel, of the tribe of Benjamin, a Hebrew born of Hebrews" (Phil. 3:5). The author of Acts has Paul say that he was "a Pharisee, a son of Pharisees" (Acts 23:6). Whether or not Acts gives us reliable information, Paul was later a Pharisee ("as to the Torah a Pharisee," Phil. 3:5); he expressed his central conviction that he belonged to God's people through zealously keeping the Torah.

By his own description, Paul was quite successful in directing his personal drives and energies by his central conviction: "... I advanced in Judaism beyond many of my own age among my people, so extremely zealous was I for the traditions of my [ancestors]" (Gal. 1:14).

His zealous devotion to the Torah and his fanaticism in defense of it led him to persecute the church. Paul saw a radical dichotomy between the Torah and the claims of the Jesus movement. By proclaiming as Messiah a deceiver of the people who had been crucified by the authorities, the followers of Jesus, Paul believed, posed a threat to the Torah—to the very foundation of Jewish identity and self-understanding, including Paul's own. Paul's fundamental belief that the Torah provided the way to be God's people meant that he must combat this movement with all his powers. So he pronounced doom upon all those who followed the one whom the Torah had cursed. Paul was confident that God and the Torah would be vindicated against those who maligned both and threatened to destroy the Torah; he felt compelled to be an instrument of God's vindication.

As a devoted and faithful member of God's covenant people, Israel, Paul's convictional world would have included the existence of God and God's election of Israel as covenant people; God's trustworthiness or truth, which enables one to believe the promises to Israel; God's role as Savior of that chosen people in the past and in the future; God's righteousness, by which the covenant is maintained and by which God's purpose for the future will be established; the Torah as the fundamental definition of God, God's relation to Israel, and God's promises for the future.

Although we have no direct knowledge of Paul's thinking during this period, we may justifiably assume that he would have regarded the Torah and the Messiah as the poles of the faith of Israel, with the Torah dominant until the coming of the Messiah, after which the Messiah himself would have preeminence. Even if Paul's earlier thinking had not included Messianic expectation, his apocalyptic thought could have allowed for the Torah to have a different place in Israel in the coming age. Although one cannot be certain of this point, some element of his thought made it possible for him later to regard the Torah as no longer binding upon those obedient to God through the gospel.

Paul's "Conversion"

Paul underwent a profound change, which transformed his perception of God's covenant, God's people, and Paul himself. He came to be driven by his new orientation as strongly as he had been driven by his old one; he became as fully convinced that he now must be an instrument of God in proclaiming the crucifixion and resurrection of Jesus as the deed of God for salvation.

In Paul's own self-understanding the key to his change is found in an encounter he had with Jesus Christ. So decisive is that encounter that he can speak of it as death and new life.

> I have been crucified with Christ; it is no longer I who live but Christ who lives in me; and the life I now live in the flesh I live by faith in the Son of God who loved me, and gave himself for me. (Gal. 2:20)

This experience is often referred to as "Paul's conversion," though some interpreters doubt that that is the appropriate way to describe what happened to him. He did not "convert" from one religion (Judaism) to another (Christianity)—such a way of putting it would have been utterly alien to Paul. Neither did he change from being "ungodly" to being "godly" or from being "immoral" to being "moral."[2] But there was nonetheless a radical change in Paul's self-perception which reflects a profound convictional change that might justifiably be called a conversion.

Even though we have very limited access to that personal encounter by which Paul was changed,[3] we do know that it reoriented his whole life. To understand what this change was for Paul, it will be useful to ask what remained the same for him, what changed, and how. Our only access to what Paul previously believed and thought is through the Paul who had changed and whose descriptions of his former life were written from his new perspective. Thus, not even Paul is able to give us an objective view of his former self. However, if we examine critically what he says, we may be able to outline the contours of that change.

It would be accurate, certainly, to speak of Paul's conversion as a reconfiguration of his system of convictions. Many of the elements remained, but instead of centering around the Torah as the fundamental reality, they now centered around Christ. But the second system of convictions is not *de novo*; it is rather a new gestalt, a new configuration of those beliefs which Paul had already held. Later chapters will explore the question of whether Paul completely rejects the Torah as embodying God's will even before the time of Christ. Even if those are correct who maintain that Paul came to see the Torah not as a positive temporary means of God's dealing with his people, but a negative means, still the covenant conviction which dominated his previous faith still dominates: God is the God who called Israel and who will save Israel through faithfulness to the covenant promise.

In my argument, then, God's covenant with Israel was the fundamental tenet of Paul's faith, both before and after his change. The reconfiguration of beliefs around God's act in Christ significantly modified his earlier beliefs in which God's covenant with Israel and their life as God's people were structured around the Torah. That structuring meant that the community of the covenant embraced those to whom the Torah spoke and whom the Torah bound to God: the Jews and occasional Gentiles who through circumcision took upon themselves the yoke of the Torah.

Paul's reconfigured convictions contained a covenant structured no longer around the Torah, but around Christ. That new understanding of the covenant contained a new understanding both of the community of faith and of the self. The community of faith was no longer confined to those to whom the Torah spoke; it contained as well those to whom Christ was addressed. Paul drew from his belief that Jesus was the Messiah the corollary belief, perhaps derived from Deutero-Isaiah, that in the new age the covenant is to be extended to Gentiles as well as to Jews. This broadening of the community alone would have prevented the Torah from being the key ingredient in his definition of the covenant community.

Previously, the self as well as the community was structured through the Torah. Unless Paul exaggerates later, in this perspective the self was understood in terms of the self's obedience to the righteousness demanded by the Torah. Paul seems to have taken with utter seriousness the prescription of the Torah that it is in the *keeping* of the Torah that one finds God's blessing (Rom. 3:13, 25; 10:5). The question of obedience or disobedience thus was the all-important question—by obedience one justified one's place within the covenant community or else forfeited that place. So intent was Paul in securing that place that his zeal was unmatched. That zeal led him, as he says, to persecute the church.

In Paul's reconfigured convictions, the self is no longer understood as being defined by the Torah and the obedience which one renders to it; rather, the self is determined by that grace expressed now in the Christ event. The Torah did not bring the Christ event into being. God's grace alone did that without the Torah, to show that salvation is by grace alone. That demonstration rendered Gentile and Jew alike before God, whereas the Torah had distinguished Gentile from Jew. The self of the Gentile and the self of the Jew are thus identical: both stand in need of God's grace, and both fully receive that grace in the gift of Christ. In Christ both are given life.

Paul's reconfigured convictions no longer allow his earlier notion that covenant separated Jews from others and placed a high standard of achievement before those who would justifiably be called God's people; now Gentiles as well as Jews receive the call to be God's people. No lasting distinction is to be made between Gentile and Jew in regard to such categories as sin, righteousness, salvation, and election. The identification of God's own is made by God's universal call and its corresponding gift.

If this reading of Paul is correct, then the change is fundamentally a change in perception of the person of Jesus, and can be accounted for only on the ground that Paul believed that he had been encountered by the living Christ. It is this conviction that reconfigures Paul's universe.

Paul's theology is the working out in words of these convictional changes. He did not immediately realize the full theological implications of his experience. Comparing the more negative statements about the Torah in Galatians with the less negative ones in Romans illustrates the development of his thought. Paul's convictional change, however, never led him to do what the gnostic heretic Marcion did in the second century: reject as demonic the Torah, the Mosaic covenant, and the God who was behind it. Though Paul came to see that his prior understanding of the Torah and his present understanding of Christ were incompatible, he did not believe that Christ nullified the Torah as God's revelation. The Torah (as well as the prophets, Rom. 3:21) points to Christ as the one to define its proper meaning. The Torah and the crucified Jesus are thus not in direct opposition as Paul previously thought; rather, rightly seen, they are compatible in the history of God's saving activity, though they remain now incompatible as the way to right relations with God.

Covenant Ideas

In its simplest terms, the covenant is "I will be your God, and you shall be my people." But there is no one single covenant in what Christians have come to call the "Old Covenant" (or "Old Testament"); rather, there are many instances of covenant-making, covenant-keeping, and covenant-breaking. Dominant covenant patterns are (1) the covenant with Abraham, a "promissory" type of covenant; (2) the Mosaic covenant, an obligatory type of covenant (including cultic and community codes); (3) the covenant with David, another promissory covenant which leads to messianism in late Judaism; (4) the "new covenant" spoken of by Jeremiah, who idealizes the future life of Israel in terms of an internalization of the covenant relationship.

Paul makes use of all of these covenant patterns. The covenant with Abraham is decisive in Paul's attempt to show that the Torah itself points to salvation by grace and faith rather than by Torah and works. One of Paul's key scriptural quotations is, "Abraham believed God, and it was reckoned to him as righteousness" (Rom. 4:3 and Gal. 3:6; cf. Gen. 15:6). Paul uses the fact that Abraham was uncircumcised when God made the covenant with him to show that Gentiles as well as Jews are to be included.

Paul does not directly set Abraham and Moses in opposition, but in his writings Abraham—a symbol of promise—conveys entirely positive overtones, while Moses—a symbol of the Torah —conveys some strongly negative ones. Abraham's promise is received in faith, giving hope, while Moses' Torah is received in pride or rebellion, giving death. The Torah not only increases trespass, it also builds a wall of separation between Jew and Gentile. Yet the Torah contains within it the promise: the new covenant in Christ is the goal (*telos*) of the Torah as the Torah understands itself through the figure of Abraham, so that all who have faith attain right relations with God.

Furthermore, ideas deriving from the Mosaic covenant are of decisive importance in understanding most of the key theological terms by which Paul expresses his convictions. "Justification," for example, presupposes the relationship established through the covenant: God's righteousness or his setting people right fundamentally means that he upholds that covenantal relationship. "Reconciliation" involves the restoration of the broken covenantal relationship. "Redemption" means bringing into covenantal freedom those who have lost their liberty by enslaving themselves to powers of sin, death, and Torah. "Expiation by his blood" interprets Jesus' death in terms of Israelite sacrificial practices prescribed in the Torah, and means the removal of those sins which threaten the covenantal bond with God. "Salvation" means the wholeness and completion which one obtains by participating in the covenant community, bound in harmony with the covenanting God. Ethical living is living within and with regard to the wholeness of the covenant community. Being "in Christ" is being in that community which shares his spirit and consequently lives out its faithfulness to his will. Thus, many of the key theological ideas of Paul presuppose the thought-world of the Mosaic covenant.

Paul's direct use of the Davidic covenant is very slight. According to that covenant, God promised David that one of his descendants would be on the throne of Israel forever (2 Sam. 7:12—16). That promise underlay Israelite hopes for an anointed king (messiah) when Israel was without a king and was subject to foreign domination. Paul attributes to Jesus the messianic role which originates from that covenant; at least once (Rom. 1:3–4, probably quoting an earlier formula) he makes direct reference to Jesus' Davidic sonship. Regardless of how one answers the debated question of Paul's use of current Jewish messianic thought in interpreting Jesus' death and resurrection, it is clear that the ideas of exaltation, lordship, and future appearances are essentially denationalized, universalized messianism. The Davidic covenant, therefore, though it plays little direct role in his proclamation of the gospel to the Gentiles, is a basic presupposition of Paul's thought.

Two corollaries of the Davidic covenant could have provided the basis for Paul's theology of mission to the Gentiles. First, Paul's belief that Jesus is the fulfillment of the covenant with David implies that now is the time for Gentiles as well as Jews to be fully included in the covenant community, for the Hebrew Scriptures and intertestamental literature assert that the messiah will rule the whole world, not merely Israel. Second, if Paul identified the Messiah Jesus with the Suffering Servant of 2 Isaiah (a point which is debated by scholars), he would have believed that Jesus is to be a light to the nations—Gentiles— and a covenant to the peoples—Gentiles (Isa. 42:6). The covenant background of the Davidic messiah and possibly the Suffering Servant influenced not only Paul's Christology but also his belief that he, as Apostle to the Gentiles, stood in the forefront of God's work of redeeming the whole world.

Paul makes more obvious use of the idea of the "new covenant" from Jeremiah 31, a radically inward covenant, not written on tablets of stone but upon the heart. Such inwardness is reflected in Paul's claim to be a minister of a new covenant which is "not in a written code but in the Spirit; for the written code kills, but the Spirit gives life" (2 Cor. 3:6). Jeremiah anticipated a new covenant based not upon the people's performance but upon God's forgiveness. Paul almost never uses the term forgiveness, perhaps because it can suggest a pardon without transformation; he speaks rather of redemption, setting free from the power of sin. Despite the change in terminology, Paul derives from Jeremiah the notion that the new covenant deals effectively with the human problem that led to the breaking of the old covenant.

Israelite covenant traditions thus play a major role in Paul's thinking. He affirms those elements of covenant traditions which help him universalize the gospel; he ignores or else transforms those covenantal traditions which are most closely tied to Jewish exclusivism. In both ways he emphasizes his conviction that in Jesus Christ there is neither Jew nor Gentile, but one new humanity.

Convictions and Thought-World

To what extent was Paul's "death" the end of one intellectual world and the beginning of another? The language with which he speaks about his central convictions certainly changed. He now speaks about everything in his life in terms of his commitment to Christ: "For me to live is Christ" (Phil. 1:21). All worldly realities and all religious convictions as well as all his plans and his speech are viewed and expressed with reference to Christ. We cannot determine the extent to which Paul had earlier expected the Jewish messiah or the messianic age, but now Jesus' identity as messiah and his return in the near future dominate Paul's thought and speech. Even if Paul had previously expected a messiah, he had not expected a crucified messiah. When he speaks of the crucified Jesus as being "foolishness" and a "scandal" to Greeks and Jews, he understood very well how they felt, for he had shared both those attitudes.

But while his convictional world underwent considerable wrenching change, his intellectual and cultural world did not change fundamentally. He remained a Jew who had grown up in a world where cultures mingled and mutually enriched one another. The book of Acts contains a believable tradition that Paul was the son of devout Pharisaic parents who lived in Cilicia in Tarsus. Thus Paul was a citizen of two worlds, the Jewish and the Hellenistic; the latter is an amalgam of cultural traditions from the Greek west and the diverse east.

Scholars have long debated what chief ingredients made up Paul's intellectual background, whether he was predominantly Palestinian Jewish or predominantly Hellenistic in his orientation. This perplexing riddle has resisted a neat solution by New Testament scholarship. Paul is sometimes portrayed as being thoroughly imbued with the kind of Jewish thinking which emerges as "rabbinic," drawing upon the Torah and its interpretations in the Pharisaic schools.[4] He is sometimes portrayed as a "renegade Jew," a Jew of the Hellenistic world who has lost sight of the joyous and warmer celebration of the Torah as the gift of God which, it is asserted, was characteristic of Palestinian Judaism. Schoeps, for example, thinks that Paul belongs to Diaspora Judaism and that he shared its emphasis upon a mission to the Gentiles as well as its understanding of Judaism in terms of moral law "disconnected and isolated from the controlling reality of the covenant."[5] Martin Hengel argues that the central idea of the atoning death of Jesus has close affinities with Hellenistic thought, and need not be accounted for on the basis of Hebrew Scriptures and Judaism.[6]

The difficulty of identifying Paul solely with Palestinian Judaism, Hellenistic Judaism, or Hellenism itself underscores what is generally affirmed in current theory, if not always in scholarly practice: Hellenism and Judaism were not separated compartments in Paul's day. For four hundred years the two had been interpenetrating each other; both were among those intermingling cultural movements of Paul's time. One cannot draw sharp lines between Judaism and Hellenism, nor between

Palestinian Jews and those Jews dispersed to various towns and cities from Babylonia to Rome. Hellenism had penetrated and deeply influenced not only Diaspora Judaism but also Palestinian Judaism, while Judaism in turn had significant impact upon the Hellenistic world.

If Paul's background was an amalgam of this complex religious and intellectual world, it is not surprising that his letters echo Hellenistic philosophy, Greco-Roman mystery religions, Jewish piety, and Rabbinic exegesis. Paul was himself not primarily a systematic thinker. He would not have asked whether an idea was Judaic or Hellenistic. He was an eclectic thinker and writer who used linguistic expressions as they were readily available. His only concern was whether an expression or an idea could be utilized in the proclamation of the gospel. Paul's enormous drive to preach Christ, to found churches and to nurture them did not afford him the leisure to forge into consistent intellectual clarity the welter of ideas, rhetorical devices, and linguistic expressions which were common currency in the worlds among which he lived. He was less interested in consistency than in being "all things to all [people], that I might by all means save some. I do it all for the sake of the gospel ..." (1 Cor. 9:22–23).

No attempt will be made in what follows to treat comprehensively the full range of issues involved in the question of Paul's cultural and intellectual background. An assertion will be made that Paul's fundamental conviction that God renews the covenant through Jesus Christ does not obliterate his complex intellectual heritage, but provides a unity to all he says.

Paul as Letter Writer

Paul is known primarily because of letters which he wrote during his missionary travels. Thirteen letters in the New Testament have been ascribed to him. Most scholars today do not believe he wrote them all, but everyone agrees that many of them are authentic. Paul's letters were genuine letters, not formal treatises in the form of letters. They express the Apostle's personal concerns, reveal his thinking, and contain many insights into the nature of the man and his work. But they are not merely private correspondence. With the possible exception of Philemon, they were written to congregations, not to private individuals.

We have no way of knowing how many letters Paul wrote, but the ones which have survived are a substitute for the Apostle's own presence, and they speak from the conviction that he has a God-given authority within the church and a God-given mission to perform through his letter writing as well as through other aspects of his ministry.

Letter writing was quite common in Paul's day. Paul's letters follow the standard form of the day, although he makes adaptations to suit his purpose. For example, he enlarges the traditional greeting, using it to express his own distinctive theology and open the way to major concerns which have prompted him to write. In Romans, the greeting includes his claim to be an apostle and a statement of his commission to bring about faithful obedience among all Gentiles. This opens the way for him to speak later about his intent to visit Rome as part of his apostolic work.

Writing was a task of specialists in Paul's day. Even people who could read and write often had the task done for them. Paul usually dictated his letters to a scribe, though sometimes he added his own greeting and signature at the end: "I, Paul, write this greeting with my own hand" (1 Cor. 16:21); "See with what large letters I am writing to you with my own hand" (Gal. 6:11). Sometimes the scribe added his own greeting, indicating that Paul utilized the services of gifted people in the church: "I, Tertius, the writer of this letter, greet you in the Lord" (Rom. 16:22). The practice of dictating the letters helps account for their conversational tone, their informal expression, their incomplete sentences (Rom. 5:12), their corrections in mid-stream (1 Cor. 1:16).

Paul often includes his associates in his writing. In 1 Corinthians the greeting is from "Paul . . . and our brother Sosthenes." 2 Corinthians is from "Paul . . . and Timothy our brother." Galatians is from "Paul . . . and all the [brothers and sisters] who are with me." Sometimes the plural carries over into the thanksgiving, but in all of these letters Paul goes on to speak in the first person singular; the mention of others might simply be a way of sending greetings from those persons, claiming the weight of their authority as well, or identifying the scribes to whom Paul dictates the letters.

Paul's informal, conversational style often includes what seem to be traditional materials, such as confessions of faith (Rom. 1:3–4), hymns to Christ (Phil. 2:5–11), poems (1 Cor. 13), and theological formulae (Rom. 3:23–25). These materials show that Paul is not isolated from the church as a whole, but that his gospel has strong connections with church tradition. It is true that Paul cites very little of the tradition about Jesus' life and ministry such as we find in the Gospels—although there are reminiscences of Jesus' teachings in passages like Romans 12 and 1 Corinthians 7, the traditions of Jesus' words and actions are largely absent from his letters—but traditional materials deriving from the life of the church in baptism, the Lord's Supper, etc., are well represented.

Scholars have appropriately designated Paul's letters as "occasional" to indicate that he directs them to specific situations in the life of churches addressed. Paul did not write just to pass the time of day or to tell congregations he founded how things went with him. He wrote because he felt a situation needed his presence and a letter was the best substitute he had for that presence. The letters show Paul in action as an Apostle. They assume that the readers know of the situation he is addressing, so that he does not usually describe it. That created no problem for the original readers, though it sometimes leaves us with listening to only one side of a two-sided conversation.

The occasional nature of the letters means that Paul does not write theological treatises in which to express his views of various theological topics. As he writes to deal with particular situations we see his theology in action, applied to the problem at hand. Thus we do not have a writing called "The Theology of Paul" or "Credo." If we wish to formulate a "theology of Paul" we have to piece it together from scattered theological statements

and unstated presuppositions which lie beneath the surface of
the language by which he addresses the churches. That fact
makes any statement about "Paul's theology" to some extent
speculative. The organization of topics in such a theology is our
own, not Paul's; the categories are likely to derive from our
concerns rather than from his. No doubt Paul had a theology,
whether or not he ever thought it through in a systematic way,
but as far as we know he never wrote a theology.

Some would argue that Romans comes close to being an exception to the general statements made previously. There is much
to support that position, yet Romans, too, is an occasional letter,
even if it is difficult to determine precisely what occasioned it.
My thesis in this present work is that a major concern which is
expressed in Romans is the unity of Gentile and Jew in the new
covenant community established through Jesus Christ.

Purpose of Romans

Why did Paul write his letter to the Romans? A part of that
answer is easy, for it lies on the surface of the text: Paul wrote
them because he was hoping to visit them and to gain their
support for his mission to Spain. That reason is adequate for
understanding part of the letter (especially the first and fif-
teenth chapters), but it is not a sufficient explanation as to why
he wrote as he did in the rest of the letter. How does the content
of the letter serve to elicit their support? Why write so extensive
a letter, treating these particular themes? This question, too,
one can answer by saying that Paul wanted the Romans to know
his understanding of the gospel, perhaps to clear up erroneous
notions they had of him through rumors of his work. Or perhaps
he thought they really did not know much about him and wanted
to inform them.

This simple explanation is probably not completely erroneous, but it does not fully explain the content of this peculiar
letter. The continuing scholarly debate concerning the purpose
of Romans clearly indicates that the solution is not really at-
tainable. It would not be profitable to enter into a discussion of
the various proposals here, but it is incumbent upon me to let

the reader know the understanding which informs my particular attempt to understand what Paul says.

Many interpreters in the past have thought that since Romans is a theological treatise independent of the particular circumstances in which it was written, any attempt to discuss "occasion" or "purpose" is futile and unnecessary. Recent scholarship, however, tends to see the letter as a real letter, written for a particular purpose.[7] There are two basic positions concerning that purpose. One finds the occasion within the context of the Apostle's own circumstances: he is going to Jerusalem, and his anticipation of that journey and its potential consequences so fills his mind that even as he writes a letter to send in the opposite direction his thoughts are upon Jerusalem; in turn, that causes Paul to reflect again on his career up to this point, and upon the whole question of the relationship between the Hebraic tradition and his faith in Jesus as Messiah—more specifically, upon the relation between the covenant with Israel in the past and the new inclusive covenant community which he has been promoting. A second alternative focuses upon the church to which Paul writes as offering the best possibility of understanding why he writes as he does. This approach assumes that Paul knew the circumstances of the church in Rome and sought to aid in the resolution of problems there. Thus, his focus upon the relationship between Gentile and Jew derives from the fact that there was serious conflict between the two in Rome.

The two alternatives are not, of course, strictly in conflict. If the issue at Rome is the same issue which has plagued the church throughout Paul's ministry, and if it is the issue which underlies the danger he faces in Jerusalem, then all those factors converge upon Paul and provide the occasion for his writing this letter. In this event, Paul attempts to deal seriously and creatively—that is, theologically—with the conflict among the Roman believers. He does so with a mind which is filled with anticipation of what lies ahead. His conversation is not only with the Romans; it is also with those whom he will face in Jerusalem, both those Jews who have accepted the new covenant

and those who have not. Even writing to a largely Gentile
church, he addresses himself to Jews—not merely those Jewish
believers in Rome, but Jews in general and the whole Judaic
tradition of which he still regards himself a vital part. He offers
a defense of his gospel, often inserting the objections which he
has heard from those who disagree with him. The defense of the
gospel is also a defense of himself as the bearer of that gospel to
the Gentiles. Paul might even hope that if he convincingly
presents his defense to the church at Rome he can be successful
in Jerusalem, too; or that somehow the church at Rome will
come to his defense in Jerusalem. He wants to make his case as
strongly as he can that with God there is no partiality, that God
is equally the God of Gentile and Jew; but he also wants to
emphasize just as strongly that the inclusion of Gentiles is not
antagonistic to the historical and continuing place of Israel
within the plan of God for the salvation of the world.

Covenant Traditions in Romans

As Paul writes the letter, then, he is pondering the most
perplexing and divisive issue facing the expanding community.
From the early days of the Jesus movement questions about the
relation between Gentile and Jew began to be urgently raised:
Is the gospel for both? If so, on what terms? Do Gentiles need to
follow the prescriptions of the Torah in order to be part of the
covenant community? Are Jewish believers in Jesus bound to
the Torah any longer? Do Jewish believers have any special
place of importance and advantage in the church, or are Gentile
and Jew on the same level? Dispute about these questions was
not merely theoretical; feelings ran so deep that the church was
threatened with schism. Paul worked diligently to avoid that
split, which he saw as a denial of the gospel of one covenant
community, and to bring about reconciliation of the factions in
the church.

His letter to the Romans is a part of that effort. He wrote it
when he was anticipating a visit to Jerusalem for the very
purpose of presenting a symbolic offering he had collected from
Gentile churches to the Jerusalem church. He hoped all would

perceive it as a symbol of the unity of all believers. He wrote the letter to a church he did not found, but one he hoped to visit after his trip to Jerusalem.

Interpreters of Paul's letter, especially those in the Protestant tradition, have tended to see it as a theological treatise whose main theme is the justification of the sinner through faith. To be sure the concepts of sin, righteousness, faith, and grace are present in the letter, but underlying the whole, and dominant in Paul's thinking at the time of its writing, is the concern to affirm the unity of Gentile and Jew in the one new covenant people.

2

Paul Introduces Himself and His Gospel

(Romans 1:1—17)

A Called People

Paul addresses his letter to "all God's beloved in Rome, who are called to be saints" (Rom. 1:7). The terms of this address reveal the extent to which his thinking is dominated by his central conviction: in Jesus Christ God has acted to form a new covenant community incorporating both Jew and Gentile. "Beloved," "saints," "called," and "all" imply the notion of one covenant community, elected by God. Although Paul infrequently applies "beloved" to a group, he uses the term both here and at Romans 11:28. In the latter passage he calls attention to the fact that even when unbelieving, the people of Israel continue to be the objects of God's electing love: "As regards election they are beloved for the sake of their ancestors." Connotations of election and covenant are evident in such an expression.[1]

Those who are "beloved" are also those "who are called to be God's dedicated people" (1:7).[2] The word translated "dedicated people" is commonly rendered "saints." It derives from the Hebrew notion of "holy" or "sacred to God." It was not applied to individuals of outstanding piety so much as to the community of those "called" to belong to God. Paul's use of "all" intends to be inclusive: both Jews and Gentiles. They are the special objects of God's love as one community of faith, not as Jews or Gentiles, but as together comprising the "saints" or "God's dedicated people." To them both, through the gospel preached by his apostles, God has said, "You shall be a people to me, and I will be God for you."

Such election presupposes and is based upon God's grace; thus Paul appropriately addresses his standard greeting–blessing to them: "Grace and peace to you from our Father God and from our Lord Jesus Christ." Because his addressees stand within the covenant community, they may expect to continue to receive that grace which has called them; as a consequence they can experience within their fellowship that peace which comes from eliminating the barriers of hostility between Gentile and Jew.

Paul usually addresses his epistles "to the church (or churches) ..." (1 Cor. 1:2; 2 Cor. 1:1; Gal. 1:2). The absence of this usual expression has no plausible explanation[3] unless it is due to Paul's deliberately choosing terms drawn from covenant vocabulary: from the beginning he emphasizes that Jew and Gentile are one new covenant community in Jesus Christ. In that context "all" emphasizes the unity and commonality of the entire community; "beloved" carries the connotation of the chosen and covenanted people of God. He chooses these covenant terms rather than the less theological word "church." He is nonetheless addressing the church.

The language of election and covenant draws lines of continuity with God's people Israel; the covenant community is made up of Abraham's children, both the circumcised and the uncircumcised, who have faith. God's grace in calling is not conferred because of merit or of ancestral connection or ritual status; it is not the godly who are called, but precisely the ungodly whom God has justified and made his own people. It follows then that the distinctive sign of membership in the church is not historical connection with God's ancient people, nor physical proximity to a local congregation. The sign is faith. Another way of saying the same thing is that the sign is the Spirit—having the Spirit or being in the Spirit. If one has the Spirit, one belongs to Christ and is part of his body. "Having the Spirit" in this sense means uttering the confession the Spirit inspires, and manifesting the life which the Spirit produces.

It is not merely the individual, but the individual within the covenant community, who makes confession of faith and participates in God's people. In emphasizing community Paul was addressing a felt need of his own time, both in the Jewish and the Hellenistic worlds.[4] The breakdown of community within Israel is seen in its fragmentation into sects, each of which claimed to be true Israel. Dissatisfaction with the establishment in Jerusalem led to the formation of such groups as the Pharisees and Essenes, with communities not only in Judaea, but widespread in the Mediterranean world.

In the Hellenistic world the breakdown of the organic life of the city-state and disenchantment with traditional religious practices led to the formation of mystery religions promising not only purification from sins and immortality but a sense of community as well. Voluntary associations of all sorts competed with more specifically religious organizations to offer a sense of human community and well-being.

No doubt one of the reasons for the success of the church in the Roman world was its strong sense of community. To a certain extent this community was a protest movement against the moral chaos of the day, as well as against some of the values enshrined in various fellowships available to people. But at the same time, the form of the faith was deeply influenced by the felt need for community, as well as by some of the values of those communities. For example, even the mystery religions possessed a certain democratic tendency, being open to women and slaves as well as to male freemen. Paul's communities learned that democratic ideal from their Hellenistic neighbors more than from Judaic traditions.

Paul's communities evidently did not take their democratic sharing to the extent that Luke attributes to the Jerusalem community described in Acts. There is no evidence for a communalism of possessions in any of Paul's churches, even though they are admonished to assist one another as well as other communities during hard times.

The emphasis upon community shows that the gospel was not understood in purely individualistic terms. To become a believer was to join with other believers; "to embrace the gospel ... is to enter into community."[5] The freedom preached by Paul was a freedom to participate in community, rather than an individual freedom. That participation was regarded as an integral part of salvation, and not merely as its corollary. That is in part because for Paul sin is not individual wrong-doing, it is alienation from God and from human community (see below, chap. 2). Paul proclaims that in Christ all can know the unity of a new humanity as they come to celebrate the oneness given to all—whether Gentile or Jew, male or female, slave or free. The way out of human alienation was in Paul's view the reconciliation of all as one new human community, not the triumph of one group over another. Paul considered himself a minister of a new covenant (2 Cor. 3:6); his task was to be an ambassador through whom God's offer of reconciliation was extended to all. Not only Paul but the whole church was entrusted with this ministry of reconciliation (2 Cor. 5:16–21). For that reconciliation he labored and for it he enlisted the support of the church at Rome.

The church is an extraordinary human community since it derives from God's powerful initiative and its future rests in God's purposes. God's call and the human response of faith comprise its life. The church is God's gift to humanity; one participates in it as an act of faith—not as if it were created by those who belong to it nor sustained by their presence alone. It fulfills its purpose by participating in God's will to reconcile all things to himself. The church represents the new creation and bears witness to the whole world that God will bring to completion the recreating activity that has called the church into being. The specific congregations point beyond themselves[6] to the oneness and wholeness of the church as the one people of

God regardless of background, privilege, rank, or gender. Human distinctions count for nothing in the community of the new creation. All were baptized into Christ, in whom there is neither male nor female, neither slave nor free, neither Gentile nor Jew (Gal. 3:27–28).

The church in Paul's understanding is confessional, eschatological, and charismatic. "Confessional" means that whoever through the Spirit makes the confession "Jesus is Lord" is within the "body of Christ" (1 Cor. 12:3–12). "Eschatological" means that it is a community of end time, the people of God for a new age. The church's proclamation was set in that context. It served God by being the "beachhead of a new creation and the sign of the new age in the old world."[7] By being what it was, the church also served the world. "Charismatic" means that the church moves as it is impelled by the Spirit, who endows it with gifts for the fulfillment of its mission. The gifts belong to the church for the sake of its ministry, not for the enjoyment or private edification of the individual believers (1 Cor. 12).

The early church shunned any technical conceptions of office so commonly seen in other religious associations of the time.[8] It was expected that priesthood was universal since the Spirit was universal, granting gifts to all to be used for the common good. The Pauline churches thus were composed of nothing but laity; he mentions neither priests nor the presbytery. All within their possibilities were priests and officeholders because they were instruments of the Spirit.[9] To say that all are officeholders is the same as saying that none of them were. 1 Thessalonians 5:12 does not contradict this assertion: "We beseech you, brothers and sisters, to respect those who labor among you and are over you in the Lord and admonish you, and to esteem them very highly in love because of their work." There are differentiations among the gifts of the Spirit so that the church can function effectively; those who possess particular gifts are to be respected for the work they do, but they do not belong to a class or category separate from others.[10]

The Called Apostle

Paul himself, though not physically with God's covenanted

people in Rome, is united with them through his own call which is akin to theirs. He is "called to be an apostle," one "set apart," designated as God's own emissary (Rom. 1:1). His identity is provided by God's call and commission. In an earlier letter to Corinthian believers Paul spoke of the organic unity of the church by the analogy of the "one body" in Christ, for the sake of whose unity and peace God had given functional gifts: "God has appointed in the church first apostles, second prophets, third teachers ..." (1 Cor. 12:28). Paul's own specialized ministry has been given to the church "to bring about the obedience of faith ... among all the nations [Gentiles]" (Rom. 1:5). But the apostle to the Gentiles (Gal. 1:16; 2:8–10) understands his ministry to include a continuing concern for members of the old covenant community. Although Paul does not speak here about attempting to bring the gospel to Jews, the tone of the whole letter reflects a high degree of concern for them and for their participation in the new inclusive community.[11] His ministry to the Gentiles was only one part of his policy of becoming "all things to all [people], that I might by all [possible] means save some," so that, "to the Jews I became as a Jew ... to those under the [Torah] I became as one under the [Torah] ... to those outside the [Torah] I became as one outside the [Torah] ..." (1 Cor. 9:20–21).

In the exercise of his specialized ministry Paul had "often intended to come to you" in Rome (Rom. 1:13). He does not specifically say in the introduction why he wishes to visit Rome. He speaks of his obligation to preach to all, "both Greeks and barbarians," of his wish to "gain some benefit" from among them as from among the rest of the Gentiles. Paul does not specify what that anticipated benefit might be. He does indicate his understanding of the communal nature of the church by acknowledging that he as well as they may be strengthened through each other's faith. What he has in mind is more explicitly stated at the end of the letter: he hopes to enjoy their company for a time, then to have their assistance as he goes on to Spain, looking for new territory in which the gospel might be proclaimed for the first time (Rom. 15:14–29).

An "apostle is one sent on a mission by another with authority from the one who appoints and sends. In his case, Paul believes God has sent him, authoritatively commissioned to perform the task of evangelizing the Gentiles.

The Gospel and the Messiah

As usual in his letters, Paul makes clear that his gospel centers on Jesus Christ as Lord: "the gospel concerning his Son ..." (Rom. 1:3). The manner in which Paul introduces Jesus as the center, however, is unusual and no doubt reflects Paul's purpose in writing. The statement about Jesus in Romans 1:3–4 draws lines of continuity with Israel's past, as does the statement that the gospel was "promised beforehand ... in the holy scriptures"(1:2). In all probability Paul is quoting a widely used creedal formula when he characterizes Jesus as

> ...descended from David according to the flesh and Son of God in power according to the Spirit of holiness by his resurrection from the dead... (Rom. 1:3–4)

In no other letter does Paul make as much use of the idea of Davidic messiahship, which essentially means that a descendant of King David will rule Israel and restore the glory of the Davidic kingdom. Paul characteristically calls Jesus "Christ," which is technically equivalent to "Messiah" (Hebrew *mashiach* and Greek *christos* both mean "anointed one"); but the term Christ has lost its political and national understandings for Paul.[12]

Select ideas associated with Davidic messiahship are found not only at the beginning of Romans but also at the end of the theological discussion:

> ...Christ became a servant to the circumcised to show God's truthfulness, in order to confirm the promises given to the patriarchs, and in order that the Gentiles might glorify God for his mercy....
> ...Isaiah says,
> "The root of Jesse shall come,
> he who rises to rule the Gentiles;
> in him shall the Gentiles hope." (Rom. 15:7–12)

This passage, along with chapters 9—11, shows Paul's intense interest in maintaining the continuity between the church and its Judaic heritage. The gospel confirms God's promises to Israel and extends those promises to the Gentiles; it does not mean the rejection of Israel as God's people. That interest can explain Paul's deliberate use at the opening of the letter of a christological statement which is Judaic in expression. Whether there is a tension between this expression and Paul's more usual modes of speaking about Jesus can be decided only through exploring more thoroughly his christological teaching.

The formula in Romans 1:3–4 presents Jesus as he is understood on two levels: on the level of the "flesh" and on the level of the "spirit." (The statement of two levels does not reflect the "two natures" Christology of later times, according to which Jesus was fully human and fully divine at the same time. The concerns addressed in "natures" language originated in a different time and circumstance.) The two levels of this formula are to a real extent sequential: on the level of the flesh, Jesus was by birth and through his life Son of David—in other words, he was the Jewish Messiah. Whether he was recognized as such is irrelevant to his real identity: he is the "root of Jesse" (Rom.15:12). The second level, that of spirit, implies the death of Jesus, though (surprisingly for a Pauline summary of Jesus' importance) it is not mentioned: he has been "decreed[13] Son of God in power" through the resurrection from the dead. Jesus was not enthroned as Messiah before his death, but now he has been—not merely through human doing, but by divine initiative exercised through the Spirit. Although Käsemann argues that no New Testament author thought of Jesus in other than metaphysical terms, the language of this passage is adoptionistic.[14]

But does this formula really express Paul's view of who Jesus is? It does not presuppose that the Son of God existed prior to the time he "came into the world," a presupposition which seems to underlie Paul's words in other places. The "pre-existence" of Christ, as this idea is called, is usually thought to be reflected in such passages as these:

> ...though he was rich, yet for your sake he became poor....
> (2 Cor. 8:9)
> ...sending his own Son in the likeness of sinful flesh.... (Rom.8:3)

...the second man [in contrast to the earthly Adam] is from heaven.... (1 Cor. 15:47)

... God sent forth his Son, born of woman.... (Gal. 4:4)

Some interpreters think that none of these passages necessarily implies pre-existence. In Galatians 4:4–7, for instance, the language of "sending" may be in keeping with Hebraic notions of commissioning and thus apply to Jesus' earthly task rather than to the sending of the Son from the heavenly world into the earthly. The sequence suggested by the translation "sent forth his Son, born of woman, born under the Torah," is not implied by the Greek construction; the Greek has one finite verb, God "sent," followed by two participles which characterize particular aspects of that sending but without implying that they happened *after* the sending.[15] The intent of the participles is to emphasize that Jesus' life was lived under the same conditions as every other human being. Paul is especially interested in characterizing Jesus' life as being "under the Torah."[16]

If Philippians 2:5–11 is, as most interpreters think, a hymn Paul quotes rather than composes, it does not necessarily reflect his own position any more than does Romans 1:3–4. It is usually understood to reflect a "three-stage" Christology:[17] (1) Christ existed with God before the incarnation; (2) then he existed as a human (presumably with an unspecified degree of "emptying" of divine attributes); (3) then he exists in heavenly form again in a state of exaltation. However, it can be argued that the hymn contrasts Christ and Adam, and that the "form" of God is the image of God which Christ, unlike Adam, did not efface or erase by disobedience.

In spite of the fact that some of the "incarnational" passages can be understood not to imply coming from another world, the preponderance of the evidence seems to be on the side of attributing to Paul an incarnational Christology.[18] However, Paul talks less about who Jesus Christ is than about what he does; more accurately, for Paul Jesus' action (or God's action through him) reveals his real identity. To put the matter more technically, Paul's Christology is more *functional* than *essential*.

As we need continually to remind ourselves throughout our

reading of Paul, he is not primarily a speculative theologian who attempts to answer abstract theological questions; he is primarily a preacher, proclaiming the gospel of what God has done and was doing in Jesus Christ for the salvation of humanity. His own experience of convictional change and his work among the Gentiles were fundamental in all his theological language. He used whatever categories were at hand, both from his Judaic heritage and from the Hellenistic milieu in which he worked, in his efforts to communicate God's grace in establishing a new covenant community of Gentile and Jew. Since the doctrine of Christ was not a recognized problem in the churches to which Paul addressed letters,[19] he could without any self-consciousness adapt creedal formulae deriving from adoptionistic modes or from incarnational modes already utilized within the church. He did not subject those modes to rigorous examination to see if they were consistent.

Paul's view of Jesus might be summed up as follows: Jesus was uniquely God's son, who enabled others to become children of God by adoption. As God's unique son, Jesus is not a fortuitous event in history of which God has taken advantage; rather, God "sent him" to express through him God's electing grace for all humankind. Jesus does not belong merely to the past, but lives as sovereign over those who confess their faith in him, and will continue to exercise his sovereignty until he delivers the kingdom to God who will be everything to everyone (1 Cor. 15:24–28). The death and resurrection of Jesus are the central elements for Paul. He displays little interest in the events of Jesus' life, teachings, or even his convictions. If Paul had available to him the traditions about Jesus later used by the Gospel writers, he made very little use of them in his letters. So powerful for him is the death/resurrection the rest hardly matters! Yet it is important to him that Jesus lived as a human being, subject to the Torah and to the full range of pressures for good and evil, and that he remained obedient even to the extent of death. That human obedience is not primarily used by Paul as an example (he seldom used Jesus as an example to be emulated), but as a sign that God was active in him for the renewal of human life.

The Theme of the Letter

The theme of the whole letter is stated in Romans 1:16–17. These verses are a genuine part of the introduction, climaxing what has been said as well as leading into what follows as the first major point to be developed. "I am not ashamed of the gospel" is an understatement, given the way Paul has introduced himself and his gospel. Although some interpreters think the mention of Rome in verse 15 makes Paul self-conscious due to the lack of worldly impressiveness of the gospel, the statement probably should not be taken as apologetic.

Much of Paul's theological vocabulary is introduced in Romans 1:16–17. Key terms include "the gospel," "salvation," "faith," and "righteousness of God." The gospel is the good news of God's active power through the death and resurrection of Jesus. That power effects salvation, i.e., it makes whole, well, or complete. There is a correspondence between the old covenant and the new at this point: the old (Mosaic) covenant was consequent upon the power of God manifest in the act of liberating Israel from Egypt; so also the new covenant is grounded in God's act of liberation in Jesus Christ. The saving activity of God is prior to human response, but it is completed in that response. Thus Paul says, "for all who have faith." "Faith" is the affirming and accepting response to the covenant offered in Jesus Christ. Since from Paul's standpoint salvation, or wholeness of life, is impossible outside the covenant relationship, salvation necessarily involves reciprocity: faith is Paul's term for that reciprocal human response to God's initiating grace. The gospel is thus a revelation of the "righteousness [= justification] of God." "Righteousness" presupposes reciprocal covenantal relationships already suggested by the phrase "salvation to every one who has faith," and is thus God's activity in establishing and maintaining a covenantal relationship with the people of God. "Righteousness" is therefore neither primarily *juridical* (i.e., God justifies by pronouncing, "not guilty") nor *eschatological* (i.e., God will set things right at the end of the world when he will save the righteous and consign the wicked to hell) but *relational* (i.e., people are set in a right, covenantal relationship with God by God's own act). This interpretation of righteousness is confirmed by the fact that Paul says it is revealed "from faith to faith," (or perhaps better translated, "out of [God's covenantal] faithfulness for [the purpose of establishing] faith").[20]

The meaning of the gospel as it applies to Gentile and Jew as one new humanity set right with God is more fully presented in the body of the letter.

3

Gentile and Jew: Alike in Covenant Breaking

(Romans 1:18—3:20)

Paul has affirmed in Romans 1:16–17 that the gospel is God's saving power to all who have faith, to the Jew first and also to the Greek; God's righteousness acts through faith. He surprises the reader by his next move: instead of speaking about God's grace at work for salvation, as the reader might expect, he speaks of God's wrath against those who have denied God and God's will. If this section were not included in the letter, would we perceive that something is missing? Could one not as easily move from 1:17 to 3:21, where the theme of God's righteousness is continued? "Now the righteousness of God has been manifested apart from the Torah . . . , the righteousness of God through faith. . . ." In the intervening paragraphs Paul expresses an almost unrelieved series of images of human depravity and wrong-doing: idolatry, various forms of immoral actions, judgmental attitudes, and false claims for preferred treatment by God. Inter-preters debate the reason for this turn. Does Paul feel compelled to show all humanity the need for salvation by pointing out the reasons why God should not save but on the contrary should condemn and destroy? Does he wish to contrast the righteousness of God with the sinfulness of humanity? Does he do so in order to prepare the way for the gospel?

Paul's purpose in this section is evidently not to convert his readers to faith in Christ, since he has already addressed them as "God's beloved" and "saints," and has said that their faith is being proclaimed in all the world (1:18).[1] Nonetheless, the early chapters of Romans do have a recognizable evangelical tone. That tone could be due to the fact that Paul's evangelical preaching has a pervasive effect on all his theological discourse. It could even be that Paul has inserted part of a sermon which he often preached in his evangelical work among the Jews, overlooking for the moment the fact that his readers represent a different audience.[2] Regardless of how one explains the evangelical emphasis, this section is not aimed at winning converts.

My thesis is that Paul intends to demonstrate the lack of distinction between Gentile and Jew, that his message is related both to the situation in Rome and to his journey to Jerusalem. This section is therefore part of Paul's social ministry of uniting all in one new covenant in Jesus Christ. That covenant is offered precisely to those whose conduct has not qualified them for it, since Jew and Gentile alike have failed to respond to God's grace which has always surrounded both. If both are now shown to be objects of God's wrath, it is because both have already been objects of God's grace. Wrath, then, is an expression of redeeming grace.

Gentile and Jew: No Distinction

Interpreters usually give this section (Rom. 1:18—3:20) a label such as "the universal need for the gospel," or "the sinfulness of all humanity." Paul is thought to be chastising first the Gentile world for its idolatry and consequent immorality, and second the Jewish world for disobedience to the Torah, pride, and a judgmental attitude toward others. Thus, it is thought, Paul shows the universal need for God's grace and forgiveness.

That interpretation correctly recognizes Paul's assertion of universal human sinfulness, but it misses the central point: Paul wishes to affirm that there is *no real distinction* between Gentile and Jew, a point to which he returns dramatically at 11:32: "For God has consigned [everyone] to disobedience, that he may have mercy upon [everyone]." This affirmation of non-distinction in sinfulness has as its larger purpose the affirmation that there is no distinction in salvation! There is one new covenant that unites Jew and Gentile as the one people of God.

The situation described in 1:18—3:20 is thus a human predicament, not a Gentile or a Jewish predicament. That point is reflected in the way the passage is both bracketed by and punctuated with the affirmation that everything applies to "both Jew and Gentile."

The first side of that bracket is established explicitly in the theme sentence (Rom. 1:16–17): the gospel is God's power "for salvation to every one who has faith, to the Jew first and also to the Greek." The bracket is completed by the summary in 3:22–23 which leads into the positive statement of God's saving action in 3:24: "There is no distinction [between Gentile and Jew]; since all have sinned and fall short of the glory of God, they are justified by his grace as a gift."

The lack of distinction between Gentile and Jew is further seen in the assertion of impartiality of divine judgment:

> [God] will render to [each] according to [each one's] works.... There will be tribulation and distress for every human being who does evil, the Jew first and also the Greek, but glory and honor and peace for everyone who does good, the Jew first and also the Greek. For God shows no partiality. (Rom. 2:6–11, possibly quoting Ps. 62:12 and Prov. 24:12)

The issue of "salvation by works" raised by the wording of this statement should not deter us from seeing Paul's main point: no distinction between Jew and Greek in either condemnation or approbation. The only concession allowed is that of priority of the Jews: "the Jew first." That priority is not a matter of God's partiality but due only to God's historical working; however, it is finally reduced to a chronological priority and has no ultimate distinguishing force.

This lack of distinction is shown further in the assertion that

Jews do not excel their pagan neighbors (Rom. 3:9–10) even though they have had the significant advantage of having been entrusted with the oracles of the faithful God (Rom. 3:1–3). Both Jews and Greeks without distinction are captive to the power of sin, for as Paul will argue later (Rom. 7:1—8:11), the Torah does not provide freedom from sin's power.

Paul's emphasis upon lack of distinction between Jew and Gentile is confirmed further by his culminating description of human sinfulness, which rounds out the whole section. For his final indictment Paul chooses texts from Hebrew Scripture which he regards as being directed to those "under the [Torah]" (Rom. 3:19) and which repeat the assertion that none are excepted from human sinfulness.

> *None* is righteous, *no, not one*;
> *no one* understands, *no one* seeks for God.
> *All* have turned aside, together they have gone wrong;
> *no one* does good, *not even one*. (Rom. 3:10–12, italics mine)

In the context, with its heavy emphasis upon lack of distinction between Gentile and Jew, these statements must be regarded not so much as an attempt to assert the depravity of each and every particular human being (though they may have such implications) as to assert the commonality of Jew and Gentile. The negative side of this commonality serves the positive side, which has already been expressed in the theme verse: The gospel "is the power of God for salvation to every one who has faith, to the Jew first and also the Greek" (Rom. 1:16). The positive side is taken up again in 3:20. The negative side, however, is not merely the dark backdrop against which to see more clearly the light of the gospel itself. In removing the ground of boasting Paul implies good news: establishing a ground for boasting is unnecessary. The declaration that none is righteous contains within it the good news that God's grace is not dependent upon human righteousness. Thus Paul does not simply present bad news as a preliminary to good news; he presents bad news within the context of good news, so that the bad news itself may be heard as good news. God's "No!" to humans is also God's "Yes!" and both the no and the yes are addressed equally to Gentile and Jew.

Covenantal Dimensions

In asserting that there is no distinction between Gentile and Jew, Paul affirms his fundamental conviction that God has provided one new covenant for Gentile and Jew on the same basis: since they are alike in being recipients of God's grace, they also must be alike in being in need of that grace. That assertion goes counter to the major thrust of Paul's past religious convictions, but he believes that it neither contradicts God's historical dealings with Israel nor necessitates the renunciation of God's covenant with Israel. Rather, the gospel is the means by which God will bring to completion the promises to Abraham and the Mosaic covenant.

Paul's affirmations about both Jewish and Gentile sinfulness are thus radical and also traditional, for he builds his theology of the new covenant community upon the traditions of God's covenant with Israel. In doing so he employs an understanding of covenant not widely accepted in his time. Historically the notion of covenant had been utilized to distinguish one group from another—Jews as God's covenant people, as distinct from the others, "Gentiles." To Israel God had said, "You shall be a people for me, and I will be God for you." Especially in post-exilic Judaism, election to be God's covenant people had implied separation from the Gentiles ("the nations") who were regarded as hopelessly sunk in idolatry and immorality.

The strong separatist tendencies of post-exilic Judaism were theologically grounded. Believing that the national disasters they suffered at the hands of the Assyrians (who destroyed the northern kingdom of Israel in 722–21 BCE) and the Babylonians (who destroyed the southern kingdom of Judah with its capital at Jerusalem, and along with it the temple of Solomon in 587–86 BCE) were God's punishment of the people because they had "become like the nations" (Gentiles), post-exilic Judaism tended to draw within itself to seek its identity and security. Separatist tendencies combined with a coincident emphasis upon the purity of God's people also led to internal fragmentation, as various groups (e.g., Pharisees, Essenes) considered themselves to be God's faithful covenanters and others to be apostate.

Paul would have known the tendency of separatists to find their identity and security in distinctiveness from others, and he would have known, too, the arrogance which so frequently accompanies that tendency. In his Pharisaic past he had embodied both. In his desire to perpetuate purity of thought and practice within Judaism he had opposed what he regarded as the apostate messianic group who centered their life around the crucified Jesus. He might also have experienced something of the "uneasy conscience" which W.D. Davies attributes to some Pharisees concerning their own narrow attitude toward Gentiles.[3]

With his change of conviction about Jesus and himself, Paul incorporated a new set of attitudes regarding "insiders" and "outsiders." We have no way of knowing precisely what Paul's attitudes toward Gentiles were before his apostolic call. He might have shared the broader outlook of many Hellenistic Jews toward their pagan neighbors; he might have engaged in proselyte activity among the Gentiles. But given his staunch adherence to the Torah, he could have accepted on equal terms only those whose dedication to the Torah was similar to his own. When he joined the messianic movement associated with Jesus, his closest associates included those who had already begun to preach to Gentiles as well as to Jews. He came to believe that he was living in the new eschatological time in which God extended the covenant to include Gentile as well as Jew.[4] The logic of that conviction led Paul to affirm that if the gospel is for Gentile as well as for Jew, then there can be no distinction; the new covenant must be offered to both on the same basis.

It is true that Paul does not speak specifically in this passage about the covenant in relation to Gentiles (or to Jews either, for that matter), but the concerns motivating Paul's writing, as well as presuppositions behind much of his language, are essentially covenantal. The "lack of distinction" which pervades this passage could indicate that the covenant with Israel has been negated. But as Romans 9—11 will make plain, Paul intends not to deny the covenant with Israel but to include the Gentiles within God's covenantal promises. By bracketing human sinfulness with God's grace in the gospel, Paul effectively places both Gentile and Jew within God's covenantal concern: even though both have neglected to affirm God's grace by covenantal faithfulness, both are still objects of that grace.

Covenantal ideas are reflected also in the way Paul grounds his analysis of the human predicament in a theology of creation. By using creation themes, Paul stresses the relational or covenantal character of human existence. Human sinfulness as Paul understands it consists not primarily of bad deeds, but of broken covenantal relationships. The corruption of human life which he depicts in 1:18–32 is grounded in human alienation and separation from God. Objective knowledge of God and the good which God wills have not resulted in human fulfillment, well-being, and happiness, because humans have failed to acknowledge God as creator or to live in a reciprocal and faithful relationship with God. Alienation and the failure to live faithfully are the cause rather than the consequence of ignorance and licentiousness.

The relationship broken from the human side is acknowledged by the terrible reality of God's giving up. For Paul this "giving up" expresses God's wrath or judgment. Paul employs that traditional covenantally derived language[5] to apply to the Gentiles as well as to the Jews. Both Gentiles and Jews had possibilities of acknowledging, honoring, or giving thanks to God—in other words, of expressing personal relationship in appropriate ways—but both Jew and Gentile have refused to live covenantally.

In grounding his argument in creation before he mentions Israel in particular, Paul stresses God's common relationship with humanity rather than historical manifestations to Israel. In taking this approach Paul shows a kinship with the wisdom tradition reflected, for example, in the Wisdom of Solomon. But unlike the author of that book, who was roughly his contemporary, Paul does not go on to divide the world between the righteous (the Jews) and the unrighteous (the Gentiles). He does utilize the Torah to distinguish between Gentile and Jew, but

the Torah finally makes no difference since it does not successfully restrain the rebellious impulses and actions which characterize both Gentile and Jew. As he does again in Romans 5:12–21,
Paul characterizes *human* sinfulness, not *Gentile* sinfulness
alone, nor does he portray Gentiles as essentially worse than
Jews.

Covenantal ideas are involved, further, in the association of
general sinfulness with idolatry. Paul characterizes both Gentiles and Jews in ways that suggest both are guilty of idolatry.
Actually in this passage it is difficult to know precisely about
whom Paul speaks. Standard interpretation has been that in
1:18–32 Paul addresses Gentile sinfulness, using the two types
of actions and attitudes which Judaism generally associated
with the Gentile world: idolatry and immorality. Then he condemns the Jews for their failure to keep the Torah and for their
arrogance toward the Gentiles. However, Paul does not identify
the object of his descriptions until 2:17, suggesting that Paul's
intent is quite different from the common assertion.

In 2:1 Paul affirms that no one, Gentile or Jew, has a standpoint
from which others may be condemned. The judgmental person
should first pass judgment upon the very self that is doing the
judging, "because you, the judge, are doing the very same
things" (2:1).[6] Failure to give God due honor and neglecting
God's glory (1:21–23) are root causes of other manifestations of
sin in both Gentiles and Jews—in speaking specifically to the
Jews (2:23–24) Paul says they did not honor God, and as a
consequence of their deeds God's name is blasphemed. Gentiles
and Jews may manifest their rebellion against God in different
ways, but at base it is the same rebellion.

"Same things" should not be construed to apply narrowly
only to the list of wrong-doing and wrong-thinking in 1:29–31;
idolatry is also included, for in Paul's view the essence of idolatry, which is the tendency toward self-deification, is present in
Jew as well as in Gentile. That tendency may be expressed
through immorality and idolatry, which Paul and others regarded
as characteristic of Gentiles, but it may also be expressed through
the boasting of religious persons about their privileged posi-

tion as God's special people, a boasting which Paul associates with the Jews of his day. Both express the same human predicament of alienation and rebellion.

To call boasting, which Paul associates especially with Judaism, a form of idolatry might stretch the term for those who consider it only a minor vice. To Paul, boasting is the radical antithesis of faith, as he shows especially in 3:27–31. To boast is to have "confidence in the flesh" (Phil 3:3), in the merely human. To boast, then, is to regard oneself as self-made, which amounts to worshiping the creature rather than the Creator. Such self-deification prevents a covenantal relationship with God. Covenantal faithfulness becomes an impossibility when the reality of God is denied. Paul believes that one terrible consequence of that boasting in the self which had once been characteristic of his own way of life is that it denies the possibility of the common covenant relationship of Gentile and Jew with God and with each other.[7]

In accusing the Jews of idolatry and immorality, he reflects not only the requirements of the Mosaic covenant (Exod. 20:4–5) but also prophetic and post-exilic writings which contain a constant warning that Israel's continued temptation to and practice of idolatry was at the root of all her sin against Yahweh. More importantly for his argument in Romans, he is drawing the lines of connection between the Gentile world as perceived by the Jews and the Jewish world itself. "There is no distinction. . . ."

Paul further reveals a covenantal/relational understanding of human sinfulness by the way in which he speaks of "knowledge" of God. The Gentiles as well as the Jews "knew" God (Rom. 1:21), but they did not honor, give thanks, or "acknowledge" God. On the contrary, they became senseless and given to foolish thoughts. Ignorance is, for Paul, not the natural human condition but one acquired through the rejection of what is known. This way of speaking of knowledge is at base covenantal, as is seen in Hosea's speaking of God's people being destroyed for lack of knowledge, a lack which derives from their refusal to live as God's covenant people.[8]

"Acknowledgment" of God is both relational and moral, with

the moral dimensions—in either the negative or the positive sense—growing out of the relational. To acknowledge God, in Paul's terms, encompasses both honor and thanksgiving in recognition of God's "eternal power and deity," which are perceived in the works of creation. As a social term "honor" implies a relationship in which worth and standing are recognized. To honor is to recognize the character and quality of the person in relationship; to dishonor is to violate the relationship. Similarly, to give thanks implies recognition of right relationship and expresses personal gratitude appropriate for one who recognizes the gifts of the Creator.

For Paul, then, within creation itself there exists a bonding, covenantal relationship which precedes the covenant with Israel and which, like the covenant with Israel, is in need of renewal. By the act of creation as well as by the historical deliverance of Israel, God has made a binding covenant with humanity. God's judgment as well as acts of salvation through the gospel presuppose that covenant given in creation and broken through human rebellion.

Paul did not originate the notion that creating the world gives God claim over it as well as concern for all in it. Rather, Paul utilizes traditions found in wisdom and apocalyptic and prophetic writings in a unique way to assert the commonality of Gentile and Jew in a primal relationship with God which transcends any historical differences which have originated through God's dealings with Israel.

The covenantal dimension of Paul's convictions is seen further in the nature of God's punishment of idolatry: God "gave them up." Paul's act of proclaiming the gospel makes it clear that the giving up is neither final nor complete, for God's setting right is available again to all through faith. In the interim, however, God has responded to human failure to acknowledge relationship by turning away from humanity. The covenant relation implied by creation is thus lapsed fully: from the human side, by rebellion, from the divine side by abandonment of the rebel. God no longer protected them from themselves, and they became "detestable like the thing[s] they loved" (Hos. 9:10).

Paul's connecting of right human–human relationships to right divine–human relationships also reveals covenantal patterns of thought which go back as far as Genesis 2—3. There rebellion against the terms of relationship established by the creator resulted in the break between husband and wife, as the man no longer rejoiced in the one given to him, but instead blamed her for his own failure and rebellion. Implicitly he blamed God—thus he neither thanked the Creator nor rejoiced in the presence of the other. His relationship as a whole was in disarray. So, too, Paul draws out moral implications of the break in covenantal relationship with God by speaking of the brokenness of human relations. The connection between the two is most clearly evident in Paul's description of human sinfulness as "lusts of their hearts," "dishonorable passions," and "a base mind" (Rom. 1:24, 26, 28). A perception of the reality of God as Creator of oneself and others results in behavior which affirms and expresses common bonds of humanity between oneself and the other; rejection of that perception and of those bonds makes the other an object of lust and self-aggrandizement. Self-deification (idolatry) and self-gratification (immorality) are twins: both are ways of denying the bonding in love which brings human life to fulfillment, both are expressions of the brokenness and alienation which so readily permeate human life.

Since idolatry and immorality are fundamentally and essentially one, it might seem possible to collapse all sin into social sin; yet Paul does not eliminate the theological understanding of human existence in favor of a purely humanistic one such as may be found in Hellenistic philosophy. He retains the logical and chronological priority of human rebellion against God as the source and origin of broken human relationships.[9] In terms of the deeper logic of Paul's thought, however, there is no chronological sequence: turning from God and turning from human community are the same turning. So also, as we shall see, is the returning: the "renewal of your mind" involves the "sober judgment" of oneself in relation to other participants in the "body [of] Christ" (Rom. 12:2–5). Thus Paul's understanding of human existence is thoroughly covenantal from beginning to end.

The list of evil deeds and thoughts given by Paul in 1:29–31[10] is not to be understood as his description of conditions at Rome, nor as his personal observations of human behavior. The list has some things in common with such lists in popular Hellenistic philosophy: with Hellenistic Jewish tradition reflected in Philo, 4 Maccabees, and the Wisdom of Solomon; and with the Jewish doctrine of the two ways. But none of the available parallels is exact; "various streams unite here which flowed together even before Paul in Hellenistic Judaism."[11]

In keeping with Hellenistic Jewish moralists[12] Paul singles out sexual misconduct as especially expressing the corruption of human life; homosexual misconduct is exemplary in Paul's eyes of the misuse and perversion of the Creator's intent and purpose. Paul goes beyond the Genesis portrayal of the brokenness in human relationships when he cites homosexual passion, but one should notice that homosexuality is only one manifestation of the perversion of God's creation which Paul sees originating in the denial of God. The list of sins which he gives in 1:29–31 concentrates on non-sexual misconduct toward others. The failure to acknowledge God has as its consequence the perversion of interpersonal relationships; "social rather than religious offenses" predominate.[13]

In arguing that Paul's perspective as reflected in Romans 1:18—3:20 is covenantal, I have used that term rather broadly. Although Paul does not speak directly of the covenant here, I have sought to show that the language of covenant is implicitly present, that the logic of a covenantal understanding of relationships structures the language by which Paul expresses the human situation with its problems and promises. Paul's linguistic inheritance from Judaism and early Christianity is such that covenantal concepts underlie his theological expressions even when explicit covenantal language is not present. This hypothesis finds confirmation in the present passage, in which the interpersonal relationship between God and humans, as well as the nature of the human interpersonal relationship, is derived from the pattern established in the past covenantal theology of Israel.

Paul's innovation is seen in the way in which he interprets the covenant tradition inclusively, so that there is no distinction between Gentile and Jew. Alike in covenant breaking, they are alike also in covenant renewal. Paul does not reject that which is central to Israel's life and thought—from within the tradition he radically revises it, always being careful that the basis for revision is found within the tradition itself as that tradition has been reinvigorated by God's act in Jesus Christ.

Universal Depravity and Damnation?

I have noted above that Paul emphasizes universal sinfulness in Romans 1:18—3:20 in order to put Gentile and Jew on the same footing before God, rather than to express "original sin" and universal depravity. However, I suggested that Paul's statements might also imply the depravity of every particular person. We need now to examine that issue.

At first reading, there may seem to be no issue at all, for does he not plainly say, "No one is righteous, no, not one"? Does he not also say, "Since all have sinned and fall short of the glory of God they are justified by his grace as a gift . . ."? Again, lest the point somehow be lost, he repeats it in other words: "For no human being will be justified in [God's] sight by works of the [Torah], since through the [Torah] comes knowledge of sin" (Rom 3:20). It appears that apart from the gospel of God's justifying grace demonstrated in the death and resurrection of the Messiah there is nothing in the world except sin and its retribution. All humans both by their deeds and by their internal corruption merit God's condemnation.

On the basis of such strong condemnation of all humanity, one would certainly seem justified in believing that in Paul's eyes every particular Gentile and every particular Jew is an unrighteous sinner before God. But to place the emphasis there is to miss Paul's main point, which is that being part of the community of the Torah does not make one fundamentally different from the Gentile. Whether Paul even believes in the essential sinfulness of every human being is a question raised especially by 2:6–16, in which he implies that some Gentiles and some Jews "seek for glory and honor and immortality" and do so by their "patience in well-doing"; God will reward them, Paul says, by the gift of eternal life. Further, he argues that Gentiles doing by nature what the Torah requires show that the Torah's requirements are written on their hearts, a description strikingly similar to Jeremiah's expectation of the situation which will prevail under the new covenant which God will make with Israel in the future![14]

This passage has posed serious problems for interpreters who have thought Paul's major intent in 1:18—3:20 has been to demonstrate universal human depravity of the sort associated with "original sin." If that were Paul's intent, 2:6–16 would make no real sense and could be dismissed as an occasion in which Paul temporarily adapted himself to those Jewish ways of thinking in which judgment is by works. C.H. Dodd, even though recognizing that "Paul should not be understood as propounding a rigid theory of . . . total depravity," nevertheless thinks Paul is speaking here "as a good Jew, and meeting his Jewish hearers on their own ground."[15] In that case one might need to excuse Paul's lack of consistency by saying that he, like any of us, has occasional lapses. However, if his *real* argument is not focused upon human depravity as such but upon the lack of distinction between Jew and Gentile, there is not necessarily any lapse at all. Just as he can utilize the Jewish characterization of Gentiles and expand it to include Jews, just as he can utilize the Torah's condemnation of those under it to show that Jews, too, are under God's just judgment, so he can also utilize the apocalyptic judgment of every person according to deeds for the same end of showing that "God shows no partiality" (2:11).

One must conclude that Paul is not presenting universal human sinfulness or total depravity as the backdrop for the gospel. Rather, he is arguing that Jew and Gentile are alike in covenant breaking, in the tendency to self-idolatry, in the moral failures which characterize human life and in the well-doing which too infrequently but nevertheless really is found there, in being the objects of God's just judgment, and in being the recipients of a knowledge of God which could and should lead to self-fulfillment. He is, in other words, preparing the way for

the presentation of one new covenant in Christ which will bind
Jew and Gentile together as one new people of God, renewed by
God's grace and empowered by the Spirit to fulfill God's will in
ways that neither Gentile nor Jew has yet been able to accomplish.

The Nature of the Human Predicament

The preceding discussion has attempted to demonstrate (1)
that the human predicament is fundamentally the same for
Gentile and Jew, "for there is no distinction"; (2) that Paul
understands that predicament in relational or covenantal terms;
and (3) that Paul's primary interest is not in arguing for original
sin or total depravity in the sense that those doctrines have
since come to be understood. In presenting these points, I have
already said a great deal about the nature of the human predicament; in the present section I shall pull together these various
strands of thought into a coherent whole.

Sin is a very general and undefined term by which Paul
sometimes refers to the human predicament. It is a summary
word, not an analytical one. Paul first uses sin in Romans 3:9, to
describe the common plight of Gentile and Jew. From 1:18 to 3:8
he has been describing that plight but has used quite different
language; now he characterizes it as being "under the power of
sin" (Rom 3:9). Paul presents the particular manifestations of
human problems rather than labeling them. Later, in chapters
5—7 (in which Paul's point is not primarily to talk about the
human problem but rather to talk about the new situation in
contrast to the old) he uses the term "sin" thirty-six times. It is as
though he regards sin as a useful summary term for the past life
of alienation from God in contrast with the new situation which
exists as a consequence of the death of Christ, but as less useful
when speaking analytically or descriptively about the human
problem itself. Taking our cue from Paul, we might also look for
other terms to describe the human predicament more precisely
than the word "sin" would do.

One obvious point to begin with is that sin is not at all
equatable with "irreligious" or "impious." Both the Gentile and
the Jew as Paul observed them were very religious. The Gen-

tiles worshiped wrongly, but they worshiped! The Jews worshiped the one who had given them the Torah and the covenant relationship, and who singled them out as the chosen people. The problem with both Jew and Gentile was the problem of living: *how* they lived, and *why* they lived as they did. The problem was not merely that Gentiles made idols and engaged in perverse sexual relationships, or that the Jews acted in a proud and condescending manner while not really behaving more morally than Gentiles did; the primary problem was that human life is always one of alienation and fragmentation.

Paul knew from his own experience that religious zeal is no sufficient guard against alienation; indeed, it may only serve to make one extremely "sinful." His fanaticism in the promotion and defense of his religious convictions was, he came to see, only an expression of his alienation rather than its cure. No more than the Gentile idolatry had his zeal for the Torah brought peace with God, with others, or with himself. He had to die to that self structured around religious devotion before he could know the reconciling power of God's grace.

Neither is sin equatable with immorality. Paul has a great deal to say about various expressions of immorality, and he avers that those whose characteristic style of life is to be morally and religiously corrupt will not participate in God's kingdom (e.g., 1 Cor. 6:9–10), for such behavior shows that they are unrighteous. But although immoral acts are sins, those acts themselves are not the problem; acts can demonstrate a lack of righteousness but not its presence. While moral reformation is in Paul's view a proper and necessary consequence of knowing God's grace, proper conduct does not either *make* one right nor demonstrate that one *is* right. One may be blameless according to very high standards of right behavior which the Torah engenders and still not be in a right relation with God, neighbor, and self.

Far from being the antithesis of sin, both religion and morality can be sin's most ardent supporters and its most serious expressions. For Paul the essence of sin is lack of faith, lack of the "acknowledgment of God," unwillingness to let God be God.

That refusal manifests itself at least as insistently in religion and morality as in any other elements of human experience. Paul concludes after reflecting on his own moral and religious attainments in light of the gospel that there is no distinction between Gentile and Jew. The celebrated religion and morality of Jews may mask an alienation as severe as the idolatry and immorality of which Gentiles are regularly accused.

The essence of sin is a distorted understanding of one's self; it is alienation from God, from others, and from one's true self. Sin, then, is not first of all a way of *acting*; it is a way of *being*. That way of being includes living in hostility, living as "enemies" of God. Such an alienated life does not manifest strength when it rebels against God; rather, it manifests weakness—weakness to establish the life one intends, and the ability only to lose the life that one has sought, and then to cover up that loss in a multitude of ways, including immorality, religiosity, boasting, and pride.

Conclusion

One of the major thrusts of Paul's letter to the Romans is the message that the gospel provides the solution to the human problem. In the next chapter we will be concerned with the way in which Paul presents the gospel as the answer. One's reading of that presentation depends in large measure upon one's reading of the nature of the problem expressed in Romans 1:18—3:20.

If sin is understood primarily as a matter of *deed*, then the solution will be understood in terms of changing one's deeds. In traditional Hebraic terminology, that means repentance: cease to do evil, learn to do good. If sin is defined primarily as *power* —as the control over human life by an alien outside force over which one has no personal control—then the solution will also necessitate power; salvation in this case will involve the success of God's power over the enslaving power. If sin is seen primarily in terms of a *condition* in which human life is lived out, then the solution will be understood in terms of a change of condition.

All three of these understandings of the human problem have

been part of Paul's presentation in 1:18—3:20; however, it is the understanding of sin as a condition of alienation that is most central in Paul's thought. Alienation leads to wrong acts, and to subjecting oneself to enslaving forces which apparently are beyond one's control. I believe that Paul's covenantal theology is revealed in this understanding as clearly as at any other point. If I am correct, then I will expect to see Paul's presentation of the gospel as solution in corresponding terms. Indeed, as I shall argue, Paul does present the gospel as the action of God in establishing a new covenantal relationship in Jesus Christ to replace the broken relationship which has resulted in alienation, hostility, and weakness, and which is expressed through immoral actions and inappropriate or blasphemous religious behavior.

4

One New Covenant for Gentile and Jew

(Romans 3:21—4:25)

Paul has presented thus far what has often been viewed as a dismal and pessimistic picture of universal human sinfulness. I have argued that Paul's real interest has not been in establishing universal human depravity as such but rather in maintaining that Jew and Gentile are on the same footing before God and that in the gospel both are offered a new covenant relationship. That interest is confirmed by the fact that Paul ended his analysis by speaking specifically of those under the Torah, insisting that by "works of the [Torah]" no human being will be set in a right relationship with God (Rom. 3:20). In order to make his point effectively, Paul ended his discussion of Gentile and Jewish sinfulness by concentrating on the situation of the Jews: what the Torah says in condemning sin is said to those under the Torah (i.e., to the Jews), not to those outside it (i.e., Gentiles). This specific assertion prepares the way for the next stage of his argument, which contrasts the Torah and the prophets with the new way of right relations with God apart from the Torah, the

way of the new covenant expressions of God's grace. The point of
the earlier section is reiterated in Romans 3:23: "For there is no
distinction [between Jew and Gentile], for all have sinned and
still fail to attain the glory of God" (my translation).

Paul has affirmed earlier (1:16) that the gospel is the "power
of God for salvation to every one who has faith, to the Jew first
and also to the Greek." He expounds upon that theme in 3:21–31,
illustrates it in 4:1–25, reflects upon the wonder and implications of it in 5:1–11, and relates it to the whole of humankind—
past, present, and future—in 5:12–21. My present chapter examines the language by which Paul presents the meaning of the
gospel as the redemptive event. It will examine first the vocabulary Paul uses in his summary statement in 3:21–31, especially
the terms justification, redemption, and expiation; and second
his use of Abraham as the best example of one whose rightness
with God was through faith (Rom. 4:1–25). It will show that
Paul sees the death and resurrection of Jesus as the inauguration
of the new covenant, and that the language by which he understands that event is derived from covenant traditions. The central purpose of Paul in this section is to show that the new
covenant in Christ binds Gentile, as well as Jew, to God.

JUSTIFICATION/RIGHTEOUSNESS

One of the key words in this section—indeed, in all of Romans—
is the term "righteousness" or "justification." It is not evident
to the English reader, but in Paul's language the terms translated by English cognates of "right" (righteousness, righteous,
right) and "just" (justify, justice, justification) all come from
only one root (Greek *dik*). Throughout the first stage of his
argument in Romans 1:18—3:20 Paul made extensive use of
the notion of "righteousness": the divine demand for it, the
human failure to achieve it, the consequences in human corruption of that failure, and the inevitability of divine judgment
upon human unrighteousness. "Righteousness" figures just as
prominently in Paul's presentation of the positive results of
divine action for human salvation. The gospel involves the
revelation of God's righteousness, his gift of grace which sets

humans right. Paul's understanding of the event of Jesus Christ as effective for salvation is tied up closely with righteousness: "Since all have sinned...they are justified [set right] by his grace" (Rom. 3:23–24). Yet, as crucial as it is for Paul and for our understanding of his theology, Paul neither defines the term nor gives any direct clues as to its meaning. He obviously takes for granted a common ground of meaning which he shares with his readers. It is possible, of course, that he takes too much for granted and that his Gentile and Jewish readers in Rome might understand somewhat different things according to their backgrounds.

Righteousness as Ethical Quality

An examination of Paul's use of "righteousness" (*dikaiosyne*) and its cognates shows that in fact the meaning is not always exactly the same. At times the context of the adjective "righteous" (*dikaios*) suggests that ethical qualities are uppermost in his mind. For example, in maintaining that Jews as well as Gentiles are "under the power of sin" he quotes from either Psalm 14:1ff or 53:1ff to the effect that "no one does good, not even one." Paul understands that to mean "none is righteous," and goes on to enumerate the despicable acts which demonstrate the truth of the accusation (Rom. 3:9–18). While it is true that some of the terms he uses concern the fundamental relationship with God ("no one understands, no one seeks for God"[3:11]), for the most part "righteous" here pertains to ethical qualities and actions. Again in Romans 5:7 Paul uses "righteous" (*dikaios*) to describe the sort of person one would "hardly die for" and parallels it with "good." Whether or not "righteous" and "good" are synonyms here, the term "righteous" has a positive ethical connotation, as it does in 1 Thessalonians 2:10, where he describes his own behavior before the Thessalonian church as "holy and righteous and blameless." In light of this usage of the term, it would be possible to think that when Paul speaks of "the righteousness of faith" he means that moral quality which faith produces in life.

Righteousness as Juridical Category

There are, however, other uses of "righteousness" which make it unlikely that its primary meaning is ethical. In nonbiblical Greek usage, this root was associated with decisions and standards expected in courts of law. In that context righteousness or "justification" meant acquittal, the declaration of innocence. If Paul's meaning is determined by this background, he would be saying that God pronounces the person of faith "not guilty." This juridical meaning is in the forefront in Romans 2:12–16, where Paul warns Gentiles and Jews of the standards of judgment which God will apply when he "judges human secrets by Christ Jesus."

> All who have sinned without the [Torah] will also perish without the [Torah], and all who have sinned under the [Torah] will be judged by the [Torah]. For it is not the hearers of the [Torah] who are righteous [*dikaios*] before God, but the doers of the [Torah] who will be justified [*dikaiōthēsontai*]. (2:12)

Here being "righteous before God" and being "justified" are parallel terms, both indicating God's pronouncement of acquittal concerning the person at the time of judgment.

Juridical overtones may be heard, too, in Paul's appeal to scriptural texts in support of his belief that "justification" is through faith and not works. In Romans 4 he uses the example of Abraham to show that the Torah itself anticipates the righteousness of God manifest in the gospel: "For if Abraham was justified by works, he has something to boast about..." (Rom. 4:2). Here "justified" carries the connotation of acquittal: Abraham is pronounced justified or acquitted by God. That meaning is further suggested by the next verse: "Abraham believed God and it was reckoned to him as righteousness."[1]

The term has juridical overtones in so far as Paul refers to the notion that God is a judge who evaluates the situation of the person before him. It becomes clear, however, that for Paul God does not deal with human beings in a detached and rational manner the way a modern judge might be expected to. Rather Abraham's belief/trust in God manifests a relationship with God in which such "reckoning" is no longer appropriate. It is not as though God rationally evaluated Abraham's faith and decided it was the equivalent of righteousness, so that by faith Abraham earns salvation. Neither did God rationally evaluate Abraham's faith and decide that it was an acceptable substitute for ethical righteousness. In either case faith would itself merit a verdict or a conclusion from God: but Abraham's righteousness was "reckoned as a gift."

"As a gift" expresses what Paul implies throughout this passage: whatever standing Abraham had before God or whatever relationship he had with him depended not on Abraham but on God. That point is made by an analogy from the world of work: "to a workman his wage is not thought of as a gift but as an obligation" (Rom 4:4, translation mine). Work and wage belong to the same realm; to an entirely different realm belong faith and grace. If "justification" and "reckon" belonged to the realm of work and wage, then they would be separate from faith and grace. Paul has already claimed that works of Torah can be no basis for justification (Rom. 3:20) and that the Torah brings to account those under it. Paradoxically, justification and reckoning are brought into the realm of grace and are thereby transformed. Abraham believes in one who "justifies the ungodly." But how could Paul believe God acts that way when he could read in his Greek Bible, "You shall not justify the ungodly"? (cf. Exod. 23:7). He believes God does for humans what they cannot do for themselves or for each other; thus God's justification is an act of sheer grace. It was so for Abraham, and for that reason he has nothing to boast about before God (Rom. 4:2). It will be so for those who in faith accept the new covenant in Christ. There is no one to condemn, for God's grace will justify or acquit (Rom. 8:34).

When justification is thought of as a gift which is given to the ungodly, then obviously any juridical meaning the term might have had has been radically changed. The nature of that change is seen in God's dealings with David:

> Blessed are those whose iniquities are forgiven, and whose sins are covered;
> blessed is the [one] against whom the Lord will not reckon
> ...sin."   (Ps. 32:1–2, as quoted in Rom. 4:7)

In citing this Psalm, Paul follows a Rabbinical practice of using one scriptural text to elucidate another. These two texts are held together by the common term "reckon." In the Psalm God's reckoning is equivalent to forgiveness; Paul implies that the same forgiving, gracious work of God is meant in the Genesis passage, too.

> The conclusion to be deduced from this . . . is that the "counting of righteousness" is equivalent to the "not-counting of sin." It becomes clearer and clearer that justification, or the counting of righteousness is neither the just evaluation of human merit..., nor the imparting of virtue, but forgiveness or acquittal. The (person) is justified, whose iniquities have been forgiven and whose sins have been covered over.[2]

The only objectionable part of Barrett's statement is his final understanding of justification primarily as acquittal, and his equating of acquittal and forgiveness. It is precisely at this point that interpreters of Paul generally acknowledge at least implicitly that the juridical meaning of justification/righteousness is unable to bear the weight of Paul's theology, and so veer away from the meaning even while retaining its linguistic expressions. Such interpretations then may seem forced or unclear.

Righteousness as Covenantal Reality

Most scholars recognize that juridical categories of Greek thought and ethical categories of Greek and Hebrew thought do not provide an adequate interpretative base for understanding Paul's use of righteousness. But what has not been sufficiently recognized is the determinative place of covenant ideas in Paul's use of righteousness. Spivey and Smith, for example, maintain,

> The model Paul has in mind is the law court, with God the righteous judge. Thus it is a *forensic* righteousness, the verdict of righteousness pronounced over a person on trial. Quite clearly, then, this righteousness is less an ethical quality than a relationship.[3]

But how does one derive this emphasis upon relationship? Surely it does not come from the forensic or juridical dimension of the term. In fact, one could argue that juridical and relational aspects are contradictory to one another—or at least should be so, if the judge is in fact "just" and impartial. Precisely at this point the covenant thought behind Paul's understanding becomes critical if we are to interpret him accurately. The idea of relationship does not derive from the juridical background but from the covenantal.[4] In fact, the forensic meaning of righteousness derives from the relational: when God's people act contrary to the terms of the covenant, God will judge them in righteousness.[5]

A covenant background provides the context for understanding that justification/righteousness is not primarily ethical or juridical, but relational.[6] What it means for God or humans to be righteous is defined by the covenant relation. Action which maintains and upholds that relation is righteous; action which denigrates or disrupts that relation is unrighteous. This is Paul's fundamental theological point: the action of God in Jesus Christ is the means by which God maintains and upholds that relationship established with Abraham and his descendants, both Jews and Gentiles.

For Paul there is no question but that God has always been righteous, has always acted in such a way as to uphold the covenant relationship given in creation. Even when God "gave them up," that did not mean that God ultimately ceased to maintain a right relationship with the human world. That giving up was only a temporary situation and was itself part of God's judgment which has renewal as its ultimate end.

In a similar way, Jewish failure to live within the covenant did not nullify the covenant, for it depends upon God's faithfulness which no amount of faithlessness on the part of Israel can cancel (Rom. 3:3; cf. 11:28–29). God will, indeed, act to uphold the covenant. In fact, Paul says, that action has already taken place:

> But now the righteousness of God has been manifested apart from the [Torah], although the [Torah] and the prophets bear witness to it, the righteousness of God through faith in Jesus Christ. . . . (Rom. 3:21–22)

The "now" emphasizes that God has made a new and decisive manifestation of faithfulness in maintaining the covenantal relationship. That manifestation is "apart from the Torah," not dependent upon it, not connected to it.[7] Paul dissociates the new manifestation of righteousness from the Torah for two reasons: (1) the Torah, he believes, has for the Jew become the way of making oneself right with God through "works"; (2) the Torah applies only to Jews, who not only tend to "rely upon the Torah" but also to "boast of [their] relation to God" (Rom. 2:17) in contrast to that of the Gentile "sinner." The new manifestation of righteousness is not aimed at the Jew, but is "for all who believe, for there is no distinction" (Rom. 3:22, punctuation mine).

How is God's righteousness manifested? Paul reflects a Hebraic outlook in thinking of God's revelation primarily in terms of action: God's acts reveal the being and character of God. The revelation of God's righteousness in Jesus Christ may be understood in one of three ways. First, if Paul understood righteousness primarily in ethical terms, then he meant that the ethical qualities which God intends for human life are revealed in Jesus and that by faith in Jesus one may come to have in one's own life those same qualities. Second, if righteousness is primarily a juridical term, then Paul meant that acquittal is made possible by the event of Jesus, possibly by his "paying the penalty" for sin to relieve the person of faith from having to pay it. Various substitutionary doctrines of atonement have been based upon this or related notions. Third, if righteousness is primarily neither ethical nor juridical but covenantal/relational, then Paul is affirming that through Jesus the covenant has been renewed, and the person who shares in the faith of Abraham receives and participates in the covenant—God's grace gives human beings a new relationship with God and others.

There are apparent advantages to the interpreter of Paul who accepts either the ethical or the juridical meaning of justification/ righteousness, for either leads to a certain clarity and simplicity of thought. One can understand how Paul might have believed that by faith one grows more and more into the ethical likeness to Jesus, so that one finally is acceptable to God. One can also understand how God might accept a penalty paid by one on behalf of another, and let the latter go free. It is more difficult to see what Paul might mean by the ambiguous language of covenant and relationship. Just how does Jesus' death establish that new relationship? This may be the more difficult alternative to understand, but it has the most to commend it and in the end might also prove to be the most theologically promising and satisfying.

To understand the relational dimension of justification, we must see how "faith" is involved. Paul's full expression is, "The righteousness of God *through faith* in Jesus Christ." (Rom. 3:22, italics mine). If the basic meaning of justification/righteousness is covenantal and relational, then it is in some sense reciprocal. To say this does not necessarily mean that the covenant depends in equal or even in similar ways upon the actions of God and humans. God reestablishes covenant relationships in Jesus Christ as an act of sheer grace: there is nothing one can do to establish that relationship or even to assist God in doing so. Yet the very use of relational metaphors necessarily implies some sort of reciprocity. Faith is the term by which Paul speaks of that reciprocal human movement which responds to God's initiating grace. A fuller view of faith will be evident in Paul's discussion of Abraham in chapter four; for now we may say that faith is conviction; it is stance, or orientation of life, rather than a set of beliefs. It is the opposite of the orientation Paul describes as "sin" or alienation. For Paul, faith is the stance which acknowledges with believing reception that God's grace in Jesus Christ is at the root of one's existence in the world. Faith is acknowledging and receiving God's grace revealed in past promises and acts; faith is affirming the covenant relationship God offers; faith is holding fast to God in confidence so that one can become a reliable member of the community of God's people; faith is confidently entrusting oneself to God's trustworthiness; faith is the commitment of the self to belong to God.

If Paul's language implies any explanation of *how* Jesus' death brings about justification it is along these lines: God's love, demonstrated by the giving of God's Son for sinners (Rom.

5:8), elicits the response of faith. Paul may well have in mind a passage like Deuteronomy 7:6ff, in which God's love, electing Israel, and keeping covenant are all intermixed and stated with an intention of eliciting Israel's faithful response. Or he may have in mind the way Hosea anticipates that God's love for "adulterous" Israel will, through constancy and discipline, bring her back to faithfulness.

Paul believes that "God's love has been poured out into our hearts" (Rom. 5:5, my translation). Such a statement includes God's initiating action and the internal response which it generates. It is a shorthand statement which is to be understood in light of Romans 5:9 ("we are now justified by his blood") and 1 Corinthians 11:25 ("This cup is the new covenant in my blood"). God's love is "poured out" through the pouring out of Jesus' blood, through which justification takes place. Note that justification and "new covenant" are really parallel terms in these two passages, and both are the consequence of Jesus' shedding his blood. "Pouring out" is the action side of the covenant which is initiated by God's grace in Jesus Christ; "into our hearts" is the subjective realization and eager reception of the grace which has been offered. That reception is associated with the presence of the Holy Spirit (Rom. 8:15), which shows that for Paul even the receptiveness of faith is grounded in the act of grace and not in the responding self.

Righteousness and Eschatology

Those who interpret justification/righteousness as a juridical term and apply it to the final judgment offer the advantage of integrating justification with eschatology. And that is no small advantage, for Paul's theology is permeated by his belief that the end-time is near. When he speaks of the doers and not the hearers of the Torah as the ones who will be justified, his apparent reference is juridical/eschatological (Rom. 2:13). However, the future tense in Romans 3:20 much less clearly has a genuine future reference, for the whole passage of which it is a part presents the situation in the present due to what God has just done in Jesus Christ; thus, it should be viewed along with the many instances in which justification is expressed as something which has already happened:

> Abraham was justified. . . . (Rom. 4:2)
> Therefore, having been justified. . . . (Rom. 5:1, my trans.)
> Therefore now that we have been justified. . . . (Rom. 5:9, my trans.)
> You were justified. . . . (1 Cor. 6:11) [8]

Righteousness no doubt has an eschatological dimension, but the key element in that dimension is not acquittal at the final judgment—it is being within the context of God's new covenant people so that whatever the future brings will not sever one from that relationship. There is no reason to fear the great assize in the future, since the only ones who could prosecute and condemn are God and Christ, and God has already called, justified, and glorified the elect. Thus the future judgment as well as any other potential future threat is removed by God's love freely bestowed through Christ (Rom. 8:30–39). Far from focusing attention on the juridical/future eschatological aspects of justification/righteousness, Paul calls attention to the new standing which has been given in Christ. That new standing both transforms the present and secures the future, so that the future does not need fearful attention in the life of faith.

The "righteousness of God" which has been revealed apart from the Torah (Rom. 1:17; 3:21–22) does not mean that future acquittal is to be grounded on faith, but that a new covenantal relationship with God is now available through faith. The promise to Abraham which did not come through the Torah but has now come through faith is not the acquittal to be pronounced at the end, but the present relationship with God which fulfills promise and removes wrath (Rom. 4:13).

The Unity of Jew and Gentile

One further consideration supports the claim that justification/righteousness is not primarily juridical but rather covenantal/relational. This consideration revolves around the issue of *why* Paul spoke of justification by faith. Is justification by faith the center and heart of Paul's gospel? Or it is primarily polemical? Does Paul introduce justification only in Romans because of the problem of the relationship between Gentile and Jew, and in Galatians because some there sought to impose the Torah as an essential part of the gospel? Some interpreters recognize that Paul might have introduced justification by faith in these two books both because it was central and because of the particular problems in those churches.[9]

One of the major points Paul makes in Romans is that there is no distinction between Jew and Gentile—that both need the Gospel of God's grace and both are equal recipients of his gracious act of salvation in Christ. On the basis of the Torah they would not be equal, for Jew and Gentile are divided by the Torah. The equality and community of Gentile and Jewish believers is a major concern of Paul's also in writing to the Galatians. He found Peter's behavior appalling when he withdrew from table fellowship with Gentile believers in Antioch (Gal. 2:11). He argues that they "are all (children) of God, through faith. . . . There is neither Jew nor Greek, there is neither slave nor free, there is neither male nor female; for you are all one in Christ Jesus" (Gal. 3:26–28).

Krister Stendahl has argued persuasively that this concern to affirm the unity of all in Christ is one of the underlying motivations in Paul's use of justification by faith.[10] That argument has confirmation in Romans 3:27–31, where Paul uses the oneness of God, who is God of Gentiles and Jews as a clenching argument for justification by faith:

> Or is God the God of Jews only? Is he not the God of Gentiles also? Yes, of Gentiles also, since God is one; and he will justify the circumcised on the ground of their faith and the uncircumcised through their faith. (Rom. 3:29–30)

In Romans 4 he attempts to demonstrate that Abraham is the father of all who have faith, Gentile as well as Jew (cf. the similar argument in Gal. 4).

Stendahl may well exaggerate when he calls Romans 1—8 a preface to chapters 9—11, which he says form the center of gravity of the Epistle, but he correctly points to the connection between justification by faith and the issue of equality of Gentile

and Jew and their relationship to each other and to God
(especially in Rom. 3:28–29; 1:16–17). Stendahl can also be
correct when he suggests that "Paul's doctrine of justification
by faith has its theological context in his reflection on the
relation between Jews and Gentiles, and not within the problem of how *man* is to be saved...."[11] If this line of thinking is
correct, then justification by faith answers the question "How
is God's plan for the reconciliation of all humanity to be effected?"
rather than "How can one be acquitted at the last judgment?"
Paul's main concern is how to bring Gentiles as well as Jews
into that relationship with God which is promised in God's call
to Abraham. The chief answer, and the primary meaning of
Jesus' death as a justifying act, is this: Jesus' death is the
inauguration of the new covenant, as it was promised to Abraham
and reaffirmed to Jeremiah. Jesus' death reveals God's righteousness and covenanting grace; it manifests that righteousness
in covenant-making and covenant-keeping to which the "Torah
and prophets bear witness" (Rom. 3:21). That death also elicits
the response of faith and thus completes the basic notion of
covenant: "I will be your God and you shall be my people."

Many recent interpreters have argued that "participatory
categories" play more important roles than juridical or sacrificial categories in Paul's understanding of the saving event.
"Covenant" emphasizes participation in the people of God. Being
"in Christ" provides another metaphor for expressing the relational dimension central to Paul's thinking (see chap. 6). When
Paul speaks of Christ as "our righteousness" (1 Cor. 1:30) and
affirms that "in him we become the righteousness of God" (2
Cor. 5:21), he means that we become related to God as covenanted
people through the event of Jesus Christ. "In Christ Jesus you
are all [children] of God.... For as many of you as were baptized into Christ have put on Christ...[and] are Abraham's
offspring" (Gal. 3:26–29). Against the background of covenantal
theology, Christ is presented as the means by which one becomes
part of God's covenant people: children of God, Abraham's offspring, righteous (i.e., in right relation). Paul is here speaking
especially to Gentile Christians, and his inclusion of them

as "children of God" is extraordinary, confirming again that "justification" is Paul's way of expressing the reality of the one new covenant which God has established with Gentile and Jew alike.

REDEMPTION

In the succinct statement of Romans 3:24–25, Paul speaks of God's justifying grace as being "through the redemption which is in Christ Jesus." Paul does not use the language of redemption as frequently as that of justification, but redemption is nonetheless an expressive word that provides insight into Paul's concept of God's saving activity in Jesus Christ. Conceptually redemption is closely related to another term which Paul uses more frequently and which provides the essential clue to the basic meaning of redemption. That term is "freedom." *To be redeemed is to be set free.*

Interpreters have taken a wide variety of approaches to the term "redemption": (1) It could derive from the idea of a ransoming sacrifice by which the deity is offered a substitute life for the one set free. (2) It could derive from the act of manumitting a slave or the ransoming payment by which a prisoner of war is set free. (3) It could derive from an act of rescue by which captives are set free. Given Paul's grounding in Hebrew tradition, the most likely meaning is that set of covenantal ideas connected with God's redemptive activity on behalf of his covenant people Israel.

God "redeems" Israel from slavery in Egypt (Exod. 6:6), "delivers" them from oppression or danger, guards them as chosen people; because of their refusal to be God's people they are punished with exile in Babylon. God does not cease to be their redeemer but sets them free again to begin anew as covenanted people. Isaiah especially built upon that social and political historical act as he anticipated God's redemption of Israel from the Exile in Babylon. God is Israel's creator and redeemer who will act on Israel's behalf through the political events associated with the rise of Cyrus the Great, who set free captured and exiled peoples including the Jews.

The political and historical dimensions remain strongly attached to the notion of liberation or redemption used in the New Testament. In Luke 24:21 we read, "We had hoped that he was the one to redeem Israel" (cf. the question asked of the risen Jesus: "Lord, will you at this time restore the kingdom to Israel?" [Acts 1:6]).

In its background, then, "redeem" or "liberate" is a quite comprehensive term; originally "political" more than "spiritual" (a rather meaningless distinction in early times), it connoted God's setting the covenant people free from anything that oppressed or that hindered their well-being. Especially significant for the interpretation of Paul is the covenantal context of Exodus and Deutero-Isaiah, in which God is spoken of as exercising power by redeeming or liberating the covenant people.

Paul's fundamental conviction, however, goes beyond that which motivated him earlier in his career. He became convinced that God has established in Jesus Christ a new covenant community made up not only of Jews but of Gentiles as well. Paul's central assertion in Romans, "There is no distinction" between Gentile and Jew, applies to redemption: both Gentile and Jew are liberated from their past in order to be God's people in the present, following God into the future prepared for them. The Exodus motif is obvious, with one major difference—it is not merely the *physical* descendants of Jacob (Israel) but the *spiritual* descendants of Abraham, whether or not they are physical descendants of Jacob, who are included in this new covenant community. Further, as Paul says in Galatians, within the new community all are children of God without distinction; whether previously classified as male or female, Jew or Greek, slave or free, all are now one community in Jesus Christ (Gal. 3:26–29). The newly liberated community has thus been set free from national distinctions and rivalries as well as from its socially determined categories.

Even if the social and political aspects of liberation do not remain central for Paul, at times receding almost to a place of insignificance behind a dominant interest in spiritual libera-

tion, they nevertheless are included in Paul's evangelical proclamation of liberation from sin, the Torah, and death.

Paul's Use of Liberation

"For freedom Christ has set us free" (Gal. 5:1). This seeming
redundancy expresses one of Paul's major concerns not only in
writing to the Galatians, but in his whole theology. Freedom
"is the central theological concept [by which Paul] sums up the
Christian's situation before God as well as in this world."[12]
This theme of freedom is sounded frequently in Romans. But
while Paul's metaphor is political, his emphasis is not upon the
freedom that one has as a right before political authorities or
as a natural potential one has by birth; rather, the freedom of
which he speaks is deliverance from a previous state of internal bondage.

The nature of that deliverance from bondage begins to emerge
as one looks at Paul's statements about the one who has performed
the act of liberation: "Jesus Christ ... gave himself for our sins
to deliver us from the present evil age" (Gal. 1:4). The assertion
that Christ gave himself for our sins reflects the cultic idea of
self-sacrifice, and may be related either to cultic ransoming or
to the notion in Jewish theology that the sufferings of the
righteous may atone for the sins of others.[13] The idea of rescu-
ing from the present evil age, however, comes from a different
line of thought, one which is probably more dominant in Paul's
own mind.

Paul shares the view of Jewish apocalyptic literature that
the present age has come to be dominated by supernatural
powers which hold human life in bondage and which keep humans
separated from God and from the life God intends for them.
Paul reflects such an idea when he reminds the Galatians that
"when we were children, we were slaves to the elemental spirits of the universe" (Gal. 4:3). There is some dispute as to the
meaning of *stoicheia* in this passage. It can mean "basic elements," "fundamental principles," or the "elemental spirits"
which the "syncretistic religious tendencies of later antiquity
associated with the physical elements."[14] The last is most likely

in Paul, who believed that as a result of human sinfulness the world had come under the control of supernatural powers opposed to God and that humans were helpless to destroy those powers or to free themselves from them without the aid of God. God did intervene in Jesus Christ, and triumphed over those forces, setting humans free. Christ took the form of a slave (Phil. 2:7), subjecting himself to those powers which enslave humanity; he let himself be crucified, but through that crucifixion he really deceived and disarmed those powers, for

> God has highly exalted [enthroned] him and bestowed on him the name which is above every name, that at the name of Jesus every knee should bow, in heaven and on earth and under the earth, and every tongue confess that Jesus Christ is Lord....(Phil. 2:9–11)

It follows that if "the rulers of this age understood this [secret and hidden wisdom of God]...they would not have crucified the Lord of glory" (1 Cor. 2:8), for their action led to their defeat. Having now been established as a legitimate and powerful ruler, Christ will continue to exercise his power until the end, "when he delivers the kingdom to God the Father after destroying every rule and every authority and power" (1 Cor. 15:24). When that victory is accomplished, then "creation itself also shall be liberated from the corrupting bondage in which it lies, to attain the freedom which springs from the glory of the children of God."[15]

This mythical language reveals that when Paul is speaking of redemption/liberation he is not making the kind of simple, one-dimensional statement which could be associated with the cultic or commercial ideas noted above. Instead, the term involves a rather comprehensive mythological worldview. I shall return later to some of the implications of that fact in chapter 6. For now, let us keep in mind the simple thought that for Paul, Christ is the one who sets free from whatever powers in the "present age" keep us separated from God and "enslaved" to evil.

A second dimension of liberation is stated in Galatians 4:4–5: "When the time had fully come, God sent forth his Son, born of woman, born under the [Torah], to redeem those who were under the [Torah]." Being under the Torah is part of being under "the elemental spirits of the universe." The Torah is not one of those elemental spirits, but it is utilized by the powers of sin and death. Thus, the Torah is part of the present evil age from which Paul believes humanity is now being liberated in Christ.[16]

The implication is that the Torah did not bring liberation from the evil age—indeed, it functioned within the pattern of enslavement which characterized that age. Nor did the Torah enable one to be renewed by the presence and power of the Spirit so that God's will could come to expression in life. But what the Torah could not do, and what one under the Torah could not do for oneself, has now been done: "For freedom Christ has set us free."

Freedom from the Torah is undoubtedly Paul's most radical teaching, and one that created the most difficulty in the church of his day. Its implications have rarely been accepted in the two thousand–year history of the church. The Torah meant not only rules, but the whole structure of Jewish religious belief and practice. This structure has much to commend it: its generally humanitarian concerns, its high level of morality and piety, its monotheistic belief. Paul was no stranger to the accomplishments of that noblest of religions available. And yet he proclaimed freedom from it in a way that alarmed many of his own day and still alarms those who take religious institutions seriously. Freedom from the Torah in its boldest, starkest terms means freedom from all those structures, rituals, and forms by which Judaism organized its life. Paul's motive was to make Gentile and Jew one, and to expose the life of both Gentile and Jew to the unmerited grace of God. He advocates freedom from religious systems in order that both Gentile and Jew might be free for covenantal faith.[17]

Paul was aware that religion can be an alienating force, indeed, among the most alienating of all human activities. Paul knew the problem in an intensely personal way, and he knew it remained a problem among Jewish and Gentile

believers in Rome. A major reason for his writing to the Romans
was to deal with the divisiveness of the religious positions of
many who promoted their views as identical with God's.

Paul's proclamation is that in Christ all can know the unity
of a new humanity as they come to celebrate the oneness given
to all—Gentile or Jew, male or female, slave or free (Gal. 3:28).
The way out of human alienation was not, in Paul's view, a
triumph of one group over another, but the reconciliation of all
as one new human community. It was that for which he labored
and for which he enlisted the support of the church at Rome.

There is yet another dimension to the liberation which Paul
celebrates: freedom from sin. That dimension finds more explicit
expression in Paul's letter to the Romans than in Galatians:
"You were slaves of sin...but having been liberated from sin
you have become enslaved to righteousness....Now having been
liberated from sin and having become enslaved to God, you
have consecration as your result" (Rom. 6:17, 18, 22, my
translation).

Freedom from sin is related to freedom from the Torah, as
Romans 6:14 makes plain: "For sin will have no dominion over
you, since you are not under [Torah] but under grace." "Sinful
passions" are "aroused by the Torah"; sin finds "opportunity in
the commandment." Even though the Torah itself is not sin,
and even though the commandment is holy and just and good,
and even though the commandment promises life, because of
human weakness in the presence of sin's dominion, the Torah
does not bring life but death, not freedom from sin but slavery
to sin (Rom. 7:5, 8, 12, 10, 13).

But since sin was in the world exercising its death-producing
power before the Torah was given (Rom. 5:12–14), one cannot
identify captivity to sin with captivity to the Torah. The Torah
reckons sin, intensifies it, and even provokes it, but freedom
from the Torah would not amount to freedom from sin. Even if
the Torah were removed, humans would still be "flesh, sold
under the power of sin" (Rom. 7:14, my translation). That situation has not arisen because of the Torah; rather, the Torah
was ineffective because of that situation in which humans already
existed (cf. Gal. 3:21).

How has Christ set humans free from this condition? Again Paul is not expressly clear on the "how." By using the commercial analogy of "sold under the power of sin," Paul may suggest the payment of ransom as a means of setting free—though ransom is not used explicitly. In Romans 7:24 he uses the symbol of "rescue," again suggesting the analogy of the cosmic battle which Christ won in his resurrection. Since sin is in an essential sense a rebellion against or disobedience to God, freeing from sin is freeing from that disobedience or an eliciting of faith(fulness) on the part of the hearer of the gospel. Though these analogies are not easily unified conceptually, each expresses part of Paul's understanding of the human situation in relation to God: from a state of alienation, separation, and rebellion; from a state of disobedience and guilt; from a situation of loss of inner resource to grasp the life God offers, the person of faith is restored to a covenant relationship to God which involves both a new standing and a new understanding.

Sin and death are closely allied in Paul's thinking. To be under the dominion of one is to be under the dominion of the other. Thus liberation from sin is also liberation from death. "Death" does not signify for Paul merely the cessation of earthly existence—that in itself can even be viewed as desirable (see Phil. 1:21). Rather, death signifies the triumph of sin, the destruction of the life which was intended to be lived in relation to God and others, the final reality which nullifies hope for those oppressed by sin and the law. When sin and death are present together, there is no future, only despair that what could have been the fulfillment of divine destiny is lost. Paul believes that the sin and death introduced by Adam into the whole human community belong to the past. In Christ all are given life. The present then is the arena in which the past is being transformed into the future. Death *reigned* but grace and life *will reign*.

Paul's use of sin and death is apocalyptic.[18] Jewish apocalyptic writings made a radical disjuncture between this age and the age to come: to this age belong sin and death, to the age to come belong righteousness and salvation. Paul modifies that dualistic structure and affirms that not only righteousness and grace but in some sense also life have come into this age. A new

creation is occurring; new life is given.[19] That new life is thus
not merely a future hope for individuals but also a present
reality in the human community. As those forces producing
alienation, oppression, and hopelessness are being overcome
within a new covenant community, life is becoming present.
Freedom from death thus includes new life in a reconciled and
reconciling community. Because Paul believes in the coming
triumph of God, he sees all human struggles, including that
between Gentile and Jew or that between Rome and Israel, in
that light. Human action begun in alienation and hate can
only produce death. God's initiation of a new human community has the potential of transforming death into life.

Romans 5:9 suggests that liberation is also from wrath
[=judgment]: "Now that we have been put in a right relation
(with God) at the cost of his (Christ's) blood, much more shall
we be rescued from the wrath" (my translation).[20] The meaning of being "rescued from wrath" is stated in other terms in
Romans 8:1: "There is therefore now no condemnation for those
who are in Christ Jesus." Sin, Torah, judgment, and death are
for Paul all part of one reality from which the person of faith
has been, is being, and will be set free. Sin, Torah, judgment,
and death all belong to the old age which is passing away.
Their opposites belong to the new age which has already begun
through God's act of liberation in Christ and which is on the
verge of coming in its fullness: "...salvation is nearer to us
now than when we first believed; the night is far gone, the day
is at hand" (Rom. 13:11–12).

On the surface Paul's proclamation of freedom seems much
more personal and spiritual than it does social and political.
Sin, death, law, and supernatural powers are the enslaving
forces from which the person of faith is offered freedom. The
paucity in his writings of any overt concern with political events
and political freedom is surprising, especially when one recalls
that it was during his active ministry that the events were
taking place which led to the Jewish wars against Rome in
66–70 and the consequent destruction of the nation and the
temple. Of those matters we learn nothing from Paul.

Precedent for Paul's apparent disengagement from political affairs appears in the mood of much Hellenistic religion and philosophy. For example, Stoic thought tended to concentrate upon the person, not the state, and to preach a kind of personal freedom regardless of the political situation. The interest of philosophy was "decreasingly the freedom of the citizens or the state," and increasingly a "much more radical freedom, namely, that of the individual set apart and under the law of his own nature or of human nature generally."[21] Hellenistic religions also tended to concentrate upon the cultivation of the interior life. Spiritual freedom from sin, concern for immortality, mysticism, ecstasy, and emotionalism engaged the attention of adherents to Hellenistic mysteries much more than politics. Perhaps Paul has been drawn away from the traditional Jewish approach of combining of religion and politics by the mood of his day.

However, while most of Paul's interpreters regard him as having no real interest in political or social issues, the absence of references to political events in Paul's letters does not necessarily mean the absence of concern about them in the context of his ministry. During the period in which both Jesus and Paul lived the Jews were engaged in an intense struggle for political and religious self-definition, and the two aspects were seldom very far apart. In spite of various attempts to show that Jesus himself was a Zealot intent upon overthrowing Roman domination, it is almost a settled conclusion that he was not a political revolutionary, even though crucified as one. But he was not *disengaged*. Zealotism was alienating, hostile, filled with hate, leading toward death. Jesus rejected it not out of indifference and not out of love for Rome, but out of an assessment of its negative consequences for God's people, both internally and externally: "Would that ... today you knew the things that make for peace!" (Luke 19:42).[22] Zealotism was the political equivalent of religious self-righteousness. It elevated the self with its causes and ideals to the status of an idol, and relegated those who disagreed to the kingdom of Satan.

Between the time of Jesus and Paul, the antipathy between Jews and Romans in Palestine grew, as did strife between Jews

and Gentiles throughout the Roman world. The whole situation was exacerbated by inconsistency and by frequent shiftings
of official Roman policy in regard to Jewish matters.[23] Paul
saw nothing to be gained by anti-Roman and anti-Gentile sentiment. He might well have shared such notions prior to his
conversion, for a sort of Zealotic attitude could explain his
persecution of the church, in which he saw an acceptance of
Gentiles and Gentile ways which profoundly disturbed him.
But he did an about-face and undertook a mission to Gentiles,
seeking to overcome the alienation and hatred which divided
humanity.

Paul's letter to the Romans was written on the eve of his
fateful journey to Jerusalem. There his primary purpose would
be to present an offering from Gentile to Jewish Christians— a
dynamic expression of the new human community established
through Jesus Christ in accordance with the promise to Abraham
that in him all nations would be blessed. This letter reveals the
Apostle's anticipation, fears, and hopes as he plans his journey
and his actions. He might well have known that a Zealotic
attitude was beginning to prevail in politically troubled Jerusalem. Not very long before he penned his letter, James and
Peter had faced severe pressure from Zealotic Jews, with the
result that James was beheaded and Peter was forced to flee.
As Paul wrote the letter, he also knew of the controversies
between Gentile and Jewish Christians in Rome (as chapters
14 and 15 clearly reflect); he knew of the tenuous situation of
Christians in Rome as a whole, within a society that was hostile and within a state which (as events of a few years later
proved) had the power to frustrate the fulfillment of the Christian mission. Nero's promotion of Hellenism led to resistance
by a renewed Zealotism in Palestine. The situation of the church
in Rome and of the Jews in Palestine, rather than his lack of
concern with politics, could have led Paul to admonish calm
citizenship and acknowledgment of the legitimate place of political government within God's providence. He might even have
seen the unity of the empire and the relative peace which had
been established by it as providing a hopeful arena for the

proclamation of the unity of humankind under the covenant established in Christ.

There is in all this mix an understandable basis for Paul's seeming disengagement from politics. Yet the disengagement is more apparent than real. On the negative side he offers no solace to those who would identify the cause of God with a program of revolution, nor to those with a sectarian definition of the human community, nor to those with a hatred of others in the name of God. On the positive side, he holds up a vision of a new humanity, one reconciled by God, inclusive of Gentile and Jew, and expressive of a gracious love that binds all together as the one people of God.

A Comprehensive Freedom

Paul intends his proclamation of freedom to be comprehensive, not only in that it is addressed to all but also in that it relates to the total human condition. In other words, Paul understands the freedom given by Christ's act of deliverance to be freedom from everything which thwarts the fulfillment of God's will and keeps human life frustrated. To sum up:

1. The person of faith is delivered from sin—from objective slavery to sin, from alienation, and from consequent subjective compulsion to sin. Positively stated, one is freed for righteousness, for right relations, for doing God's will, freed to realize one's capacity for doing good.

2. The person of faith is freed from Torah—from the external commands and prescriptions of the Torah and from the internal tendency to establish a ground for boasting of one's accomplishments; freed, therefore, from religion as a human way of establishing right relations with God; freed also from rebellion against God, which may be only the obverse side of religion. Positively stated, one is free for faith, for looking to God who delivers one from the deadly cycle of sin, Torah, and more sin.

3. The person of faith is freed from wrath—from the objective situation of condemnation because of wrongdoing and from the subjective situation of guilt and consequent fear. Positively

stated, one is free for peace with God, for hope, for rejoicing "in our hope of sharing in the glory of God" (Rom. 5:2).

4. The person of faith is freed from death—from the objective situation of confronting the end of life and from the subjective power of inner corruption. Positively stated, one is free for the life of obedience which the Spirit empowers, free for the continuously renewing presence and power of God who promises life and fulfills that promise.

Paul's covenantal thinking is apparent in his association of that freedom with adoption, an association he expresses in Galatians 4:5: Christ came "to redeem those who were under the [Torah], so that we might receive adoption as [children]. And because you are [children], God has sent the Spirit...." Again Paul uses the covenant idea of adoption to express God's grace in Jesus Christ. God intends and promises Abraham descendants, not slaves. The Torah produces slaves, but the gift of God in Christ is the freedom of adoption. The gift of adoption has begun to be realized through the personal address to God inspired by the Spirit, "Abba! Father!" (Rom. 8:15). The complete fulfillment still lies in the future, and the whole creation yearns for its realization, for in that realization the purpose of God for creation itself will be realized, and the "bondage to decay" will give way to the "glorious liberty of the children of God" (Rom. 8:21).

SACRIFICE

A third important term Paul uses in Romans 3:24–25 to speak of God's saving act in Jesus Christ is "expiation," or "means of removing sin." This terminology clearly derives from the sacrificial practices established by the Torah: "... God put [Christ] forward as a means of expiating sin through his blood."[24]

Paul found sacrificial concepts already in use in the church for interpreting the meaning of Jesus' death, and he sometimes uses them, but those concepts do not dominate his understanding of the cross. The term translated here as "means of expiating sin" (Greek: *hilasterion*) is nowhere else used by Paul; it probably derives from church tradition. It and its cognates are used by other New Testament writers with the meaning "mercy seat" (Heb. 9:5), "to make expiation" (Heb. 2:17), "expiation" or "propitiation," in the KJV (1 John 2:2, 4:10), "be merciful" (Luke 18:13). The word itself is thus rather ambiguous. Paul could mean that Jesus is a *sacrifice* for sin, or the *place* where the blood of sacrifice is sprinkled, or a *means of rendering God favorable* to sinful humanity, or a *means by which God purges* human sinfulness. The added phrase, "in his blood" or "by his blood" leaves no doubt about the sacrificial meaning of the term. Since Paul uses the word only here, we would do well to ask what other indications there are that he thought of Jesus' death as a sacrificial one, and how he understood that sacrifice.

Sacrifice and Communion

The best clue for understanding the meaning of sacrifice in Paul is found in his use of the traditional sayings concerning the Lord's Supper, which reflect a sacrificial understanding of Jesus' death and associate that sacrifice with covenantal notions: "This cup is the new covenant in my blood" (1 Cor. 11:25). Paul's interpretation of the symbols of cup and bread is revealed in the way he changes the traditional usage of them. In 1 Corinthians 11:23–25 he quotes the traditional formula which places the word about the "bread" before the word about the "cup," but in 1 Corinthians 10:16 Paul refers to the cup before the bread[25] in a passage in which he is not quoting tradition but interpreting it. The change in order signifies an important point of interpretation: the two elements of the Lord's Supper are not merely parallel references to Christ's sacrificial death, as they probably are in the Synoptic tradition,[26] and perhaps in the tradition Paul knew.

Paul's interpretation reflected in his reversal of the order in 1 Corinthians 10:16 connects the sacrificial element with the covenantal element much more explicitly than any of his other texts, and shows that for him the chief importance in the Lord's Supper is its establishment of the covenant community. "The cup of blessing which we bless, is it not a participation [*koinonia*] in the blood of Christ?" The sacrificial death of Christ is for

Paul the establishment of a covenant through him, so that those who partake are linked through him with God as God's own people. The sacrifice of Christ is thus paralleled to the blood of the sacrificial animal with which the Mosaic covenant was sealed. The tradition Paul quotes makes that connection explicit: "the new covenant in my blood." If Paul (and perhaps the tradition, too) has in mind the event described in Exodus 24, then he may think of the accompanying burnt offerings and peace offerings which were made before the "blood of the covenant" was thrown upon the people. The ideas of purification and consecration thus would be included in his understanding of Jesus' death: that death is atoning in the sense that it is the means which God provides for the removal of human sinfulness which separates from God; it is a consecration in that it makes the recipients "holy" or set apart as a people for God.[27] This interpretation suggests, then, the notion of expiation (removal of sin) rather than propitiation (the satisfaction of God's justice or the removal of his wrath by a propitiatory sacrifice).

But Paul's main emphasis, at least in the Corinthian context, is upon the community as the body of Christ. This emphasis is seen in his reversal of the order of the elements in 1 Corinthians 10:16:

> The cup of blessing which we bless, is it not a participation [*koinonia*] in the blood of Christ? The bread which we break, is it not a participation in the body of Christ? Because there is one [loaf], we who are many are one body.

It also appears in his admonitions in 1 Corinthians 11:26–34:

> Any one who eats and drinks without discerning the body eats and drinks judgment upon himself. (vs. 29)

Paul interprets the meaning of the community in terms of the Lord's Supper.[28] The sacrifice of Christ not merely brings a person into an individual relation to Christ; it also establishes the covenant community of God's people. Paul interprets the traditional saying "This is my body" to refer to the church. "Discerning the body" means to perceive the connection between belonging to Christ and belonging to the church; failure to appreciate one's connectedness to the covenant community shows that one does not belong to Christ, and thus subjects one to judgment. Paul is upset with the Corinthians not because they are defiling a holy rite, but because in disregarding their common unity in Christ as members of his body they are fragmenting that covenant community which God had established through Jesus' sacrificial death.[29] The Corinthian enthusiasts who liked to congratulate themselves on their knowledge and their spiritual attainments needed to be reminded that they had not arrived at such a state of spiritual perfection that they could ignore without peril their need for the renewal of the covenant between themselves and God symbolized by the Lord's Supper; nor could they ignore their need for and responsibility within the community which draws its nurture from a common participation in the one body of Christ.

Thus, Paul's distinctive contribution as he interprets the tradition of the Lord's Supper concerns his understanding of covenant. New covenant ideas were already associated with the Lord's Supper in the tradition Paul received; Paul emphasized the communal aspects of that covenant and used the Lord's Supper to interpret the meaning and necessity of community. He anticipated that interpretation by his comments in 1 Corinthians 10:16–17, and in chapter 12 he built upon it, further explaining what the body of Christ formed through the new covenant in his blood meant for the Corinthian church.

This interpretation provides the best clue to the meaning of blood in Romans 5:9:

> Therefore now that we have been justified [i.e., set in a right relationship] by his blood, how much more certainly shall we be saved through him from the wrath. (my translation)

If I am correct in arguing that justification/righteousness is a covenantal term, with the dominant meaning of "set in a right relationship with God," and if I am correct in associating blood in 1 Corinthians 10–11 with the sealing of the covenant between God and humans, then the meaning of the present passage becomes apparent: it is through Jesus Christ, through his life given in death, that the new covenant relationship is established.

Sacrifice and Justification

The striking similarity between Romans 3:25 and 5:9 shows the close connection between justification and expiation:

"... expiation by his blood. ... " (3:25)
"... justified by his blood. ...." (5:9)

Are "justification" and "expiation" synonymous in Paul's vocabulary? Since Paul uses expiation only once (Rom 3:25), and since he is probably quoting a traditional formula, we may rightly conclude that the term is not a part of his own usual mode of expression. Justification/righteousness, however, is distinctively Pauline terminology. Are justification and expiation then interchangeable? In one sense, yes: both have to do with the benefits of Christ's death, and the benefits primarily center on the relationship with God spoken of with covenant terminology. They differ in the way in which they image those benefits. "Justify" is primarily personal; it refers to the establishment of a covenant relation with God in which one knows one's own identity and responsibility. "Expiation" is more cultic and at least potentially impersonal: its imagery is that of purging or removing sin, the result of which is that the person whose sins are removed may now stand without fear in the presence of God. The imagery of purification (including cleansing, washing) is not dominant in Paul's rhetoric,[30] though it has foundations both in Hebrew Scriptures and in early church tradition. The cultic vocabulary of purification is far less important to Paul than the vocabulary of personal commitment. Inasmuch as "blood" is a cultic term, Paul finds little occasion to use it, and then primarily in passages based upon traditional language. Paul's own preference is for language dominated by the active, volitional element (faith, trust, obedience) rather than by the passive, cultic elements.

One could, of course, argue that since cultic removal of sin in Israelite and early Christian understanding involves repentance and personal forgiveness, it too is not merely an impersonal, mechanical procedure. However, there is *some* reason why the language of forgiveness finds so little place in Paul, and the reason may well be that in his understanding forgiveness implies a "letting off" more than a renewal; for him the cultic expression may suggest the same notion.[31]

A Sacrifice "for Us"

Finally, we need to inquire whether and in what sense the language of sacrifice may be seen behind Paul's assertion that Christ died "for us":

> Christ died for the ungodly. (Rom. 5:6)
> While we were yet sinners Christ died for us. (Rom. 5:8)
> One has died for all. (2 Cor. 5:14)
> ... one for whom Christ died. (Rom. 14:15; cf. 1 Cor. 8:11)
> ... who died for us. (1 Thess. 5:10)[32]

The question of the meaning of "for us" is a much disputed one, and the answer has an enormous impact upon one's understanding of Paul's theology (or vice versa). Much of traditional theology has interpreted "for us" in a substitutionary manner: "Christ died for us" means that he died as a substitutionary sacrifice (his death "instead of ours"); that sacrifice was propitiatory in that it made an offering to God which was necessary for the forgiveness of sins; that sacrifice has removed God's wrath which was justifiably directed toward sinful humanity.[33]

Leon Morris contends that "for (*huper*) us" is no different from "instead of (*anti*) us," and that the substitutionary sense is found equally in both expressions.[34] Harald Riesenfeld too thinks that "the sense 'on behalf of' is something very close to 'in the place of,' 'instead of,' 'in the name of.'"[35]

"Very close to," yes; "identical to," no. The New Testament passages Morris points to (1 Tim. 2:6 and Mark 10:45) for proof of the equation of *huper* and *anti* are post-Pauline and show further theological development in the direction of substitionary sacrifice. Morris finds evidence in some Pauline passages for the identification of *huper* and *anti* as an argument for the substitutionary sense of *huper*. An examination of those passages fails to convince. According to 1 Corinthians 15:29, people in Corinth were being baptized "for [*huper*] the dead." It is the case that the living were being baptized and the dead were not; but the primary point is not the substitution of one for the other but rather that the one is doing something on "behalf of" the other, "for the advantage of" the other, "for the benefit of" the other. In Philemon 13 Paul says he would like to have Onesimus serve him "for" (*huper*) Philemon. Perhaps "instead of" is the natural translation; however, Paul does not suggest that although Philemon *ought* to do the service himself, he can send Onesimus as a substitute; he means that no more than he means that he himself is a substitute "for Christ" in 2 Corinthians 5:20. Representation, acting in the name of another, rather than substitution, is the correct meaning.

Morris also contends that *huper* has a substitutionary meaning in John 10:11 and 11:50; and Romans 16:4. An examination of those passages fails to support his contention. In John 10:11 "the good shepherd lays down his life for (*huper*) the sheep." One could argue that unless the shepherd puts his life on the line, the sheep might be destroyed, but his life is not a *substitution* for theirs. One sees here the evident limitation on any metaphor. John 11:50 comes close to suggesting substitution: "one man should die for (*huper*) the people" rather than "that the whole nation should perish." Perhaps Johannine irony means just that, though the more likely ironic meaning is that Jesus' death is for the well-being of the people in a way his enemies could not understand, rather than that his death is a substitutionary sacrifice "in the place of" theirs. Romans 16:4 is the least convincing—and the only Pauline!—passage cited by Morris: Prisca and Aquila "risked their necks for (*huper*) my life." It was on Paul's behalf that they took their risks, but not as a substitute for him. He might have died if they had not been willing to do so, just as the sheep might have died if the shepherd had not been willing to risk death, but in neither case is the one "death" a substitute for the other. If these passages demonstrate anything, it is the weakness of Morris' position!

Paul clearly understands Christ's death as being "for us" in the sense that it is "for our benefit," but how and why does his death benefit the believer? Whether or not Jesus' death was viewed by Paul and/or the pre-Pauline church according to the model of the suffering servant of Deutero-Isaiah is a much controverted issue. In Isaiah 52—53 the servant's suffering is "for our transgressions" and "for our iniquities." Many argue that the "for our sins" of 1 Corinthians 15:3, which Paul says he derives from tradition, is based on that passage. Certainly there is a conceptual analogy between the two regardless of the question of the literary influence: just as the servant is recognized by others after his suffering to have benefited them by that very suffering, so Christ is seen after his suffering to have died "for us," that is, "for our benefit." His death has reference and relation to "our sins," so that his self-giving is seen as a sacrifice "for us." The prepositional phrase here does not imply substitution; that would require a different proposition: *anti*, "instead of." But one would probably be correct in seeing that the contexts of the phrase invite or even imply the metaphor of sacrifice as a way of understanding the meaning of Jesus' death. To push beyond that point and to attribute to Paul a substitutionary doctrine of the atonement on the basis of his use of *huper* would stretch his language beyond his apparent intent.[36]

The language of sacrifice is explicit in 1 Corinthians 5:7: "For Christ our passover lamb has already been slaughtered."[37] Paul offers no argument or interpretation of this identification of Jesus with the passover lamb; probably it was a "stock tradition" in the Christian community which the Corinthians would readily understand.[38] The Passover festival in Israelite practice was preeminently an occasion emphasizing covenant community; the ritual focused attention upon the past when they were identified as God's people and as God's people were led out of Egyptian bondage to freedom. Paul uses the metaphor here to remind the Corinthians whose they are and the kind of community they should consequently be. Although he does not explain the metaphor, he evidently has in mind that the community owes its origin and thus its allegiance to the crucified and exalted Jesus.

In Paul, ideas of substitution and propitiation certainly are not dominant in understanding the meaning of sacrifice, just

as they are not in Hebrew Scriptures. Such ideas are not necessarily ruled out, but nowhere are they necessarily the correct
interpretation. Rather, sacrifice has its home within the covenant context and derives its meaning therefrom.

Paul, then, is much more likely to mean "expiation" (removal
of sin) than "propitiation" (removal of wrath) in Romans 3:25.
That is not to say Paul has no notion of God's wrath; he clearly
does, as we see in Romans 1:18, 2:8, etc. Sacrifice, however, is
not presented as the means of appeasing wrath. Paul does not
speak of God turning and venting wrath upon Christ instead of
upon the sinner; he does not say God accepts Christ's death as a
sacrifice instead of ours. Expiation involves the removal of
wrath only in this sense: in removing sin from human life, it
removes the barrier of alienation and rebellion which in Paul's
view are constitutive of sin. With the condition of human life
thus changed (expiation), the occasion for wrath (judgment) is
likewise changed. If the interpretation suggested above is correct, the sacrifice is God's way of dealing with sin (removing
it), not Christ's way of appeasing God's wrath.

Paul views the death of Jesus as that event in which God
expressed grace which calls all humankind to relationship. It
is the basis and the occasion for the formation of a covenant
community of God's people: "I will be your God, and you shall
be my people." As the demonstration of God's grace, which is at
the same time "the grace of our Lord Jesus Christ," it is like a
sacrifice in which sin is removed and a right relationship
established.[39]

Paul's Focus: Covenant

If in my attempt to interpret Paul's theology I have dealt at
length with his understanding of God's saving act in Christ,
this does not mean Paul's own main concern in this section of
the letter is to explicate the meaning of that event as the remedy to human sinfulness. The saving act is presented in the
briefest fashion in Romans 3:25–26, using for the most part
traditional language without any real explanation. Christ's
death as the saving event is thus presumed more than it is

developed. The real focus of Paul's concern is upon the way God has covenanted with Gentile and Jew on the same basis, by grace through faith.

That point is clear when one notices how the formulaic statements are set in the context of the assertions that there is no distinction between Gentile and Jew: Romans 3:22 makes it plain that in regard to rightness with God "there is no distinction"; 3:29–30 follows up the summary of God's act in Christ with the further assertion that since God is one, there is no distinction between Gentile and Jew, and that faith is the means by which all are set right with God; 4:1–25 presents the example of Abraham, who is the father of all who believe, whether Gentile or Jew.

To point out Paul's concern with the issue of Gentile and Jew in this context is not to deny that he is vitally interested in God's act of salvation in Jesus Christ; certainly it is not to suggest that Paul's interest in the theology of the cross is minimal —far from it, as my explication of that theology has attempted to show. But it is important—more important than has generally been recognized—to see how Paul's theology of the cross is utilized in his solution of concrete social and religious problems within the human community.

As Paul makes clear in writing to the Corinthians, Jews have no reason to celebrate with religious pride their superiority over the Gentile; nor do Gentiles have reason to vaunt their intellectual virtues over the Jews. The crucified Messiah makes all one; the cross renders human religious or cultural accomplishments null and void as measurements of human worth. God graciously gives the new covenant in Jesus Christ to all alike; thus all alike may respond in grateful and obedient faith to the offer of life in a new covenant community in which God is binding all humanity together.

Abraham as Ancestor of Jew and Gentile

To support his claim that in salvation as well as in sinfulness there is no real distinction between Gentile and Jew, Paul appeals to two basic elements of Jewish thought: monotheism, the foundational theological affirmation; and Abraham, the one in whom the race is founded. Monotheism is appealed to briefly but cogently in Romans 3:27–30; Abraham is treated more fully in Romans 4:1–25, which thematically refers back to and justifies the assertions of the earlier verses.

Paul argues in Romans 3:27–30 that if righteousness were to be gained through the Torah, then righteousness would be available to Jews only, for the Torah was given through Moses only to them. That fact could be taken to mean either that a different god is god of Gentiles, or that God is one but partial to Jews. Paul will accept neither of these alternatives. The first denies a fundamental tenet of Judaism ("The LORD our God is one," Deut. 6:4), while the second is an expression of the arrogance of which at one time Paul might have been guilty, but which he now rejects as antithetical to his own call as an apostle. The one God deals with all alike: all are justified through faith.[40] Such a claim, Paul asserts, does not deny the validity of the Torah; rather, it confirms it, as the example of Abraham clearly shows, for in the Torah itself Abraham is said to be right with God through faith.

In Romans 4:1–25, where Paul argues for his claim that Abraham's righteousness was based on faith, he makes four main points. First, in 4:1–8 Paul shows that Scripture confirms what he claims, for it says that Abraham's faith "was reckoned to him as righteousness" (4:3, quoting Gen. 15:6). I have dealt with this passage above in discussing whether Paul thinks juridically when using the term "justification." I have argued that covenantal rather than juridical ideas are dominant, and that Paul comes close to equating justification, forgiveness, and covenant, so that Abraham's being right with God amounts to forgiveness, or the restoration of the alienated to a position of harmony with God. Had it been a matter of Abraham's deed establishing his righteousness, then, Paul says, he would have something to boast about; as it is, his situation is comparable to that of David whose sin was forgiven (Rom. 4:6–8, quoting Ps. 32:1–2) and who thus is the recipient of sheer grace.

Second, Paul argues that the blessing of right relationship and forgiveness is intended for Gentiles as well as for Jews (Rom. 4:9–12). His argument is that God's blessing took place before Abraham had been circumcised, and thus circumcision could not be in any way the basis for it. Circumcision was received by Abraham as a distinguishing mark, a confirmation of the right relationship which faith established even while he was uncircumcised. This sequence was purposeful on God's part, for it allowed Abraham to be the ancestor not only of Jews, but of Gentiles who, like Abraham, have faith in God. Since it was Abraham's faith and not his circumcision that was decisive, those circumcised should not rely upon the confirming sign but rather follow the real example of Abraham, his faith; further, they should recognize their kinship with all who share Abraham's faith, whether circumcised or not.

The other side of this point is that the uncircumcised (Gentiles) have no advantage over the circumcised. If in writing to the Galatians Paul seemed to suggest that circumcision is not merely unnecessary but also detrimental, he avoids that interpretation here. Under the pressure of the intense Galatian debate about circumcising Gentiles, Paul did say derogatory things about this sacred Jewish rite. In writing to the Romans that debate is in the background. Here he puts faith as the primary quality, but there is no contradiction between being circumcised and having faith. Both here and in Romans 11 Paul removes the ground from under those Gentile believers who are disparaging Jews and Jewish believers in Christ. Abraham is the ancestor of both Jew and Gentile.

Third, Paul disputes the logic of the claim that the promise to Abraham was anticipatory of the Torah and in actuality based on it, as some Jewish interpreters claimed (Rom. 4:13–15. See the quotation from Ecclesiasticus p. 00). Paul argues that the way of faith is to be the way of all whether circumcised or not. Since righteousness is pronounced on the basis of faith before anything else was possible, Torah and circumcision (which both come later) cannot be inserted as the basis of that relationship. Paul regards the originating promises of Genesis 12 as the foundation and summation of all other promises; thus the promises of Genesis 15, 17, and 22 cannot mean that the promise is conditional on Abraham's circumcision or his obedience to commands.

To attempt to base the promise upon the later Torah is to make faith empty and the promise void, for two implied reasons. First, if the promise depended upon the Torah, the situation would be hopeless, for the Torah brings condemnation; it condemns transgressions and thus produces wrath, that objective condition of standing on the negative side of God's promise of life. As Paul sees it, grace involves promise and faith, whereas Torah involves demand and performance. For Paul, therefore, hope is grounded in grace, not in the Torah. Second, since the Torah (and its requirement of circumcision) relates to Jews only, to base the promise on the Torah would constrict God's grace and promise to Abraham. Paul understands Abraham's being the father of "many nations" to include Gentiles as well as Jews: "many" is understood Hebraically to mean "all": Abraham's heirs include the whole world of Gentiles and Jews.

Finally, Paul argues that Abraham's faith is analogous to faith in the resurrection of Jesus (Rom. 4:16–25). Abraham faced a situation in which faith seemed to be nullified by death. It is true that Abraham was not dead, but as far as the possibility of producing heirs in accord with the promise was concerned, "his own body... was already dead because he was about a hundred years old" (4:19, my translation). Life by him from Sarah's barren womb was as hopeful as life from the tomb of Jesus. But Abraham considered that situation in faith, and did not waver in his conviction that God was still fully able to do what he had promised. What was written about Abraham is thus applicable equally, and was indeed intended to apply equally, to those who still believe in the one who brings life out of death.

Paul's appeal to the analogous experience of Abraham may be put in a broader perspective. Abraham's special importance for Paul is seen in the fact that Paul used Abraham more extensively and positively than any other figure except Jesus.

Abraham is for Paul the key person in Scripture, an unambiguously positive figure whose response to God's initiating grace is always that of faith. In him Paul finds embodied that relationship with God which has come to fruition in Jesus Christ. Grace and faith, not Torah and circumcision, are the essential ingredients in the relation of God and humankind; and those realities are manifested in the patriarchal beginnings of God with his people.[41] In Romans 4 and Galatians 3 Paul engages in his most vigorous attempt to justify his doctrine of justification by faith through appeal to Scripture. In each instance he does so by appealing to the scriptural protrayal of Abraham.

Paul's appeal to Abraham is not accidental; Abraham was used in both Palestinian and Hellenistic Judaism in Paul's time as the great example of right relation with God. For example, the apocryphal book of Ecclesiasticus (or Wisdom of Jesus Ben Sirach) says of Abraham:

> Abraham was the great father of a multitude of nations,
>   and no one has been found like him in glory;
> he kept the law of the Most High,
>   and was taken into covenant with him;[42]
> he established the covenant in his flesh,
>   and when he was tested he was found faithful.
> Therefore the Lord assured him by an oath
>   that the nations would be blessed through his posterity;[43]
> that he would multiply him like the dust of the earth,
>   and exalt his posterity like the stars,
> and cause them to inherit from sea to sea
>   and from the River to the ends of the earth. (44:19–21, RSV
>   Apocrypha)

Jewish lore developed this tradition even more, especially focusing upon Abraham's sacrifice of Isaac as an exemplification of his unwavering trust and fidelity.[44] Some Rabbinic passages link the deliverance from Egypt with Abraham. This linkage may be expressed in terms of Abraham's deeds:

> R. Banaah says: "Because of the merit which Abraham their father did [bizekut mitsvah], I will divide the sea for them."[45]

It may be expressed in terms of his faith:

> [R.] Shema'yah says: "The faith with which their father

> Abraham believed in Me is deserving that I should divide the sea for them."[46]

Or it may be expressed in terms of God's promise to Abraham:

> R. Eleazar . . . says: Because of the merit [*bizekut*] of our father Abraham did God bring Israel out of Egypt, as it is said: "For He remembered His holy word unto Abraham His servant," and, "He brought forth His people with joy." (Ps. 105:42f)[47]

It is clear from such passages that God's covenant promises to Abraham played a large role in Jewish reflection upon their identity and history as a people. Paul does not make explicit mention of God's *covenant* with Abraham, but refers rather constantly instead to God's *promise* to him. That fact is probably due to the general tendency by Paul's time to identify "covenant" with the terms or stipulations of the covenant (i.e., with Torah), or perhaps with circumcision as the sign of the covenant. The quotation from Ecclesiasticus makes this identification, possibly deriving it from the priestly account in Genesis 17:9–14, where covenant seems to be identified alternately with God's promise to Abraham and with circumcision. Paul omits those passages which suggest the importance of circumcision within the context of the covenant.

Whether or not Paul thought explicitly in terms of covenant when speaking of Abraham, he makes use of what scholars today call the promissory covenant which God established with Abraham. Paul emphasizes that Abraham would receive his promised inheritance on the basis of God's gift alone: "The promise to Abraham and his descendants...did not come through the [Torah] but through the righteousness of faith" (Rom. 4:13; cf. Gal. 3:18: "God gave it [the inheritance] to Abraham by a promise").

Paul obviously has in mind passages from the Genesis account of Abraham, as well as some of the Jewish lore about Abraham. According to the Genesis account, God called Abraham and gave him promises. There is nothing in Genesis to suggest that those promises were elicited by Abraham's actions or character— they were, as Paul says, given ("graced") to him. In the various instances in Genesis in which the covenant with Abraham is

made and the promises given, the promises include (1) descendants as innumerable as the stars in the sky (Gen. 15:5) or as
the dust of the earth (Gen. 13:16) comprising many nations
[= Gentiles, 17:4]; (2) a land which will be in the possession of
his descendants forever (17:8); (3) a "blessing" which will be
realized by many nations [= Gentiles, 12:3]; (4) the very presence of the covenanting God ("I will be their God" [Gen. 17:8];
"I will establish my covenant ... to be God to you and to your
descendants after you" [17:7]).

Paul utilizes those promises selectively in ways that support
his conviction that in Christ God is fulfilling them through
inaugurating a new covenant which embraces both Gentile
and Jew.

1. The promise of descendants is fulfilled through those who
share Abraham's faith; they are his children and God's children. Abraham is the "father of all who have faith," whether
they are circumcised (Jews) or uncircumcised (Gentiles) (Rom.
4:11–12). Paul does not mention Isaac by name in Romans 4,
demonstrating that his interest is not in the past historical
fulfillment of that promise but in its present applicability to
the unity of Gentile and Jewish believers.[48]

2. Significantly Paul does not mention the promise of land to
Abraham, in keeping with his universalizing of the promises
and the hope that attaches to them. He transforms the promise
of land as he emphasizes that Abraham's seed will inherit the
whole world (Rom. 4:13). For Paul, that inheritance now belongs
to Christ, who is the eschatological heir of all things; for the
seed of Abraham *is* Christ and those who belong to him (Gal.
3:16,29).

3. The "blessing" which God pronounces upon Abraham Paul
implicitly understands as the blessing of forgiveness which is
pronounced upon the circumcised and the uncircumcised (Rom.
4:6–9). In Galatians 3:6–9 that understanding is more explicit:
Scripture "preached the gospel beforehand to Abraham," the
gospel of God's acceptance of all those whose faith is like that of
Abraham.

4. Implicit in all of Paul's writing is the conviction that the

covenanting God who promised Abraham to be the God of
Abraham's decendants has now in Christ chosen anew; that
new people is made up of circumcised and uncircumcised, of
Jew and Gentile, of slave and free, of male and female. None of
those ordinary distinctions either qualifies or disqualifies one.
Faith is the only identifying criterion of those for whom God is
God. Faith itself is sufficient indication that God's electing
grace is present, creating a people for God who are Abraham's
real descendants. Such action is nothing less than bringing life
out of death (Rom.4:16-25).

Conclusion

Romans 3:21—4:25 often seems confusing to ordinary readers. Paul uses a vocabulary which confounds by its strangeness,
he apparently takes liberties with the text of Genesis, and he
reflects concepts about which we know little. Scholars do not
agree on how to interpret this point or that, and there appears to
be no way to resolve their differences.

In the midst of such confusion it will be helpful to remember
that Paul's basic convictions are actually quite simple and may
be easily grasped by any reader. One can summarize in two
words the convictions which underlie what Paul says here:
grace and *faith*.

Grace is for Paul the primary reality of God's dealings with
humankind. Grace is a personal and relational word which
expresses God's goodwill and helpfulness toward humanity. For
Paul, God's grace is not generated by God's act in Christ, as
though without Christ's sacrifice God would be wrathful; rather,
God's gracious favor is expressed through that act, as God seeks
to overcome all that alienates human life and diminishes human
well-being. Because human existence is fundamentally relational, and because the possibility of mutually satisfying
covenantal relationships is given with human existence, life is
essentially good.

Grace is prior to human alienation and wrongdoing, so that
sin is a denial of grace, living as though grace were not a reality.
Grace is thus not *ad hoc*, not an expedient God resorts to when

all else has failed. Grace is fundamental to God's character from beginning to end; as such it is extended to all, and its effectiveness is known to all who will receive it.

Faith is the recognition and reception of grace. Faith sees life as a gift of God's grace, and seizes upon that gift in gratitude. Faith sees the cross itself as God's gift. What could be seen as a tragedy, as a miscarriage of justice, even as a justifiable execution of a troublemaker, is perceived through faith as paradoxically a gift of grace itself. Faith rejoices in the miracle that the cross is followed by resurrection, that life comes out of death because God is a God of grace. Faith rejoices in the liberating power which sets free, a power which miraculously is present even when death makes its ultimate assault on that freedom.

Faith responds to grace and acknowledges that faith itself has been made possible by the grace which has invaded the human realm with the power of new life. Faith accepts that new life within covenant relationships and lives it out in community with others.

Thus justification is by grace through faith: God's grace acts to set humans in a right, covenantal relation with God and with others; in faith—in acceptance, trust, and commitment of self—that new covenantal definition of life is accepted with rejoicing. Salvation—wholeness, completion of life—is the comprehensive term to describe what happens in human community as a consequence.

5

The New Covenant as Grace and Peace for All

(Romans 5)

Interpreters have long debated the place of Romans 5 in Paul's overall plan for the letter. Does this chapter sum up what has gone before, begin a new major section which moves from justification (the beginning of a new life) to sanctification (the realization in personal life of the results of justification), or serve as a bridge between two major sections?

A connection with Romans 1:18 — 4:25 is seen in the opening phrase, which points back to what precedes and assumes the completion of a prior point: therefore, "since we are justified ..." (Rom. 5:1). The word "justified" itself makes connection with the foregoing discussion (cf. 1:18; 2:13; 3:4, 20, 21–31; 4:1). Further, within the chapter there is considerable reiteration of two themes found in 1:18—4:25: the magnitude of human sin and helplessness which made God's act so astounding, and the wrath (judgment) of God which deservedly falls upon human sinfulness.

On the other hand, there are disjunctions between chapter 5

and the preceding section. Some themes have been dropped: Paul's stress on the distinction between *knowing* and *doing* God's will; his emphasis upon the lack of distinction between Gentile and Jew, which my analysis of the preceding chapters has especially emphasized; and his enumeration of the particular sinful human acts. Several themes absent from earlier chapters are introduced: peace, reconciliation, rejoicing in hope, the gift of the Spirit, Adam as contrasted with Christ, the increase in human sin as a consequence of the Torah, and hope for the future. Some of these new themes do reflect back upon earlier themes and could be said to be mere changes in vocabulary (Adam, peace with God), while some anticipate themes to be returned to and developed more extensively later (Spirit, hope for the future, connection between the Torah and sin).

From these considerations, I believe one is justified in speaking of chapter 5 as a "bridge": it forms a transition not only in thought, but also in mood, though not as completely as was suggested by the traditional shift from "sin" to "salvation" (see Rom. 6; 7). My analysis will divide the chapter into two major parts: verses 1–11 and 12–21.

RECONCILIATION AND HOPE (Romans 5:1–11)

Reconciliation

In his succinct statement in Romans 3:24–25 Paul speaks of God's saving act in terms which I have interpreted primarily in covenantal/relational rather than cultic, forensic, or commercial terms. Covenantal interpretation finds support in the new term Paul introduces in chapter 5: "reconciliation." Although Paul uses reconciliation infrequently, the ideas involved in it may be Paul's most creative and original linguistic expression of the saving act.[1] Along with "justification/righteousness," the concept of reconciliation in the New Testament is almost entirely limited to Paul and Deutero-Pauline literature.

Paul makes special use of reconciliation in Romans 5:10–11 and 2 Corinthians 5:16–21. The major theme of Romans 5:1–11 is assurance for the future, assurance which is affirmed by the love of God revealed in the self-giving of Jesus. This amazing

gift of God is placed in contrast with the conditions of those to
whom it was given:

> ... we were still weak. (5:6)
> ... Christ died for the ungodly. (5:6)
> ... while we were yet sinners. (5:8)
> ... while we were enemies. (5:10)

The change in the human condition is expressed in terms of
relationship:

> ... we have been set in a right relationship by faith. (5:1, my
> translation)
> ... we have peace with God. (5:1)
> ... God's love [for us] has been poured [out] into our hearts. (5:5)
> ... we were reconciled. (5:10)
> ... we rejoice in God. (5:11)

The relationship with God had been one of enmity, but now is
one of peace; it had been one of alienation and fear, but now is
one of rejoicing in the presence of the other.

In 2 Corinthians 5:16–21 Paul speaks of his own ministry
under the new covenant as one of reconciliation. That ministry
is essentially dependent upon the act of God in Christ, reconciling the world to himself. Paul is engaged in proclamation because
he is convinced that "one has died on behalf of [huper, for the
benefit or advantage of] all." As a consequence of that death,
all have died in so far as they have come to live no longer for
themselves but for him who on their behalf died and was raised
(2 Cor. 5:14–15). Reconciliation is thus associated with the idea
of dying and rising with Christ (cf. Rom. 6:1–11; Gal.2:20). In
verse 17 salvation is expressed as being "in Christ" and as
being a "new creation"; in verse 21 as well as in verses 14–15
sacrificial ideas are used.

Although the term "reconciliation" does not derive directly
from Hebrew Scripture, it expresses the personal quality of
Israel's covenant relationship with God. Reconciliation implies
the restoration of a previous condition and as such builds upon
the idea of a covenant within which God and Israel once lived
in a harmony which was subsequently disrupted. One of the
most moving models of changing relationship may be seen in

Hosea: God betrothed Israel in faithfulness, but though God remained faithful, Israel became "adulterous" and pursued other lovers (gods); God is depicted as torn between love and hate for faithless Israel (Hos. 9:15)—in fierce anger God could, "like a lion," tear Israel to pieces (5:14), but God's heart recoils against that destruction and grows "warm and tender"; God, who is not like humans, will not come to destroy (11:8–9); rather,

> I will heal their faithlessness;
>   I will love them freely,
>   for my anger has turned from them. (Hos.14:4)

Even if Paul does not have Hosea specifically in mind when he talks about the overcoming of enmity and the establishment of peace and reconciliation, he does reflect the tradition in which the relationship between God and the chosen people is expressed in very anthropomorphic terms of love, alienation, and reconciliation.

A much-discussed issue among Paul's interpreters is, who is reconciled to whom, and how? In all Paul's uses of reconciliation, the direct expression is that God "reconciled us" to God's own self. This language implies that humans were at enmity with God, and that the expression of God's love in the cross has overcome that enmity. God is the reconciler rather than the reconciled.

However, the issue is not to be resolved that easily. While it is true that Paul places all the blame for the broken relationship on the human side and all the credit for restoration on God's side, the anthropomorphic terms in which he thinks and writes should make one wary of ruling out too quickly any change within God. Especially is this the case with his language about "wrath" or "wrath of God" as a way of expressing the judgment which sinners must face in life and in death. Further, when Paul speaks of "peace with God" (Rom. 5:1), which those who are set right have, he is not merely thinking about the new subjective state which persons of faith have but of their new objective standing now that "through him we have obtained access to this grace in which we stand" (Rom. 5:2).

All of this language makes sense in the context of covenantal relationships: God's attitude and conduct toward Israel is that of electing grace, and God maintains that attitude through all the wanderings and rebelliousness of the chosen people. But, as is so poignantly seen in Hosea, God is spoken of as having human emotions as well as human form. God's love ignored and spurned can turn to hate, and so God is personally torn by ambivalent feelings for the chosen people. In that context, judgment is not merely the expression of impersonal laws of retribution, but rather of God's hostility toward sin, even toward the sinner. While it is true that Paul attributes human emotions to God less than Hosea does, we would be amiss to disregard the personal reaction of God to human rebellion.

Reconciliation thus involves more than bringing humans around to accepting God's grace. While it is true that reconciliation is two-sided, some ways in which that truth is often presented can be misleading. Some say there is a tension between God's love and justice, and that God's love cannot cancel out God's demand for justice to be done by paying the penalty for sin; others maintain that without sacrifice God cannot forgive; or that God's wrath must fully express itself before it can be laid aside. Paul does not express such notions. He does suggest, however, that just as God's wrath is aroused by faithlessness, it is overcome by repentance, returning to faithfulness. God does not desire sacrifice, but covenant loyalty and steadfastness. The change in God is effected in response to human change, not as a consequence of an act outside human consciousness.

Paul extends those covenant relationships which are healed in Jesus Christ to include the Gentile as well as the Jew. God is in Christ inaugurating a new fulfillment of the covenantal promises, choosing humanity anew; God is "reconciling the world to himself" (2 Cor. 5:19). To be sure, universal reconciliation does not exclude the Jews. Of them God says, "this will be my covenant with them when I take away their sins" (Rom. 11:27). But that covenant of reconciliation is also for Gentile on equal terms. This manifestation of God's grace elicits faith instead of rebellion. When grace affirms and faith responds, reconciliation is reality; Paul sees this reality becoming present through the proclamation of the gospel of Jesus' death and resurrection "for us."

The "Atonement"

In the previous chapter I elaborated upon some of Paul's terminology for speaking of the saving effects of Christ's death and resurrection: justification/righteousness, expiation/sacrifice, blood/redemption. I discussed the rich variety of language associated with reconciliation. It is time now to consider how to interpret this variety of expression. Does each term stand for a distinct part of the saving action of God? Are the terms to be arranged sequentially so that they are separate acts in the drama of salvation? Or are the various terms merely redundant expressions of the same reality? It is my conviction that one best understands Paul's varied language by regarding the terms as metaphorical expressions which help to elucidate the meaning of Christ's death "for us." The different metaphors point to different dimensions of God's saving act in Christ, look at that event from different angles, speak of it in different forms:

1. Christ's death and resurrection is an act of *justification*, of establishing right relationships. It inaugurates a new covenant fulfilling the promises to Abraham, the intent of the Mosaic covenant, and Jeremiah's prophecy. Just as God brought life out of death by giving childless and "dead" Abraham and Sarah a son, in order that the covenant promise could continue, so God has brought life out of Jesus' death, continuing the promise of "seed" to Abraham.[2]

2. Christ's death and resurrection is a *redemption*, an act of liberation like a slave's release from bondage. Humans who have been enslaved to sin, death, and the Torah are set free from all that bound them. Now they may live as free people before God. The metaphor of redemption recalls God's original act of liberating the Hebrew slaves from Egypt. That act stood in the context of the covenant, carrying forward the promise to Abraham and reestablishing his descendants as God's people. Christ's death and resurrection functions as a new Exodus which sets God's people free from sin and death, brings together the

broken people of God, and forges a new community.

3. Christ's death is a *sacrifice* adequate for restoring right relations with God. This metaphor is drawn from the Jewish sacrificial system. The Jews, however, did not generally look upon sacrifices as means of procuring God's favor, as though God would be angry unless appeased by sacrifice. Rather, they looked upon sacrifice as the God-given means by which covenant was established and maintained, community experienced and affirmed. Following Jewish ideas, Paul is saying that Christ's death is like that sacrifice in which the worshipers offer themselves anew to God, and communion is reestablished through the means God has provided. Connected with this metaphor of sacrifice is Paul's use of the term "blood." In Exodus the covenant between God and his people was sealed by the blood of a sacrificial animal sprinkled upon the altar and upon the people. When Paul uses the term he is thinking not that God's anger must be appeased, but that a new covenant has been sealed between God and his people; the Lord's Supper is a symbolic representation of that covenant sealing.

4. Christ's death and resurrection is a *reconciliation*, the restoration of a friendship which has been broken through the wrongdoing of one friend against another. The image is that of the wronged party reaching out so that the enmity which exists can be overcome.

To speak of these terms as metaphors, however, is to acknowledge that there is no clear theory of the atonement to be uncovered in Paul's writings—an acknowledgment that Christian theology has been reluctant to make, but which exegesis shows must be made. Increasingly biblical scholars recognize that Paul uses traditional language which lacks the internal logic of a clearly worked-out theory. Even those who, like Rudolf Bultmann, tend to find a strongly substitutionary cast to Paul's language would not argue that he has a *theory* of atonement.

In various ways many interpreters of Paul emphasize the "participatory" nature of Paul's language: Paul presents Christ's death and resurrection in ways that suggest that Christ participated in human life so that humans can participate in his. A good example of that language is found in Galatians 2:20:

> I have been crucified with Christ; it is no longer I who live, but Christ who lives in me; and the life I now live in the flesh I live by faith in the Son of God, who loved me and gave himself for me.

The crucial point about such a passage is not that Christ "gave himself for (*huper*) me" in a substitutionary sense, but that in an act of divine grace he placed himself in the position of sharing fully in the human experience of suffering, sin, and death in order that humans might participate fully in the glory, righteousness, and life of Christ. Such language derives from a covenantal understanding of the divine-human relationship: God initiates the relationship by moving toward the chosen people in order to generate a reciprocal human movement toward God. The covenanting God does not remain aloof from the human condition, but expresses grace by becoming involved in the people's situation. The change in the human condition is the result rather than the cause of that divine involvement. Paul broadens the covenant community when he asserts that in Christ God says to all—Jew and Greek, male and female, slave and free— "I will be your God and you shall be a people to me."

Past, Present, and Future

Attention to the element of time in 5:1–11 provides insight into Paul's theological outlook. Time is not the same as verb tense, though tenses often suggest elements of time; rather time has to do with Paul's perspective on past, present, and future as those dimensions of human experience are understood in light of the death and resurrection of Jesus.

To a real extent 1:18—3:20 speaks not about the present but about a past which has been rendered inconsequential by God's act received by faith. Human sin may well be a present reality for Paul—indeed it is—but Paul's outlook on the world is not properly understood as one of misanthropy toward those wicked people outside the church who inhabit the world. Rather, the gospel of God's grace brackets all that sinfulness; God has caught the world up in a new cycle of redemption which makes all things new.

Consequently, in Romans 5 the most decisive thing about the past is not human sinfulness, but the death and resurrection of Jesus. For Paul the past contains weakness (vs. 6), ungodliness (vs. 6), sin (vs. 8). Such terms describe the human condition in its pastness, but so do other terms which not only are past but also continue into the present and determine the future:

> We are justified. (vss. 1, 9)
> We have received access to grace in which we [now] stand. (vs. 8 my translation)
> God's love has been poured [out] into our hearts. (vs. 5)
> The Holy Spirit . . . has been given to us. (vs. 5)
> We were reconciled. (vs. 10)
> We have now received our reconciliation. (vs. 11)

Paul thus describes the human past as composed of weak, ungodly people who have missed the way of God's covenant people. The second aspect of the past continues into the present and reaches toward the future: God has established a new, right relationship with people, whether Gentile or Jew, whose alienation is overcome by God's love, who stand within God's grace, and who rejoice in the experience of knowing God's presence.

Both past and present lead into the future, for hopelessness has been replaced by hope. Paul, however, says very little in our current passage about the future; he will say more, especially in chapters 8—11. Essentially he says here that the future will bring salvation: we shall be saved from wrath, we shall be saved by Christ's life (cf. 5:21: grace will reign through righteousness to eternal life through Jesus Christ). The future is less a matter of speculation than a matter of assurance given by the nature of God's past action and by the confirming experience of renewing grace in the present.

Hope for the future finds expression in verses 3–5, which form a sort of parenthesis anticipating the fuller expression in chapters 8—11. This parenthesis does not develop the content of hope any more than does the general affirmation that "we shall be saved"; rather, it anticipates and responds to questions that might be put to Paul by one inclined to doubt his optimism: Does not our present experience of suffering nullify the hope which you have affirmed? How can one piously hold on to hope in a world where hope is continually contradicted by the present? Paul certainly is not unaware of the realities of the present; he has already penned that catalogue of human suffering which had been compiled during his years of missionary endeavor:

> Five times I have received at the hands of the Jews the forty lashes less one. Three times I have been beaten with rods; once I was stoned. Three times I have been shipwrecked; a night and a day I have been adrift at sea; on frequent journeys, in danger from rivers, danger from robbers, danger from my own people, danger from Gentiles, danger in the city, danger in the wilderness, danger at sea, danger from false brethren; in toil and hardship, through many a sleepless night, in hunger and thirst, often without food, in cold and exposure.... (2 Cor. 11:24–27)

At first glance Paul's optimistic outlook in Romans 5:3–5 may resemble the Stoic's passionless determination in face of adversity: "suffering produces endurance, and endurance produces proven character, and character produces hope...." That sequence is what Stoics also believed could result from suffering rightly accepted. Right acceptance for the Stoic included a recognition that there really is no such thing as evil in this world—only imperfect perception which causes some things to appear evil; thus suffering patiently endured proves one's solid character and confirms one's hope in the best of all worlds.

To a certain extent Paul's language here follows the Stoic affirmation, but he departs from it at a crucial juncture: "God's love has been poured into our hearts through the Holy Spirit." The relational dimensions of human experience which constitute the core of Paul's understanding of human life place him at far remove from the impersonal, sometimes cold and formal outlook of the Stoic. Paul rejoices in suffering because he rejoices in God. Suffering is not one of life's joys, but the one who has experienced God's grace renewing human existence can rejoice in that renewal, affirm its reality in the midst of suffering, and know that the outcome is still within the sphere of grace. Paul rejoices in suffering because he is convinced that the ultimate reality is grace, not evil or nothingness.

CHRIST AND ADAM (Romans 5:12–21)

The famous contrast of Christ and Adam which dominates this section of Romans has been utilized widely in Christian theology as a summary statement not only of Paul's Gospel but of the whole of biblical revelation. Karl Barth, in his essay on Christ and Adam, expressed that viewpoint very powerfully.

> This is the history of man and of humanity outside Christ: the sin and death of a single man, of Adam, the man who in his own person is and represents the whole of humanity, the man in whose decision and destiny the decisions and destinies, the sins and the death of all the other men who come after him, are anticipated.

> Human existence, as constituted by our relationship with Adam in our unhappy past as weak, sinners, godless, enemies, has no independent reality, status, or importance of its own. It is only an indirect witness to the reality of Jesus Christ and to the original and essential human existence that He inaugurates and reveals. The righteous decision of God has fallen upon men not in Adam but in Christ. But in Christ it has also fallen upon Adam, upon our relationship to him and so upon our unhappy past.[3]

Adam as Ancestor of Jew and Gentile

Because of its theological import Romans 5:12–21 seems to invite interpreters to isolate it from its surroundings and to regard it as a gold mine from which it is appropriate to extract nuggets. Much good theology (and much that is not so good) has derived from such an approach. But in order not to miss what Paul has to say in this important paragraph we need to understand why Paul included it in writing to the Roman church. The question of the intent and purpose of Romans as a whole arises as critically here as at any other point. If we regard Romans as primarily a theological treatise in which Paul systematically, carefully, and logically lays out his gospel for the Roman Christians (and for *all* Christian readers), then we might regard 5:12–21 as a logical summation of all that has gone before: human sinfulness has been shown to be universal (1:18—3:20); God's act in Christ has done for us what we could not do for ourselves (3:21–31); insofar as we have appropriately responded with a faith like Abraham's we have been justified (4:1–25); chapter 5:1–11 has begun to look forward to the Christian life, a theme which will continue in chapters 6—8.

There are, however, problems with this approach, not least of which is the fact that chapters 6—8 do not deal only with the development and nurturing of Christian life; they still contain a great deal of argumentation concerning the nature of sin, death, and the Torah, which have not really been overcome by the grace which has produced faith. Such an approach also runs aground by regarding chapters 1—8 as the *real* letter, with chapters 9—11 as a kind of theological appendage and chapters 12—15 as general moral maxims, rather loosely (at best) attached to the earlier parts of the letter.

Much recent scholarship has recognized that Romans is a genuine letter, and while there is considerable debate about its exact occasion and purpose, its occasional nature is certainly to be accepted. If I have been correct in my approach, the central issue concerning Paul as he writes is the problem of the relationship between Gentile and Jew within God's plan of salvation. It is quite possible to see that issue reflected in the structure and argument of chapters 5—8 as a whole, and in Romans 5:12–21 in particular.

Jouette Bassler has argued convincingly that "divine impartiality" dominates Paul's thought in Romans 1:16—2:29, is strongly reflected in chapters 3—4 and 9—11, and influences the admonitions of chapters 14—15. However, she says, "The question of Jews and Gentiles disappears in chapters 5—8, where Paul explores other questions and ramifications of his concept of justification," before returning to the theme in chapters 9—11.[4] Bassler's contribution needs to be taken further, for the question of Gentile and Jew is still reflected in chapters 5—8. Beker is surely correct when he says that the Jew/Gentile issue is always in the background of Romans even when Paul does not deal directly with it. Beker perhaps overstates his case when he maintains that "Romans must be characterized as a dialogue with Jews"; Beker himself tacitly recognizes that overstatement when he modifies it:

> To be sure, Romans 5:1—8:39 cannot be characterized as a direct debate with Jews. Here Paul transcends the Jewish-Gentile question and focuses on the new reality of the lordship of Christ in the church as the proleptic manifestation of God's imminent eschatological triumph.[5]

Beker rightly sees 5:12–21 within the context of the overall purpose of Romans, though he goes too far in ascribing to Paul an anti-Jewish polemic both in 5:12–21 and in chapters 9—10, when he expresses the notion of what "Christians" have (joyous access to God, etc.) in contrast to what "Jews" have (condemnation, boasting, etc.).[6] As Beker presents it, Paul has three categories of humans: Jews, Gentiles, Christians, though the three are collapsed into two, those belonging to the old Adam and those belonging to the new.[7]

Paul, however, does not speak about "Christians"; the word is not in his vocabulary, and what it denotes is not in his theology.[8] For Paul Christ is the beginning of a new humanity, not a new religion. The way in which he utilizes human figures to illustrate his convictions shows quite clearly that universal perspective: Abraham belongs to both Gentile and Jew as the father of all who have faith (not the father of those who are "Christians"). Adam is the ancestor of all, embodying in his rebelliousness the Jew as well as the Gentile; Moses only serves to heighten the human problem, for since the Torah cannot set one right with God but can only express condemnation and provoke sinning, it cannot distinguish Gentile from Jew in any sense which produces positive results; Christ is the agent of God's universal salvation, and thus equally Lord of Gentile and Jew. Religious distinctions have been obliterated by God's act of condemnation and salvation: "There is neither Gentile nor Jew [nor Christian] ..., for you are all one in Christ Jesus" (Gal. 3:28).

One might ask, however, if Paul is still emphasizing the unity of Gentile and Jew in chapter 5, why is there no mention at all here of those terms? If he had really wanted to keep that theme before his readers, would he have done it so subtly? Note a similarity with 1:18—2:8, where no mention is made of Jew and Gentile. While using standard Jewish condemnation of Gentiles, Paul mentions neither, and at his first mention of them (2:9–10) he puts them completely on a parity. Likewise in chapter 5:1–11, he uses the inclusive symbol of humankind: Adam.

The use of Adam as a symbol for universal human need, along with the assertion of the ineffectiveness of the Torah to remedy the situation, affirms that salvation is *human* salvation provided by God's grace, not *Jewish* salvation enlarged to incorporate Gentiles within the Israelite covenant nor Gentile salvation to the exclusion of the Jews. Does that mean, then, that the Mosaic covenant is negated or obliterated? This question takes on decided seriousness when Paul discusses the fate of Israel in chapters 9—11; as I show in chapter 8, in Paul's view the Mosaic covenant is not God's ultimate act of salvation for Israel; it is an interim measure until the coming of Christ. The new covenant in Christ thus does not nullify the old in its *intent*, though as the means to universal salvation for Gentile and Jew alike it supersedes the old. A host of issues is wrapped up in this point, not least of which is the question of the purpose and place of the Torah; I will return to these issues in subsequent chapters.

Structure of This Passage

This paragraph is complex, raising many theological issues (more perhaps than it answers!), and it is easily subject to misunderstanding and debate.

Paul begins with a sentence in 5:12 which he abandons, instead entering a long parenthesis beginning with 5:12b—"and so death spread"—and ending with verse 17. Verse 18a in essence repeats verse 12a and finally moves to the points which he was making before he was diverted.[9]

(1) Just as the transgressive act of one disobedient person (Adam) led to condemnation of all as sinners, so the righteous act of one obedient person (Christ) led to the setting right in life of all. (2) The Torah did not materially change the human situation; it exacerbated it, but that very exacerbation led to an even greater abundance of grace. (3) As sin led to death, grace leads to life.

Paul's intent then is to affirm the overarching and overwhelming power of grace in Jesus Christ, not to put forward a theory to explain that human sin has its orgin in the first man, Adam. He no doubt follows, however, a great deal of Jewish theological interest in Adam which is well-documented in the first century B.C.E. and the first three centuries C.E.,[10] for his parenthesis shows clearly that he is familiar with that theology, as does his dealing with human sin in chapters 1—3.

Furthermore, his parenthetical statements touch upon additional themes: (1) Sinners are responsible for their sinning: "because all sinned" (vs. 12b). (2) Sin works its effects, including death, even if there is no specific command or law known to be violated (vss.13–14). (3) Adam is a "type" of Moses, for he possessed commandment(s) from God, just as Moses did, and in both cases those commandments led not to righteousness and life but to disobedience and death (this point leads to the obvious conclusion that Gentiles and Jews are not really to be differentiated).[11] (4) Christ is vastly superior to Adam: "much more.... much more..." (vss. 15,17). These points, while not in serious opposition to those of the non-parenthetical statements, do add considerable redundancy to the whole section and lead many interpreters to think that Paul's primary interest was upon Adam and fallen humanity.

The passage in its main thrust and parenthesis raises questions which it was not Paul's real intention to answer, but which claim our attention as theologically aware and interested readers. Among those questions I will explore the following:

1. To what degree does Paul think individual humans are responsible for their own condition of sinfulness or of righteousness? Do the typological characters (Adam, Abraham, Moses,

Christ) so determine the human situation that individuals simply are parts of a humanity whose destiny is fixed regardless of their own decisions?

2. What does Paul mean by death, and how is it related to sin and the Torah?

3. What does he mean by his emphasis upon Christ's act having "much more" effect than Adam's? Does he imply that ultimately all will receive the results of that act of grace, which increases in greater abundance than sin?

4. How do Paul's statements in this passage relate to his theme of the unity of Gentile and Jew in the one new covenant?

These are questions Paul did not set out to answer, and for the most part does not answer; but since they are legitimate questions to raise with Paul, I shall attempt to clarify them.

Individual Responsibility

Paul's argument in Romans 5:12–21 raises questions concerning the relation between Adam and other persons. Paul asserts that sin and death entered the world through that one disobedient person, and as a consequence of that entry all have become sinful. Contemporary readers who have grown up with the notion that Adam sinned and passed on to his descendants a fallen and corrupted human nature might pass over this passage without blinking an eye: is it not all there? "Sinful nature prone to do evil and slothful in doing good"; "miserable sinners"; "totally depraved"? Yet the attentive reader will ask why Paul is only now introducing Adam directly; why not at 1:18—3:20 when discussing the general sinfulness of Gentiles and Jews? If, indeed, as I have maintained, Paul did have in mind the stories of creation and fall, why did he wait until chapter 5 explicitly to mention Adam?

The chief answer lies, I believe, in this direction: the mention of Adam is useful to Paul in advancing his primary argument in 5:12–21, which is that God has now accomplished by the single act of grace in Jesus Christ the restoration of all that had been corrupted in the history of human sinfulness. Paul's real interest is not in Adam, but in Christ, not in original sin, but in righteousness. He uses Adam as an individual person because of his interest in Christ who is an individual. The parallelism required for its effectiveness an *adham* (human being) who sums up in one experience the symbolic meaning of sin and death.

By no means should one conclude thereby that Paul used Adam casually. Robin Scroggs is probably correct in asserting that "the Apostle wrestles mightily with Genesis 1—3," for his writings contain many allusions to stories recounted in those chapters.[12] Nevertheless, Paul's presentation of the human departure from God's will can be as profoundly expressed by using a general reference to humankind ("they" in Romans 1) or by using the first person singular ("I" in Rom. 7). Such variety in mode of expression shows that for Paul "Adam" is not so much the "first" as he is "every" person. Not that Paul thought of Adam as "only" a symbol—he probably thought of him as a real person—but Adam's significance is in symbolizing and embodying what happens in human beings generally. That point appears to be confirmed by the way in which Paul emphasizes individual responsibility more than corporate guilt, inherited sinfulness, or fallen human nature. That emphasis is reflected in 5:12: "because all sinned."

Paul was not the only one to wrestle mightily with the stories of Genesis 1—3 (although he is the only one whose wrestlings have found a place in Hebraic or Protestant scripture). At least from the first century B.C.E. to the third century C.E., Jewish theologians gave serious attention to the story of Adam. Two major views concerning the consequences of Adam's disobedience are summed up in these quotations:

> For though Adam sinned
> And brought untimely death upon all,
> Yet those who were born from him
> Each one of them has prepared for his own
>   soul torment to come,
> And again each one of those has chosen for
>   himself glories to come,
> Adam is, therefore, not the cause save only
>   of his own soul

> But each of us has been the Adam of his own soul.
> (2 Baruch 54:15–19)[13]

> For the first Adam, clothing himself with the evil heart,
> transgressed and was overcome; and likewise also all who were
> born of him. Thus the infirmity became inveterate; the Law
> indeed was in the heart of the people, but (in conjunction) with
> the evil germ; so what was good departed and the evil remained.
> (4 Ezra 3:21–22)[14]

Whether or not Paul deliberately entered the discussion among
Jewish theologians, he shows himself to be closest to those who
emphasize individual responsibility. Adam is indeed the one
through whom sin entered the world, and with sin death, but
Adam is not credited with establishing human nature as sinful
and guilty. Although much Christian theology has presented
Paul in that manner, such a view depends upon two erroneous
readings of the text. The first concerns the phrase in Romans
5:12 which the Revised Standard Version rightly translates
"because all sinned." Augustine (and a long line of interpreters
following him) took the phrase to mean "in whom all sinned" in
the sense that all humans were incorporated in Adam and his
act therefore determined their future.[15] There is little doubt
that Augustine's grammatical understanding was incorrect.[16]
The second erroneous reading of the text upon which the theory of fallen human nature depends is in verse 19: "many were
made sinners" by one man's act of disobedience. The verb here
can mean "appoint" or "ordain" or "cause (make) someone to be
something." Thus Augustine's meaning can justifiably be found
here; but the word (*kathistemi*) can also be equivalent to
"become."[17]

The issues of fallen human nature and original sin have
been heatedly debated by Christian theologians for centuries
(often with a lack of charity which tends to prove Augustine
correct!). They will not be solved here. In looking at this passage, from which a great deal of that debate springs, we need
first of all to remember that Paul's point is not universal
sinfulness but the sufficiency of grace. Beyond that, I suggest
the following points derived from Romans:

1. Paul does not deal with human beings as though they were individuals isolated from history and society. He takes seriously the corporate nature of human sinfulness. Sin exists within institutions and social structures, including religious ones, and thus there is no escaping its reality. Human sin has both an endemic and an epidemic quality about it. Paul affirms without reservation the universality of human sinfulness, and associates the beginning of that condition with the primal beginnings of the human community.

2. Paul takes with great seriousness the responsibility of individual persons for their own acts. Individual sin exists in the context of a world alienated from its source, and individual sin is a manifestation of that general condition. What Paul does is to bring that general situation into the personal situation and to emphasize its existential nature. "No one commences his own history and no one can be exonerated."[18] World conditions and individual choice reinforce each other in such a way that individual guilt is not denied and yet no one is free from the destructive power of sin. Sin—and death which is its consequence—"have the character of universal forces which no one escapes and to which all in their own ways are subject both passively and actively."[19] It is precisely in our active lives that we confirm the revolt which is characteristic of the world and become exponents of a force which transforms creation into chaos.

3. Adam is then to a certain extent portrayed as the determiner of that world within which individual choices take on the character of alienation and rebellion. He is also the model of that rebellion so that "each of us is the Adam of his own soul," and as such is also the Adam of other souls by passing on the world as we found it, perpetuating the conditons which made our own choices what they have been.

Death in Relation to Sin and the Torah

Sin and death are twin realities for Paul. His emphasis in this passage is the contrast between death and life: "through sin death entered the world and spread to all.... Death reigned...."

Many died. . . . Death reigned. . . . Sin reigned in death." "Death" does not signify merely the cessation of earthly existence; that in itself can even be viewed as desirable (see Phil. 1:21). Rather, death here signifies the triumph of sin, the destruction of that life which was intended to be lived in relation to God, the final reality which nullifies the promise of hope for the future and the realization of the glory of God. When sin and death are present together, there is no future; there is only despair because what could have been the fulfillment of divine destiny is lost; it is thus that the sting of death is sin, and that when sin is overcome by grace, death loses its sting—its character as threat to human fulfillment. In that sense it is destroyed.

Paul follows Jewish theology in his assertion of death's sway as a consequence of human sinfulness. As a consequence of Adam's sin, 4 Ezra 3:7 says, "Thou didst appoint death for him and his descendants." Although some Jewish texts emphasize that it was each person's sin which brought death to that person, the "basic and ultimate judgment of Jewish theologians is that death is God's decree upon all men because of Adam."[20] Paul differs from Ezra in attributing universal death to universal sinfulness, suggesting that each is responsible for each one's death.

Paul asserts the impotence of the Torah to deal with the situation in which sin and death reign over humans. He will say more in chapter 7 concerning the cause of this impotence; here he only affirms it and affirms further that God never intended the Torah to be able to give life: "The Torah came in, to increase the trespass" (5:20; cf. Gal. 3:21). He does not at this point attribute the Torah to God: he only says it "entered in," using a word which can imply sinister or unworthy motives. What could be understood as a derogation of the Torah is modified in chapter 7, where Paul affirms that it is "holy"; his main point here then is to show that the Torah is irrelevant to the actual human situation. Sin and death held sway both before and after the Torah; they did not originate with the Torah, nor are they solved by it. The Torah intensifies sin (and by implication death) but in a final sense it is not a decisive factor in the human equation.[21]

Christ and Adam: "Much More"

Fundamental to Paul's gospel is the affirmation that God's act of grace in Jesus Christ powerfully suffices to renew and restore all that has been corrupted or lost through human sinfulness. The emphasis in this passage falls not upon Adam but upon Christ. Adam—and the sin and death introduced by him into the human community—belong to the past, even though the effects are still present; Christ and the righteousness and life he brings belong to the future and are already present. The present then is the arena in which the past is being transformed into the future. Death *reigned* but grace and life *will reign*.

Since sin and death oppose God's intention for the created world, and since God's sovereignty is manifested in grace, sin and death will not ultimately prevail. The glory which has been lost is being restored; the image which has been marred is being renewed through the impact of its revelation in Jesus Christ; the enmity which has separated humans is being overcome in reconciliation. So optimistic is Paul that the triumphant reign belongs not to forces of the past but to God's kingdom of the future that he can affirm that the more sin increases the more grace abounds.

In his optimism does he affirm more than he intends or should intend? Does the logic of his assertions imply a universal salvation? Would that view be consistent with what he says elsewhere? These same questions will arise even more insistently in chapters 9—11. Let us currently examine the matter only as presented in these verses of chapter 5.

Several times Paul contrasts the effects of Adam's and Christ's acts, for the two are not strictly parallel. They are, however, parallel in the pervasiveness of their effects:

> Verse 15: *many* died . . . grace . . . abounded for *many*.
> Verse 18: condemnation for *all*. . . . acquittal . . . for *all*.
> Verse 19: *many* were made sinners, . . . *many* will be made righteous.

Since "many" is equivalent in Hebraic thought to "all," Paul makes no distinction in the extent of effects mentioned in these various expressions; even if there were a difference in meaning between "many" and "all," each time he uses the same term to speak of both sides of the equation. The difference between Christ and Adam is not to be found in the idea that Adam involves *all* in sinfulness while Christ involves only *some* in salvation.

Nor is the difference to be found in the freedom that humans have to associate with either. Paul maintains that the fallenness of the created order does not remove from humans personal responsibility for choosing that fallenness. The same can be said of God's grace: it puts the world of humans in a fundamentally different situation, but not in such a way that grace and life automatically belong to a person. In both cases one affirms one's participation by a "faith" relationship with Adam or with Christ. This point is not emphasized in this passage but is expressed in a minimal way by two phrases: "because all sinned" (vs. 12) and "those who receive" (vs. 17).

Then what does Paul mean by the contrast? How is "the free gift not like the trespass"? How is the reign of righteousness "much more" than the reign of death? How is grace more abundant than sin? He could mean that Christ's act is more *comprehensive*, that it effects more people than Adam's. This explanation is not likely, as I have argued above, unless Paul envisages a new historical age in which persons might come into a world not dominated by Adam's sin but by Christ's righteousness and thus be affected only by the latter and not the former. There is, however, no evidence that Paul saw that sort of perfection within the historical order.

Or, he could mean that Christ's act is more *powerful* than Adam's. Because sinning is easier than righteousness for humanity in its weakness, the spread of Adam's results was relatively easy; because the rescue operation was more difficult owing to the powerful forces against which it operated, Christ's act was not like Adam's, for it was an exertion of greater power.

Or, he could mean that God's act in Christ is all the more *surely* effective. It is, after all, God's world, and God's will will ultimately prevail. Thus, if it seems certain that all do and will participate in Adam's sin and death, that still is no reason for

ultimate pessimism. As Paul says, elsewhere, "Just as we have
borne the image of the man of dust, we shall also bear the
image of the man of heaven" (1 Cor. 15:49). By this statement,
then, Paul expresses a central conviction that in Christ we see
the will of God for humanity, and that the grace expressed
there provides a guarantee for the future. "Where sin increased,
grace abounded all the more" (Rom. 5:20), so that grace will
ultimately triumph.

Paul does not explicitly say here that *all* (i.e., every particular human being) will be "saved," but the optimism expressed
in the "much more" can include such a notion. At any rate,
Paul believes that the world is in a new situation as a consequence of Christ's act. The unleashing of such a powerful expression of God's grace has created the condition which will lead to
the renewal of all things. That, anyway, is his hope, and he has
seen and experienced enough of that transforming grace to
believe it can and will be effective for all.

Unity of Gentile and Jew in One New Covenant

I have acknowledged that my major theme finds no explicit
mention in this section, so that one can understand Bassler's
skipping over chapters 5—8 in discussing God's impartiality.
Yet as Beker says, Paul's interest in the Jewish-Gentile question is never far in the background. The evidence for its presence here may be summed up as follows:

1. Paul contrasts Adam and Christ, not Adam and Moses.
The Mosaic Torah only increased human sin and did not provide release from it. Death reigned from Adam to Moses and
from Moses to Christ, and thus there is no distinction between
those under the Torah and those not under it. Adam is a type of
Moses, for both signify commandment, sin, and death, so that
Gentile and Jew are alike.

2. For Paul, the new covenant involves the removal of sins
of Israel (cf. Rom. 11:27), but not of Israel only. Here in emphasizing God's grace in renewal, Paul's underlying convictions
are both universal and covenantal: God enters into a new relationship with humankind, in which the alienating and corrupting

effects of sin are overcome. Christ overcomes the sin of Adam;
he does not merely correct the failings of those under the Mosaic
Torah.

3. It is God's grace which provides the power of the new
creation; that grace is not circumscribed by, nor channeled
primarily through, the Torah, but is universal in its intent, its
operation, and its effect. If it were through the Torah it would
affect only those under the Torah, but since it is "apart from
the Torah" it is for all, Gentile as well as Jew.

6

Answers to Opponents' Objections

(Romans 6—7)

PAUL'S THEOLOGICAL WARRANTS

These chapters provide good examples of the warrants which lie behind much of Paul's theological argumentation. We see him relying upon Scripture, general observations of human behavior, and the particular experiences of believers. In chapters 1—5 Paul has wished to show that his Gospel is thoroughly grounded in Scripture. In Romans 1:18—3:20 Paul might hope that his presentation of the human predicament would ring true for his readers, that they might see themselves as being like others who in various ways rebelled against God. His argument, however, is not based on appeal to their experience. In fact, he does not specify any basis for his argument. Likewise, while readers familiar with the Genesis account of Adam's fall and with the various traditions of Jewish and Hellenistic moralists recognize Paul's use of them, he does not cite them as authority. In 3:21—4:25 he explicitly uses Scripture as his primary warrant, to show that although he now reads Scripture through a new (and correct) lens, he does read it and has not abandoned its covenants, promises, and claims. Rather, he proclaims its valid fulfillment. In chapter 5, he attempts to clinch his previous argument by his comparison and contrast between Christ and Adam, again relying on Scripture to confirm the Gospel. His Adam/Christ analogy ends with the assertion that the Torah did not correct the human situation introduced by Adam, but rather exacerbated it: The "Law came in, to increase the trespass" (Rom.5:20). But God did not leave the matter there, for "where sin increased, grace abounded all the more" (Rom. 5:20).

Those final assertions leave him two serious questions with which he grapples in 6:1—7:25: (1) Does Paul's theology of grace lead to licentiousness and immorality? (2) If the Torah resulted in more sin, is the Torah itself contrary to God's purposes? These questions put in jeopardy Paul's theology of one new covenant of redeeming grace for Gentile and Jew, and he must deal with them. As he does so, he continues to rely upon Scripture (7:7–25 alludes to Adam's fall in Gen. 3); he also uses observations of human behavior and reflects upon the ambiguous character of human existence (also in Rom. 7:7–25). More strikingly, especially in chapter 6 he supports his views by appealing to the personal and communal experience of his readers. He assumes a commonality in that experience, and thus makes little appeal to *Gentile* or to *Jewish* experience, but to the general experience of believers.

A Brief Analysis of This Passage

On the surface it appears that what I have identified as a basic concern of Paul in writing Romans—the unification of Gentile and Jew into one new covenant community—has receded at least temporarily into the backgound. Jouette Bassler seems justified in saying that the "question of Jews and Gentiles disappears in chapters 5—8, where Paul explores other questions and ramifications of his concept of justification."[1] However, chapters 6 and 7 deal with two problems which surfaced in 1:18—5:21. They were left aside in favor of the main issue, but are so potentially damaging to the position Paul advocates that he now takes them up before proceeding with his main argument.

The first issue is revealed in Paul's question in 6:1: "Are we to continue in sin that grace may abound?" That question grows out of his assertion in 5:20 that "where sin increased, grace increased in greater abundance." But the question has been in Paul's mind earlier, as 3:5–8 shows: some of Paul's opponents "slanderously charge" him with advocating a position which undermines ethical conduct and leads to licentiousness. In response to this criticism Paul argues for life of morality based not on the Torah but on the renewing power of grace at work in the community of the baptized and by means of which the baptized may move toward a completed commitment. Both the power of grace at work in the community and the possibility of yielding oneself to God as a slave yields to a master are means available to Gentile as well as to Jew; both are expressions of God's grace and the faithful response within the new covenantal relationship established by grace. Morality thus has a more effective grounding than that provided by the Torah.

The second issue in chapters 6 and 7 also grows out of 5:20: If sin increased when the Torah entered the situation, is the Torah therefore sinful? This point has also been in Paul's mind since early in the letter: note especially 3:20 where "knowledge of sin" is associated with the Torah, and 4:15, where he asserts that "the Torah brings wrath."

7:1–6 serves as a transition from the central question of chapter 6 to that of chapter 7. It is connected with chapter 6 by continuing the themes of release through death and of slavery to sin (6:15–23); it anticipates 7:7–13 by indicating that slavery to sin is intensified by the Torah, and that freedom from the Torah is an ingredient in freedom from sin.

That last assertion raises the question as to whether the Torah is sinful. Paul's answer is, "Hell no!"[2] The Torah is holy (belongs to God), but is ineffective in the presence of the human propensity toward sin. In fact the Torah by providing the knowledge of sin leads to the desire to sin; further, the Torah provides an opportunity for sin to get hold of human life. Thus, under the Torah the Jew is no better off than the Gentile; for though the Torah is from God and though its commandments do express God's intention, it cannot lead to life simply because human existence is what it is and the Torah cannot change it. The "I" of 7:4–25 refers to human existence, expressed in the personal terms of Paul's own experience. Because "I" am what "I" am, the Torah is ineffective in establishing covenant righteousness. Thus, Jew as well as Gentile need a different power for change.

The main focus of these chapters is not on the issue of the relationship between Gentile and Jew. Paul uses the concept of justification by faith apart from the Torah, however (which asserts the oneness of Gentile and Jew), to raise the questions he attempts to answer here; unless he can answer these questions adequately, his fundamental thesis regarding Gentile and Jew will be threatened.

In one sense, then, though chapters 6 and 7 do not advance the main argument,[3] they do seek to protect it at especially vulnerable places. As we shall see, in a deeper sense Paul's replies to his opponents do advance his argument because they lead into the twin themes of "Spirit" and "life" in Romans 8.

Let us now look at some of the main theological issues of Romans 6—7 in more detail.

The Relation of Sin, Baptism, and Grace

Paul celebrated the action of God in response to human sin: "where sin increased, grace abounded all the more" (5:20). This statement should be allowed to have its full impact, for it is very close to the core of Paul's gospel of grace. It reverses traditional wisdom regarding God's action, and seems to contradict a fundamental principle of the covenant: that when the people are righteous, God will bless them, but when they do evil they can expect God's wrath.

> "And if you obey the voice of the LORD your God, being careful to do all his commandments which I command you this day, the LORD your God will set you high above all the nations of the earth. And all these blessings shall come upon you and overtake you, if you obey the voice of the LORD your God....
>
> "The LORD will cause your enemies who rise against you to be defeated before you.... The LORD will establish you as a

people holy to himself, as he has sworn to you, if you keep the
commandments of the LORD your God, and walk in his ways."
(Deut. 28:1–9; see also verses 15, 28; 29:1; cf. 30:15–20)

To be sure, Paul is not the first to announce that God maintains love for the chosen people even when they act wickedly.
Hosea portrayed God as being unable, because of love for Israel,
to execute the sentence of wrath, and he spoke movingly of
God's act to win the hearts of a recalcitrant people again. But
Paul emphatically claims that it is precisely human sin that
brings forth grace.

Grace in this context is not a feeling on God's part, but the
action by which God sets right that which is wrong. The action
of grace may well include the expressions of wrath (God's judgment against human sin), but the purpose of wrath in the
context of grace is justification, not condemnation.

The boldness of Paul's assertion generates a natural reaction
from traditional religious wisdom: "If human sin elicits such a
response from God, why not persist in sin in order to increase
the supply of grace?" This rhetorical question, often raised by
objectors to Paul's theology, intends to reveal the perceived
weakness in his position: By advocating grace/faith as sufficient for dealing with human sin, Paul undercuts the call to a
moral and ethical life, opening recipients of his gospel to lives
of immorality and consequently leading them not to salvation
but damnation. His gospel is thus not good news at all, but a
dangerous break with the valued insights of the past. Surely,
his opponents claim, one may hope that ultimately God will be
merciful and "not requite us for our deeds nor deal with us
according to our iniquities," but one should not presumptuously
assume that to be the case. A moral and ethical life in obedience
to God's commands is essential in the covenant community
of God's people. To advocate a position which, intentionally
or not, undermines that essential is to err dangerously.

Paul, of course, does not disagree with the assertion that
covenantal faithfulness demands moral and ethical living. He
believes that the commandments[4] express God's will (Rom. 7:12)
and that they should come to fruition in the life of faith (Rom.

8:4). But even though what the commandment advocates is good, the commandment does not accomplish the good, for reasons he will elaborate upon in Romans 7. Ethical living needs a more effective grounding than the Torah provides.

Paul finds that grounding in the power of interior grace, signified by the act of baptism. He appeals to the general experience of baptism in order to demonstrate that the person whose affirmation of faith has led to baptism has definitively left behind a former way of life and resolutely adopted a new outlook, a new communal environment, and a new mode of conduct. Paul assumes baptism as the universal rite of initiation into the church. He does not argue for it. At one point in his polemic against the Corinthians for their partisanship, Paul claims that baptism was not a part of his apostolic commission (1 Cor. 1:17); he did engage in it, however, as verses 13–16 make clear.

Paul never explicitly presents his view of baptism, but one can glean from his writings a fair sense of its practice and meaning in the Pauline communities. In addition to the points made above (that baptism is a universal rite signifying the adoption of a new way of life), Paul's remarks in chapter 6 show that for him baptism is connected with the crucified messiah:

> baptized into his death (vs. 3)
> buried . . . with him by baptism into death (vs. 4)
> our old self was crucified with him (vs. 6)
> we have died with Christ (vs. 8)

The community of Jesus' followers probably engaged in baptism before his death,[5] but baptism took on a different character after Jesus' death. Matthew includes baptism in the commission given the disciples by the risen Jesus. The connection between Jesus' death and baptism is not far below the surface in the gospel accounts of his own baptism by John, as the allusion to the Suffering Servant in Mark 1:11 shows.[6] A connection between the gift of the Spirit and baptism in Jesus' name is drawn especially closely in Acts (see also Mark 1:8). Paul does not utilize this latter connection directly, even though appeal to the Spirit's coming to the believer at baptism could strengthen his argument here in Romans 6. He does utilize the Spirit as the power of the new life in chapter 8, and one wonders why he failed to mention it here. Does he associate the Spirit less closely with baptism than others do?[7] It is certainly possible that Paul makes less of the connection between baptism and Spirit because of the tendency in some Hellenistic communities (such as Corinth) to engage in an enthusiastic religious fervor without a corresponding ethical transformation. Whether the Corinthian experience led Paul to downplay the ecstatic elements of baptism and to emphasize the cross (see 1 Cor. 1—2), he remains consistent here in Romans 6 with that emphasis. When he does deal with the Spirit in Romans 8, he connects the Spirit with moral life and presupposes the "death" symbolized here by baptism.

For whatever reasons, Paul emphasized *death* before he emphasizes life in the Spirit. Romans 6 reveals the extent to which all his thought is grounded in his conviction that the cross fundamentally reorients the whole world. The crucified Messiah constitutes the core of his preaching; its acceptance must also constitute the foundation of the moral life. Its central impact is death to the old self as a necessary condition for new life. Abandoning the Torah as the basis for ethical life in favor of spiritual ecstasy can quickly lead to spiritual pride, arrogance, and a perverted notion of freedom (see Corinthians again). If that were the nature of Paul's proclamation he could be rightly accused of promoting sin. Connecting baptism with death as its key symbol blocks that aberration of Paul's theology.

Baptism is a burial, an ending, before it is a resurrection, a new beginning. Just as Jesus' death is God's "no" to human pride, achievement, wisdom, and power, so baptism is the "no" of faith to the merely human. Baptism symbolizes faith, that moment of passivity in which one allows God to be God in one's life and accepts that reality as an end to one's own idolatrous self-assertion. The initiation into life is death.

The ironical paradox that the gospel brings death in order to bring life is striking, especially when one notes that in 5:21 "sin reigned in death." Now we learn that death does away with sin! Just as Christ "died to sin" (6:10) as a prelude to his being raised so that he now "lives to God," so also the baptized are to experience death and new life. Death is at the center of the new life; it is the ultimate point at which sin reigns, and it is paradoxically the point at which sin is dethroned and destroyed. That logic underlies Paul's earlier assertion that where sin increased, grace increased in greater abundance. "The one who has died is *justified* from sin." This strange expression, which translators in despair render as "set free," means that precisely at the point where sin has nullified human existence sin itself is rendered powerless. "Much more does the grace of God" abound; "death reigned," but much more will "grace ... reign in righteousness" (5:15–21).

With the language of death as the symbol of new life Paul erects another roadblock against the enthusiastic response which his gospel often received among his Gentile hearers. He refuses to bring resurrection fully into present life: "we *shall ... be* united with him in a resurrection like his" (6:5, my italics). Again his Corinthian experience might lie behind the care with which he chooses his tenses. Some Corinthians believed that the resurrection had already occurred and that they had already become full recipients of its power.[8] This "resurrection" had removed them from mundane concerns about morality or consideration for others. Enthusiastically religious, they believed they had been transformed into superior spiritual beings. Paul thought otherwise, and told them so. Now, in writing to the Romans, he wishes to guard against such spiritualistic aberrations. He does so by holding out a future resurrection, and by utilizing resurrection as a symbol for moral renewal in the present: "... so that we may conduct our lives in a new way" (6:4, my translation).

Baptism is intended to result, then, not in a mystical experience but rather in a conscious self-determination by which the baptized must consider themselves "dead to sin and alive to righteousness." What takes place in baptism is to take place in human consciousness. Baptism is not merely a sacrament that happens to a person; it is a personal happening as one knowingly and willingly sets aside one mode of existence and takes up another within a new community of faith.

Yet the dying and beginning of life anew should not be regarded merely as the realization of a human possibility; they are grounded in the grace of God's act which is symbolized in the baptismal participation in the death and resurrection of Jesus. Since, as we have seen, sin is not merely wrongdoing (immorality) but also a condition of alienation and a controlling power which can possess a person, a firm resolve to do better provides no adequate basis for freeing oneself from it. For Paul, God acts to liberate, to free from a power. God reestablishes his sovereignty. Baptism *into* Christ, into his death and resurrection, joins one to Christ as Lord and to a community which acknowledges that lordship. That lordship, though, is not a mystery which conveys its benefits and moves on; it is a lordship over continuing life.

Paul's combination of indicative and imperative statements confirms that reading of the passage:

> Do not let sin keep controlling your mortal bodies so that you obey its desires; rather, put yourselves at God's disposal[9] as those living out of death, and your members to God as instruments of righteousness (Rom. 6:12–14, my translation).

The indicative refers to God's grace, symbolized in the sacrament; the imperative signifies the response appropriate to persons belonging to the community of faith. Together they contain both sides of the covenantal relationship established in Christ. The baptized have already been claimed as God's people; they also must continue to be given to God's purposes. The reality of the former is the ground of the latter; just as Christ's death was once-for-all a death to sin, so should baptism mark a once-for-all death of the baptized. But just as resurrection is still future for believers in the way it is not for Christ, so death to sin is in a real sense future also. Baptism itself confers neither immortality nor sinlessness.

The traditional Protestant division between justification (as the beginning of the life of faith) and sanctification (the consequent and necessary growth in grace) does not provide a tenable[10] explanation of the structure of Romans, but it contains an element of truth in its perception of Paul's theology: the once-for-all act of baptism must lead to a life of faithfulness grounded in the covenant which both makes it possible and defines it. The covenantal grace of God is symbolized and expressed in baptism as God's incorporation of the baptized "into Christ," "with Christ." The grace which elicits faith is the irreplaceable ground of covenant faithfulness.

Paul believes grace adequately ensures that faithfulness. The Torah is for Paul no longer the primary expression of that covenanting grace, nor any longer the guide and source for the faithful life. What the Torah aimed at is, however, fulfilled, not obliterated, for Christ is the end of the Torah (Rom. 10:4), so that the "just requirement" of the Torah can come to fruition in those whose life is conducted through the Spirit (Rom. 8:4).

Sacramentalism?

Two issues of Paul's theology grow out of the language he uses regarding baptism. The terms "into Christ," "with Christ," and "into his death" raise the question of whether Paul's concepts can be described as either "sacramental" or "mystical." Does he believe that the act of baptism in and of itself conveys God's grace and incorporates one into the mystical body of Christ in a realistic sense? Or are these terms symbolic of what happens within the consciousness of the person allied to the new community of faith?

My interpretation above tends in the latter direction. With Paul's strong emphasis upon the role of faith, it is not likely that he believed that a ritual enactment apart from faith could be efficacious. Yet it would not be accurate to describe Paul's view of baptism as a "mere symbol." In Hebraic understanding there is a close connection between symbol and reality that would make "mere symbol" an inadequate designation: the symbol is created by the reality and the reality becomes attached to the symbol in such a way that the symbol conveys the reality. Thus grace concretized in the death and resurrection of Jesus invests the symbol of baptism in his name with its power.

As symbol, baptism proclaims that grace and makes it present in the community of faith, but since that grace has as its end the reconciliation and renewal of persons, and since faith is a necessary ingredient in relational salvation, it would be virtually impossible for Paul to hold a notion that baptism is effective irrespective of what happens in the conscious life of those baptized. Paul's language in Galatians 3:26–27 suggests that baptism is the norm for those of faith and that faith is prior to baptism:[11]

> For all are [children] of God, through faith in Jesus Christ. For all those who were baptized into Christ have put on Christ. (my translation)

Has baptism replaced circumcision as a requirement for inclusion in the community of God's people? Paul's radical gospel of grace and faith would be compromised if he required baptism as a necessary rite. 1 Corinthians 1:14–17 suggests that he did not pay much attention to baptism, though it was probably practiced with his concurrence or even his encouragement. It would be in keeping with his theological position to regard baptism as a highly expressive symbol of incorporation into Christ without equating it with what it symbolized.

Is baptism then a symbol for that mystical experience of union with Christ? The language of incorporation, frequently used by Paul, is found in Romans 6 in three of its versions—"into," "with," and "in":

> ... baptized into [*eis*] Christ Jesus.... (vs. 3)
> ... buried ... with [*syn*] him.... (vs. 4)
> ... united with [*syn*] in a death like his.... (vs. 5)
> ... crucified with [*syn*] him.... (vs. 6)
> ... died with [*syn*] Christ.... (vs. 8)
> ... alive to God in [*en*] Christ Jesus (vs. 11)

The future tense also occurs: "We shall be united with [*syn*] him in a resurrection like his (vs. 5); "we shall also live with [*syn*] him" (vs. 8).

Union with a god is not an extraordinary conception in the history of religions. Many religions have cultivated an experience of union as the ultimate goal of religious endeavor. Although we may think of this as especially true of Eastern religions stemming from or influenced by Hinduism, religious enthusiasm and ecstasy were commonly pursued in the Hellenistic world of Paul's day. In the mystery religions union with the deity was expected to bring immortality. Does Paul, under the influence of mystery religions, lead the church into "mysticism"?

New Testament interpreters have debated whether Paul's theology centers in the mystical experience of being "in Christ" or in the forensic reality of justification (understood as acquittal of the sinner). If my interpretation of the covenantal nature of Paul's theology is correct, the dichotomy suggested by that alternative is a false one. Both justification and "in Christ" are relational terms derived from covenant conceptions. A strong argument in favor of this understanding may be found in Paul's parallel between Christ and Adam: "For as in Adam all die, so also in Christ shall all be made alive" (1 Cor. 15:22).

If the parallelism here is genuine, and there is no reason to doubt that it is, the sentence argues for a non-mystical understanding. "In Adam" constitutes solidarity with the rebellious, idolatrous, alienated, and hostile humanity subservient to sin and death. "In Christ" constitutes solidarity with the renewed humanity present in and through Jesus Christ: reconciled, freed from the enslaving power of sin, given new life, serving God in peace and joy. Paul's terminology builds more upon the Hebraic notions of "corporate personality" than upon mystical notions of the mysteries.[12] There is, as L. Cerfaux argues, no distinction between "in Christ" and the other prepositional phrases by which Paul expresses the relationship between Christ and the believer: "into," "with," "according to" and "through."[13] All these terms are equivalent to "belonging to" Christ, and thus are indicative of personal relationship rather than of mystical union.

To argue against a mystical interpretation is not to argue that "in Christ" has nothing to do with religious experience. Paul's experience, like that of many others in the early church, included prayer, praise, ecstatic rapture, "visions and revelations" (2 Cor. 12:1). But "in Christ" does not describe that experience nor does that experience explain the essence of being in Christ. If we were to label "in Christ" as either mystical or moral, moral would be closer to what Paul means by it, though that is a rather weak term. Better than either would be "eschatological": just as Adam stands for the old aeon of sin and death, Christ stands for the new aeon, which is in process of replacing the old, an aeon of righteousness and life. In the figure below, "in Christ" suggests the communal nature of faith. Even though Paul does not identify the church with Christ, it is at least metaphorically associated with his body. Being in Christ engages one in the covenant community which celebrates Christ as Lord and strives to live in obedience to his will. An individualistic emphasis which suggests that "in Christ" is merely personal and private will miss a central element in Paul's theology.

IN ADAM	IN CHRIST
Gentile and Jew	One new humanity
sin	righteousness
law	faith
wrath	peace
death	life
disobedience	obedience
"in the flesh"	"in the spirit"
judgment	justification

Present transition:
God's act in Christ, responded to in faith,
symbolized by baptism

FIGURE 1

Freedom and Slavery

In Romans 6:15–23 Paul uses a metaphor for the life of faith which was as inherently unattractive in his day as it is today: slavery. Slaves had no rights; they could be used, abused, or cast out at the will of their owners. Paul himself recognizes the limitations of this metaphor in chapter 8 when he says believers did not receive a "spirit of slavery which leads again to fear" but a "spirit of adoption." Why, then, at this point does Paul choose the symbol of slavery?

For two reasons, perhaps. First, the symbol provides an emphasis needed to counter the charge that his antinomianism amounts to license; it shows that the life of faith does not allow one to do whatever may seem appealing. The life of faith is a life lived in obedience to the will of God. In the introduction of the letter he spoke of the response which the proclamation of the gospel seeks to engender as "believing obedience" (Rom. 1:5). The symbol of slavery continues that emphasis.

Second, in his eschatological understanding, opposing supernatural forces struggle for dominion over humans; in that context sin is an alien power which rules human existence. Correspondingly, salvation is liberation by God, who claims a new and rightful dominion. Salvation is the extension of the lordship of Christ, under whose sovereign reign one is placed through faith and baptism. This political metaphor is natural for one whose thought is molded by Israel's history and tradition. God is the great king of Israel, whose dominion is now exercised through the risen Christ, who has been exalted to God's right hand and given the name "Lord" (Phil. 2:11). The metaphor of "servant" or "slave" becomes a natural corollary to these monarchical rather than democratic political images. Paul acknowledges, however, that his speech here is analogical and not direct (an acknowledgment which he does not make in the use of adoption): "I am giving all this in a human illustration because your understanding is only human."[14]

Paul's illustration is not in itself a model of clarity. Especially his use of obedience becomes muddled as he contrasts two ways of expressing the obedience which is a necessary form of human existence:

> either: slaves of sin (leading to death)
> or: slaves of obedience (leading to righteousness, Rom. 6:6)

> either: slaves of sin
> or: obedient to the received teaching (Rom. 6:17)

either: yield to impurity (leading to greater iniquity)
or: yield to righteousness (leading to holiness, Rom. 6:19)

either: slaves of sin (Rom. 6:20)
or: slaves of God (Rom. 6:22)

Obedience, received teaching, righteousness, and God all are mentioned as objects of right obedience, as opposed to obedience to sin or impurity. The results are also not expressed with complete consistency: negatively, the result of obedience to sin is iniquity (vs. 19), freedom from righteousness (vs. 20), or death (vss. 16, 21). Positively, obedience results in righteousness (vs. 16), freedom from sin (vs. 18), holiness (vs. 19), sanctification and eternal life (vs. 22).

Although the imagery may be confusing because it is less than consistent, and although the paragraph is redundant, Paul's point is nevertheless clear: the life of faith does not offer a license but a lordship. It is thus slanderous to charge him (as some do, 3:8) with teaching that "we should do evil in order that the good may come." Paul's intent here is to defend his gospel against that charge. This defense is, as we have suggested, not the primary purpose of the letter, but it is essential to that purpose.

Chapter 6 then primarily serves an argumentative rather than an hortatory purpose. There is some exhortation in it, especially at verses 11–13 and again in verse 19, but the exhortation primarily illustrates the nature of the moral imperative within the life of faith.

One large issue dominates his argument: does salvation by faith undermine ethical living? Is the Torah necessary to keep the person of faith from immorality? Will people be good only if goodness is commanded and defined by law? Paul answers with the logic of believing obedience (faith) which is the logic of a new life. The change from an old life to a new one requires the assent of the one in whom it has occurred. The recognizably positive benefits deriving from the change of lordship are such that no one in a right mind would change back. Thus, for Paul faith is not an insurance policy payable upon death for one who has kept its terms and paid its premiums; faith is a way of living, which once experienced will continue to be voluntarily accepted because of its inherent desirability.

But there is also more at work than an individual change of consciousness. For Paul, faith in Christ brings one into a new sphere, the sphere of Christ as a member of his body. The community of faith is a new social reality within which one lives out the life of faith as a part of an organic whole, not merely as an isolated individual. By incorporation into the body of Christ one participates in the beginning of a new creation: "Anyone who is in Christ is a new creation; the old has passed away, the new has come" (2 Cor. 5:17, my translation). Paul's argument includes the notion that "new conduct is already included in the new being."[15] That conduct is affirmed as God's will in the personal obedience which is the Spirit's gift to those within the covenant community of faith (Rom. 8:1–11).

The imperative is necessary to show that the powers which have enslaved are not dead because of baptism and incorporation into the new covenant community. The imperative guards against triumphalism which sees freedom from sin as moral perfection and against the complacency that such perfectionism can engender. Thus the imperative is a necessary part of the argument. But since the imperative is rooted not merely in human good will nor in human moral power but in the gospel of grace, even the imperative is encouragement as well as demand.[16]

The Torah and the Divided Self

Chapter 7 in Romans has significant differences from anything else we have from Paul. Those differences, along with some ambiguities in the text, create problems for the interpreter. Attention focuses especially upon the internal struggle against sin which leads to the anguished cry, "Who will deliver me from this body of death?" Does this anguish come from the so-called happy pagan, who in spite of a frivolous disregard for morality and decency is nevertheless troubled by a conscience which gives no rest? Or is it the anguish of the Jew who, celebrating God's gifts in election, covenant, and Torah, nevertheless knows moral failing and is disquieted over the inability to live according to the commands of the Torah? Or does the anguish belong to the person of faith who knows that in spite of baptism, profession of faith, the desire to do God's will, and the experience of the Spirit, sin still has inordinate power?

One problem is that Paul elsewhere describes none of our three candidates in the terms he uses here. If the Gentile suffers from guilty conscience it is not evident in that description of idolatry and immorality given in Romans 1. Perhaps it is dimly reflected in 2:15, when Paul suggests that at the judgment the Gentiles' conflicting thoughts and their consciences will condemn or excuse them for their response to the law written on their hearts, but for the most part Paul does not presuppose a guilty conscience in the Gentiles to whom the gospel is addressed.

Neither does Paul regard the Jew as being torn by this inner contradiction. The Jew in chapter 2 exhibits pride and boasting, and, even if disobedient, does not seem to be troubled by conscience; rather there is too much confidence that regardless of what the Jew does God's electing grace will continue. In describing his own life as a Jew elsewhere, Paul gives no indication of being troubled in conscience. Rather, he considered himself not only full of zeal for the Torah but also blameless under it (Phil. 3:4–6). Again there is no indication that he saw in the gospel the answer to the guilty feelings of Jews who were sensitive to their failings under the Torah.

Neither does Paul elsewhere present the life of the believer in such dark terms as those found in Romans 7. It is true that he sees the life of faith as a struggle; obedience does not become automatic for the baptized person, as the imperatives of chapter 6 show. In Galatians he admonishes his readers:

> Walk by the Spirit, and do not gratify the desires of the flesh. For the desires of the flesh are against the Spirit, and the desires of the Spirit are against the flesh; for these are opposed to each other, to prevent you from doing what you would. (Gal. 5:16–17)

It is clear that believers are not beyond the possibility of succumbing to the desires of the flesh, that they need continued vigilance and guidance so that faith will express itself in love. But if Paul does not view the life of faith in perfectionist terms, he does believe that in some significant sense the believers have been set free from sin. Thus the statements in chapter 7 seem hardly appropriate descriptions of the life of faith: "I am carnal, sold [as a slave] under [the power of] sin" (7:14). If Paul had believers in mind in writing this paragraph, believers would be the most miserable of all people, which is not the way Paul elsewhere speaks of them. The kingdom is, he says, "peace and joy in the Holy Spirit" (Rom. 14:17).

The question of identity of the "I" in chapter 7 is best approached by careful attention to the question Paul intends to be answering. Such a common-sense observation would seem gratuitous were it not for the fact that is so often overlooked. We have argued that chapters 6—7 have as their major purpose the defense of Paul's gospel against his critics. Chapter 7 specifically is an answer to a charge which grows out of his assertion in 5:20 that the effect of the Torah is an increase in the trespass. That assertion could suggest to some of his hearers that Paul says that the Torah is not from God; rather it is from the one whose purpose is to increase sin, or even that the Torah itself *is sin*. Paul directly confronts this issue in 7:7.

The question put to Paul by his opponents is neither trivial nor unfair. Its seriousness is seen in the implications of saying that the Torah is sinful: if it is, then either God has played a monstrous trick on Israel by commanding them to keep a Torah which was evil in the guise of good; or, the God who gave the Torah is not really the "God and Father of our Lord Jesus Christ," but an inferior or even evil being. If the latter is the case, then Israel's election, covenant, promises, and history are to be totally rejected as evil, and faith in Jesus is a new, true religion in opposition to the false religion of the Jews. In the second century Marcion adopted a view quite like that described, and claimed Paul as his champion.

If that seems an outrageous reading of Paul, he himself is partly to blame. In the heat of battle for Gentile freedom he says some very negative things about the Torah and what it commands:

The Torah is a "yoke of slavery." (Gal. 5:1)

Hagar, the slave woman who bears "children for slavery ... is ... from Mount Sinai." (Gal. 4:24–25)

"Christ redeemed us from the curse of the [Torah]." (Gal. 3:13)

"... the [Torah] was our custodian[17] until Christ came."
(Gal. 3:24)

"The Torah came in to increase the trespass." (Rom. 5:20)

"Sin will have no dominion over you, since you are not under [the Torah] but under grace." (Rom. 6:14)

There is no complete consistency in these statements. Though they all imply that the Torah is inadequate, inferior, and temporary, some are more negative than others. The statement in 5:20 could not be made of the child's custodian, even if custodian is not a positive image. The pressures of arguing against the necessity of the Torah might well have been responsible for Paul's negative statements. But some of them were, as perhaps he himself came to recognize, overstatements.[18] In general there is a different tone in Romans from that in Galatians. There is less defensiveness and aggressiveness. Yet, some of his strongest theoretical statements against the Torah (as opposed to emotional statements) are in Romans—especially if 5:20 is understood to express the *purpose* and not merely the result of the Torah. There is a logical connection between what Paul says in Galatians and Romans 5:20 (and the subsequent emphasis upon freedom from the Torah in chapters 6—7). But in Romans his passionate defensiveness is not so engaged; as he wrestles with the issue of whether his position has led him implicitly to define the Torah as sin, he makes changes in his approach. He examines the issue in light of the nature of human existence. In doing so he at the same time offers an apology for the Torah and also engages in a profound reflection upon the power of sin in human life in a way he does not do elsewhere.

The gist of his position is that the Torah, though expressive of God's will (implicitly then, from God; cf. Rom. 5:20: the Torah "came in") does not contain within it the power to bring itself to fulfillment (cf. Gal. 3:21: "if a [Torah] had been given which could make alive, then righteousness would indeed be by the [Torah]"). The problem of sin is fundamentally due to a flaw in human nature, a flaw which is both weakness and rebellion.

Confronted by the rebellious and weak nature of human existence, the Torah has disastrous consequences. It aroused sinful passions (7:5); it taught the meaning of sin, not merely by pointing out what actions were sinful, but much more profoundly by bringing to consciousness the desire to rebel (7:7–11). Paul cites as an example the effect of the commandment "You shall not covet...." Following a Jewish tradition that this commandment is the "core and sum of the law,"[19] Paul claims that the essential intent of the Torah is rendered impossible by the Torah itself, due to the nature of those to whom it is addressed. Paul breaks off the quotation of the commandment before it names the objects not to be coveted; the effect is to give the term its broadest possible meaning. The absence of specific objects of covetousness suggests that the core of the problem is not merely that a forbidden fruit is more desirable, but that the restriction of freedom produces rebellion. Covetousness then becomes the passion to assert oneself against God and neighbor.

The propensity of humans to rebel against a life of obedience and to assert independence from any lordship makes the Torah inadequate to deal with the human predicament. If knowledge of what is good could solve the problem, the Torah could solve it, for the Torah does express God's will. The possession of it can even enable one to be a "guide to the blind, a light to those who are in darkness, a corrector of the foolish, a teacher of children," for the Torah is "the embodiment of knowledge and truth" (Rom. 2:19–20). But the problem is fundamentally lack of obedience in the rebellious heart, and that problem is not solved by the Torah. What is needed in Paul's view is an internal change within the human, akin to Jeremiah's notion of the law written on the heart. For Jeremiah, that does not mean that the law has been memorized, but that it has been received by an obedient self whose center of willing (the heart) has internalized God's will.[20] That internalization Paul attributes to the Spirit, whose presence provides the motivating power (Rom. 8:4), and by whose presence one finds a resolution of the conflict between the willing and the doing.

Is Paul being fair to Israel's traditions when he virtually identifies the Torah with commandment, as he does here in chapter 7? As John Calvin says, he seems to forget that the Torah was based on grace.[21] In seeing Torah as commandment, creating rebellion, Paul isolates it from the grace of God's act of deliverance. In Exodus the Torah from Sinai is prefaced by the liberation from Egypt; on the basis of that creative act which gives the people life, God presents them with commands which are to express their grateful and faithful response. The commandments, in other words, have grace as their ground and grace as their context. Jews who recognized this expressed delight in the Torah; they did not regard it as an onerous burden but as a sign of God's grace.

How does Paul so completely separate Torah and covenantal grace? Is it because of his own experience under the Torah? Is it because of Gentile context? Perhaps it is some of both. Perhaps as Schoeps says, because that tendency was present in Hellenistic Judaism from which Paul came. Perhaps, as Wilckens maintains, Torah was the central issue from the beginning for Paul; his eschatological view of the messianic age led him to remove the wall of separation between Gentile and Jew. He sees humans as humans, not first as Israelites or Gentiles. For him Adam has primacy over Moses in both defining the human situation and in exposing the true nature of humanity's rebellion against God. As I have suggested there is a parallel drawn between Adam and Moses; the former is a type of the latter (Rom. 5:14).[22] The Adamic and Mosaic covenants were alike to Paul in that they both involved commandments intended to generate obedient response to prior acts of grace in creation or redemption. The Commandments, though quite different in form, were in essence the same: they involved a prohibition on *coveting* or *desiring* in the broad sense of rebellion against God by seeking precisely what was forbidden, namely freedom from God. Sin gains power in such a context, for the power of sin is the Torah as commandment (1 Cor. 15:56; cf. Rom. 5:f).

Paul rarely speaks positively of the Mosaic period (he does indicate God's grace in giving the Torah in 9:1–4), just as he does not speak positively of the Adamic period before the fall. In both cases, he believes, grace has been missed and rebellion against direct commandments has been generated. That is why Abraham can be set in contrast and can offer a positive model of the relation with God. Abraham received promises to which he responded in faith; he did not (in Paul's reading) receive commands which generate rebellion. Abraham can then provide an analogy for Christ in whom God's promises are confirmed and renewed, but who does not bring new commandments.[23]

Who Is the "I" of Romans 7?

For reasons indicated above, interpreters have found it difficult to know about whom Paul speaks here. I have argued that the question is best answered when attention is given to Paul's purpose: the defense of his gospel against his opponents. Paul's purpose then is not to describe any particular person or group, but to speak of the human reality which prevents the Torah from bringing God's will to fulfillment. More particularly he wishes to show that even though the Torah expresses God's will, when confronted with the human propensity for rebellion, the Torah actually generates more sinfulness (7:7–13). This point could be sufficiently established by this paragraph alone; but Paul's need to offer a convincing apology to show that the Torah is not sin leads him to reflect further upon the human condition.

The change from the past tense to the present in verse 14 has been used as a strong argument in favor of taking verses 14–25 to refer to "Christian experience," and verses 7–13 to refer to Paul's pre-conversion experience under the Torah. More likely the "I" is not really personal in either case. Many have argued that in verses 7–13 Paul sums up his experience in growing up: his time of innocence (when he was "once alive apart from the

[Torah]," Rom. 7:9) came abruptly to an end at around the age of twelve when he became a *bar mitzvah*. At that point he felt the force of the commandments—especially, "you shall not covet." This commandment brought his latent rebellion to the fore: "Sin sprang to life, and I died" (vs. 9, my translation). From then on, so this interpretation goes, Paul struggled to do God's will, but never felt that he had really accomplished it, and moreover, was burdened with guilt because of his failure. Only the gospel of grace in Christ saved him from despair, as he learned that he was justified by grace through faith and not by his own works.

There are several problems with this interpretation. First, it doesn't agree with Philippians 3:4–8 in which Paul speaks of his experience under the Torah; he speaks of the past as a time of pride, not of guilt. Second, the notion of an innocent childhood without the Torah is not Jewish.[24] Third, under this reading, "I was alive" and "I died" would be reduced to a process within the consciousness, whereas for Paul death and life are not merely subjective states.[25]

Verses 14–25 have also been taken to be autobiographical. Attributing special significance to the change in tenses, the proponents of this view argue that Paul reflects the difficulty which he has, even after his convictional change, in putting God's will into practice. Putting the two together, many have seen Paul's problem both in the past and in the present to be a conscience rendered guilty by his moral and spiritual failures. In this view the gospel makes its major impact by granting forgiveness, hope, and perhaps some measure of increased obedience. Krister Stendahl has argued persuasively that this model for understanding Paul is an erroneous reading of Paul through the eyes of Martin Luther.[26]

I have stated earlier that Paul can speak of the human situation either in terms of "they" (Rom. 1), or in terms of Adam (Rom. 5:12–21), or in terms of "I" (Rom. 7). In each case the problem is fundamentally the same: God's offer of life is rejected; humans become alienated, separated from God and from the fulfillment of his will; thus human existence apart from God is frustrated and doomed to death. The situation is changed only by God's grace which has now been fully made present in Jesus Christ. He is the source of a new covenantal relationship with God which brings liberation, justification, removal of sins, reconciliation. Romans 7 then is no more and no less autobiographical than Romans 1 and 5. The Genesis story of Adam is the molding influence in all three instances, and that story is read both on a general and on a very personal level. No doubt Paul speaks here of himself, but not really about his subjective consciousness. He speaks of himself as a human like all other humans; but it is not his own subjective experience which he is describing.

One further question about the "I" remains: what is the object of the willing which fails to find fulfillment? Rudolf Bultmann has argued convincingly that the struggle is not between the subjective willing of the individual person and the objective failure to fulfill that will (i.e., a tension between *will* and *deed*). Paul's anthropology, he argues, is not subjectivist. The willing of which Paul speaks is not the attempt of the conscious self to do God's will in particular commandments. Nor is the failure limited to a particular deed. *Life* is willed in all human doing, but what comes is *death*. When law meets the human self with God's demands, and the self rebels, it is not seeking death; rather it thinks that by taking charge of its own existence, by being like God, it will achieve life. But that pursuit brings death because in wanting to be independent the self is lost and dies. The deceptive power of sin lies in its utilizing the desire to achieve life to bring about death.

The "I" can find the solution to its predicament in a covenantal context in which life is perceived as a gift of grace, not as a human achievement or as a reward for adequately good behavior in response to commands; where death is not seen as a threat carried out in punishment, but as the only possible choice for those who miss life as grace. Paradoxically as Paul expressed it in 5:17, the way for humans to rule in their own lives is to renounce such rule—allowing God to be God rather than rebelling against his rule enables those of faith to "reign in life through the one person Jesus Christ." That can be so because faith receives "grace and the gift of right relationships" (Rom. 5:17, my translation). The division within the self is healed in the covenantal relationship offered in the gospel, for Gentile and Jew alike.

7

New Covenant, New Life, and the Spirit

(Romans 8)

Protestant interpreters of Romans have typically seen chapter 8 as the culmination of the letter; here Paul brings together the themes of justification and the new life in the Spirit. That interpretation reflects the traditional Protestant emphasis upon individual sin and salvation. I have argued that much more importance should be given to the issue of the unity of Gentile and Jew within one new covenant community. If I am correct, chapters 9—11, with their stress upon the final inclusion of Israel within the new covenant community, and chapters 12—15, with their admonitions for unity within the diverse church, are integral to the purpose of Romans and should not be relegated to postscript status. Nevertheless, chapter 8 does bring together many of the themes of chapters 1—7. If it is not the watershed of the Epistle, it is still a high peak.

A Brief Analysis of the Passage

Chapter 8 particularly gathers up the central thrust of

chapters 6 and 7 and takes the key points further, by connecting the new life of morality with the Spirit (reflecting the concerns of chapter 6) and by connecting the fulfillment of the Torah with the Spirit (reflecting the concerns of chapter 7). The new covenant given in Christ Jesus does not nullify the call of God for people to live a moral life—quite the contrary: because of the presence of the Spirit, God brings to fulfillment in the community of faith the "just requirement of the Torah" (8:1–5).

In sounding these themes Paul leaps without clear transitions from one to another, as one caught up in the excitement of an idea that captures life and imagination. His declaration that the Torah comes to fulfillment through the Spirit leads to the related theme of Spirit's giving life (8:6–13). Sin brings death; consequently freedom from sin brings freedom from death. Renewal of the inner life through the Spirit brings life eternal: the "Spirit is life" for persons of faith. This insight leads into the next theme (8:14–18, and beneath the surface to the end of the chapter); life in the covenant "in Christ" is a life of adoption, for the Spirit leads one to say "Abba! Father!" Thus, Spirit, ethical life, eternal life, and adoption are all interrelated themes in chapter 8. Together they push forward to the next theme, the future realization of all that God's grace is now accomplishing in human life. It is adoption that immediately provides the motive and power for speaking about the future, for children—as opposed to slaves—have a future. In 8:17 we find the transition: "if children, then heirs." 8:18–25 universalizes the glory associated with adoption, and applies it to the whole creation. 8:26–39 affirms the expectation that God will bring the fulfillment in God's own way, since persons of faith do not even know how to pray for that fulfillment. They do know, however, the inner groaning or yearning which characterizes the whole creation (8:22–23) and with which the Spirit fills them; they do know the guarantee which the Spirit gives that fulfillment is in the power of the one who predestines and glorifies and from whom nothing can separate the covenant people who are loved by God (8:37–39).

These intertwining themes of life, spirit, and righteousness in chapter 8, highly reminiscent of prophetic emphases, reveal the covenantal pattern of Paul's thought. The prophet Ezekiel presents God's promise to put a new heart and a new spirit in the chosen people; as a result they will live in accord with God's will as expressed in the statutes and ordinances and the land will become "like a garden of Eden" (Ezek. 36:26ff; cf. Rom. 8:4, 19). Israel will be God's people and God will be their God (Ezek. 37:23, 27); God will make for them a "covenant of peace," and David will be their ruler (Ezek. 37:25–26). For Paul this anticipated messianic age has dawned: the new covenant has been established; God's people are being restored; creation will be renewed; the Spirit is creating new righteousness in the community of faith.

Perhaps even more striking than his similarity to Ezekiel is Paul's use of themes from Isaiah 59. Earlier (Rom. 3:15–17) Paul had quoted from this chapter in his characterization of the sinfulness of the Jews. He also quotes from it in 11:26 in connection with the eschatological promise that the deliverer will come from Zion, ungodliness will be banished from Jacob, and a new covenant will follow the removal of sin. Thus even though there is no direct quotation from Isaiah 59 in Romans 8, one is surely justified in seeing its influence in the association of the Spirit, the fulfillment of God's will, and the renewal of life. By using these prophetic themes Paul is describing a new covenant which gives new life in a new age.

Flesh and Spirit

Paul's contrast of "flesh" and "spirit" in this chapter can lead to great confusion. The terms carry a range of meanings, not all of which are easily harmonized. "Spirit" can mean Holy Spirit or Spirit of God; in many instances, especially in Romans 8, the translator does not know whether to use "Spirit" to indicate the Holy Spirit or "spirit" to indicate the human spirit. I will discuss Paul's understanding of the Holy Spirit in the next section of this chapter. In regard to humans, spirit can mean the psychic or emotional life of a human being, with no moral or religious connotations at all: the arrival of Paul's friends from Achaia "refreshed my spirit" (1 Cor. 16:18).[1] Spirit can also refer to the attitudes or qualities that a person displays in life, such as a "gentle spirit" (1 Peter 3:4), or a "dull spirit" (Rom. 11:8). More important theologically, the spirit can also refer to the renewed life of a human being in right relationship with God: to be "in the spirit" or to live "according to the spirit."

"Flesh," too, can have a wide variety of meanings. It can refer to ordinary life without regard to its quality or its relationships: "The life I now live in the flesh" (Gal. 2:20) simply means "my present existence." But "in the flesh" or "according to the flesh" can also indicate a life of alienation which should have been left behind by those who have faith: "You are not in the flesh, you are in the Spirit, if in fact the Spirit of God dwells in you" (Rom. 8:9).

The contrast between "in the spirit" and "in the flesh" reveals the most important and potentially the most confusing meaning of these terms. The contrast is not between two "parts" which make up human beings, one part essentially good and the other part either problematic or essentially evil. Rather the contrast is between two ways of life, two fundamental orientations which are possible for humans to have. "Flesh" then is not the outward stuff of which humans are made; it is what humans have made of themselves when they have turned from God. "Spirit" is correspondingly not what humans are made of inside, but what humans are shown to be when faith is expressed in their way of life.

To be in the flesh means to exhibit an attitude of the self-reliant person who trusts in the merely human, or to have values and commitments which derive from the alienated ego and its desires. A combination of egoistic self-reliance and pursuit of self-satisfaction may best describe being "in the flesh." The life of the flesh goes beyond mere sensual gratification; it includes also "spiritual" self-gratification, or the satisfaction of one's drives to be successful. Paul's list of "works of the flesh" in Galatians contains acts which express sensuality, such as illicit sexual activities, moral impurity, licentious behavior, and excessive banqueting. But it also includes "spiritual" sins such as idolatry, sorcery, hostile feelings or actions, strife, jealousy, enmity, outbursts of rage, disputes, dissensions, and factions (Gal. 5:19–21). Such lists of vices (and virtues—see vss. 22–23) probably are derived from popular philosophy, perhaps mediated to Paul through Hellenistic Judaism. The point here is not so much the individual vices as the fact that they include both "sensual" and "spiritual" sins, thus rendering this distinction irrelevant. The strongly social character of this list of works of the flesh confirms the perception that alienation is the key ingredient in living "according to the flesh."

Living "according to the spirit" is the exact opposite of living according to the flesh; it too refers to a disposition or orientation of life, but in the positive sense of affirming God's will, of being reconciled and trusting. A person of faith can live according to the spirit, for the trusting acceptance of grace opens one up to an acceptance of God's will as good. That is why the Torah's requirement of righteousness can come to fulfillment in those who live not according to the flesh but according to the spirit (Rom. 8:4).[2]

Spirit, here, refers not primarily to the Spirit of God but to the human spirit, or to the positive human orientation to the will of God. It is akin to the notion in Ezekiel that God will put within them a new heart of flesh or a heart of spirit (a faithful disposition), or it refers in Jeremiah's terms to a new covenant written on the heart. Such a person could also be said to have God's Spirit, for when the human spirit [= human affirmation and acceptance of God's will] and divine Spirit [= the presence and power of God expressed in the human world] are in harmony, one can indifferently be said to live "according to the spirit" or "according to the Spirit." The spirit in humans then is not some higher principle or special intellectual or spiritual power or faculty, but simply the self viewed as willing, purposing, intending,[3] when God's will is the content of that mind-set. Conversely, "flesh" does not mean "lower nature" (NEB), but the human self alienated from God's will.

Throughout this passage Paul contrasts the two ways of life

(and for him there are only two) available to human beings in order to affirm the power of the gospel to transform human life. The concerns of chapters 6 and 7 are thus continued and resolved here. The life of faith is not a life of sin and more sin; rather, it is a life of faithfulness in the spirit. Therefore the accusation that justification by faith apart from the Torah leads to licentiousness is totally false. Justification by faith is the only way in which God's will can hope to come to realization. The Torah did not solve the problem of living according to the flesh. The problem of alienation expressed in idolatry and immorality was only intensified, so that flesh became even more dominant. Because of the nature of human existence already in rebellion, it could do no other. What the Torah intended in expressing God's will can come to fulfillment only in a community of faith. This strongly suggests that the intent of the Torah was the life of faith which it could not directly produce, a suggestion which appears to be at odds with the statement in Romans 5:20: "[The Torah] came in, to increase the trespass." However, if "to increase" does not mean "in order to increase" (its most customary meaning in Greek), but "with the result that sin increased" (a possible meaning in Greek), the contradiction would be largely eliminated. The Torah resulted in greater rebellion (as in Rom. 7), but God supplied his grace in such proportion ("much more") that the result has not been permanent. Rebellion is overcome in those who through faith walk "according to the spirit."

Flesh and spirit then are not two warring irreconcilable components which necessarily produce schizophrenia in human beings so long as mortal life endures. In Paul's optimistic view the triumph of grace may be known in the present existence. Although Paul resists the triumphalists at Corinth who think they have passed beyond good and evil and have achieved spiritual freedom and although he affirms his own imperfection (Phil. 3:10–14), he nonetheless believes that the life of faith "in the spirit" has brought one beyond the moral paralysis expressed in Romans 7. "There is therefore now no condemnation for those who are in Christ Jesus" (Rom. 8:1). A new life is possible and has begun within those who participate in the community of faith which God is producing through the Spirit at work with the human spirit. The way in which that renewal is due to the working of God's grace may be seen more clearly by examining Paul's language about the Holy Spirit and its work within the world.

The juxtaposition of "in the spirit" and "in the flesh" presents a dramatic either/or which suggests that for Paul one is either totally committed or totally alienated. Such language is confusing, leaving the reader uncertain about the effect of Paul's meaning. How is the past which was leading to death related to the future which is leading to life? How do both the past and the future impinge upon the actual present? Am I dead or alive? Am I a sinner or righteous? Am I justified or condemned? Reconciled or at enmity? Liberated or in bondage? Am I a person of faith or not? Paul's readers are often appropriately confused, especially if they take him seriously. Most honest people know that present life is a tension between good and evil, faith and unfaith, trust and fear, love and hate. So how can Paul speak in such either/or terms, to suggest that we are either "in the flesh" or "in the spirit"? If he really believed that one is either totally within or totally without, why would he need to direct imperatives toward believers?

Paul's language has a strongly Hebraic character in this as in many other matters. It was characteristic of Hebraic thought to put issues in either/or terms: either God is Lord or not—Israel cannot limp between two options; either Israel is faithful or faithless—a mixed response to God's call is a negative response. Jesus' teaching is filled with either/or statements: there are two gates, two ways, two masters, two treasures between which one must make a decisive choice. So Paul also speaks in terms of alternatives: either you are in the spirit or you are in the flesh. In many instances, of course, Paul speaks to Corinthians and others of the need for growth, for maturing in the faith, to indicate that the matter is not all one way or the other. Nevertheless, the radical antithesis remains characteristic of Paul's language in many places.

The radical antithesis of flesh and spirit is perceived by Paul not to apply merely individualistically but communally. Being placed in the sphere of the Spirit [=in Christ] is an event in personal history, taking place at baptism, but it transfers a person to a new realm, the realm of the community of faith. In that sense one can realistically be said to belong either to the flesh [=outside the community of faith] or to the spirit. Paul's language is reminiscent of that of the Dead Sea Scrolls, according to which one is within the society of the flesh or else a member of the community of the covenant. To be in the community does not mean total absence of evil, but it does involve participation within the community which represents God's work of renewal in human life.[4]

Such language is not meant to describe individual or group behavior so much as to prescribe what the community of faith should be. The language is that of the prophetic call, which is intended to result in decisive commitment that leads into a future of increased faithfulness. Paul is not so interested in measuring the degree of progress made by those to whom he writes, though he sometimes does praise them for their faith. Rather, he intends to call them to greater faithfulness by presenting the gospel as all-consuming, demanding a death and a new life, occupying so dominant a place in life that nothing else matters. He generally does not hold up his own accomplishments or that of others as models to be emulated; rather, he holds up God's call and revelation in Jesus Christ as an all-consuming claim upon those who hear it.

"In the Spirit"

In this chapter Paul connects many themes of his theology with the "Spirit of God" or "Holy Spirit." In its barest essential meaning, the Spirit is the presence of God effectively accomplishing God's will. The Spirit is not spoken of as mere presence but as active presence. For Paul God is present and at work for the renewal of human life, producing a new humanity; that renewal may be spoken of as a new creation, as justification, or as reconciliation. The particular terms are not as important as the reality of that renewal. Since God's active presence for human renewal is manifest in the Christ event, the Spirit is linked to the proclamation of that saving event and to the faithful response to it. So closely does Paul link the Spirit with Christ that he can say, "the Lord is the Spirit" (2 Cor. 3:17) or again, "Any one who does not have the Spirit of Christ does not belong to him" (Rom. 8:9).

Paul connects the Spirit with the confession of faith by which one comes to participate in the community of the new covenant. He explains the baptismal cry, "Abba! Father!" as being God's Spirit "bearing [joint] witness with our spirit that we are children of God" (Rom. 8:16). The confession of faith regularly made at baptism, including uttering "Jesus is Lord," can be made only through the assistance of the Spirit: "No one can say 'Jesus is Lord' except by the Holy Spirit" (1 Cor. 12:3). The point of such statements is not to advance a predestinarian belief that God selects only some to be saved, but to affirm that human salvation is assured because it ultimately depends not on human will and power, but on God. Confession of faith is a human need and it becomes a reality in human life, but it is not a human accomplishment.

Paul's intensely personal language about the Spirit's presence is especially fitting after the autobiographical terms used in chapter 7 to speak of the weakness of the flesh. But though the experience of the Spirit is intensely personal, it is not merely private. For Paul both human sin and human renewal take place within personal relationships, not merely in isolated individuals. Thus the Spirit leads not only to personal faith, but also to community. The communal context of faith is reflected in Paul's shift from the first person singular to the first person plural.[5] He used the first person singular to speak of humanity in its alienation (chapter 7); he uses the first person plural to refer to the new humanity of which the community of faith is the beginning and the sign. The "I" under the power of sin is alone; the "I" who professes faith is part of a community.

The communal aspects of the Spirit's work are revealed in the mutual responsibility members have for each other. In chapters 14—15 Paul deals with division within the church by emphasizing the commonality which all possess, which he describes as "peace and joy in the Holy Spirit." In 1 Corinthians 12 he states even more emphatically that the Spirit's gifts (*charismata*) are not individual possessions but community assets. The Spirit binds the church in *koinonia,* community; the beginning of a renewed humanity consists of a community of persons, divine and human, bound together. The Spirit strengthens that community, uniting it, making it holy (dedicated to God), and equipping it for its task of reconciliation. The church, therefore, is a "spiritual" reality because it depends upon the Spirit. "Spiritual" does not mean ethereal or out of touch with the ordinary world, but Spirit-filled and Spirit-directed. The Spirit chooses the church as the principal arena in which to carry out the work of creating humankind anew as the one covenant people of God.

Paul also emphasizes the Spirit as the source of moral renewal (8:1–10). That emphasis is elicited by the need revealed in chapters 6—7 for demonstrating that freedom from the Torah does not lead to immorality. The norm and guide for conduct is "living [literally, "walking"] by the Spirit." The Spirit produces transformed living in which God's will comes to fulfillment in those who walk no longer "according to the flesh but according to the Spirit" (Rom. 8:4). The Spirit effects a life expressed through renewed relationships more than a life of piety expressed in religious activity. The new life created and given by the Spirit is to be expressed in concrete living. It is not a prize possession to be placed in a case and admired, nor an insurance policy to be kept in a safe-deposit box. Rather, the new life involves a new set of relationships in which self and community are freed for a life of faith expressing itself in love. Concrete manifestations of renewal within community will claim Paul's attention in Romans 12—15.

Paul associates hope for the future with the Spirit. That motif was introduced as early as Romans 5:5 with the statement that "hope does not disappoint us, because God's love has been poured into our hearts through the Holy Spirit which has been given to us." In 2 Corinthians Paul speaks of the Holy Spirit as a guarantee or down payment which God has given as an assurance of the future fulfillment of that which has been begun in promise (2 Cor. 1:22; 5:5). A similar idea is expressed in Romans 8:23 with the image of the "first fruits of the Spirit," a metaphor deriving from the practice of offering the first fruits of the crop to God in the confidence of an abundant harvest. By these images Paul affirms that the Spirit's presence in renewing human life demonstrates that the new age has been inaugurated; that demonstration carries the promise that the new age will come to full realization. Paul's optimism for the future then is grounded in the experience which the community of faith has in the past and in the present. God's present active power gives sure confidence that the future is securely in God's hands.

The Spirit does not bring release from present suffering, but impels believers into it, for the Spirit's witness that "we are children of God, and if children, then heirs," contains the proviso "we suffer with him in order that we may also be glorified with him" (Rom. 8:16–17). Present suffering prevents confidence for the future from becoming triumphalistic. But if the Spirit does not nullify suffering, neither does suffering nullify the confidence which the community may have for the future. In Paul's mind the Spirit is connected with a universal yearning to experience the fulfillment of God's purposes:

> I consider that the sufferings of this present time are not worth comparing with the glory that is to be revealed to us. For the creation waits with eager longing for the revealing of [God's children]." (Rom. 8:18–19)

Paul presents a picture of both human and non-human creation yearning for the renewal of all things. Creation is groaning in labor pains as it anticipates the appearance of God's children. "So also we ourselves who have received the first fruits of the Spirit groan within ourselves as we accept with satisfaction our adoption, which is the liberation of our bodies" (8:22–23, my translation). The Spirit participates in the yearning by assisting the believer, who hardly knows how to prepare in anticipation of the future restoration.

In Paul's view, all creation feels the separation, alienation, and corruption which human sin has entailed and seeks to be free from it. Even in the midst of their rebelliousness, humans know that rebellion brings not freedom but enslavement, know in their inmost being that it is not God's laws and will which are being violated but rather their own persons and the communities in which they participate. They know that in pursuing life on their own terms and according to the lusts of their hearts, they have missed life. Not only do they know, they experience abandonment by God, contradictions between their knowing the good and their choosing and achieving the bad. And if they acknowledge their deepest longings, they also know the need to be delivered from such a self given over to death.[6] They have a yearning to be free.

Humans and the non-human creation are not alone in their yearning, for the Spirit of God shares in the process, bringing before God the inarticulate groans which express the human need and longing for complete renewal. "The Spirit helps us in our weakness" (8:26); literally, the Spirit "takes hold on the other side," assisting in lifting the burden. The Spirit does so by putting meaning in human sighs which by themselves they would not have. Thus God, too, participates in the yearning for renewal which God is now accomplishing. In all this—human yearning, the longing of creation, the intercession of the Spirit—God works for good in those who by loving God show they are called according to God's will (8:26–28).

The New Age and the Created Order

When Paul personifies creation and presents it as a participant in the pain and hope of the human community (8:19–23), it is difficult to know precisely how he views it. He evidently draws on two elements of Jewish tradition:

(1) The Fall, which involved not merely human life but natural creation as well. In the story of the Fall, alienation characterizes not only relationships within the human community and

between humans and God but also between humans and nature as well: the ground is cursed, and brings forth thorns and this-tles. That theme is also found in later Jewish literature:

> And when Adam transgressed my statutes, what had been made was judged. And so the entrances of this world were made narrow and sorrowful and toilsome. (4 Ezra 7:1ff)

> Although things were created in their fullness, when the first man sinned they were corrupted, and they will not come back to this order before Ben Perez (the Messiah) comes. (Gen. Rab. 12:6)[7]

(2) The renovation of nature, which is part of the apocalyptic thought:

> "For behold, I create new heavens and a new earth;
> and the former things shall not be remembered
>   or come into mind....
>   they shall plant vineyards and eat their fruit....
> The wolf and the lamb shall feed together,
>   the lion shall eat straw like the ox;
>   and dust shall be the serpent's food.
> They shall not hurt or destroy
>   in all my holy mountain,
>   says the LORD. (Isa. 65:17–25)

> I shall transform the heaven and make it a blessing of light forever. I shall (also) transform the earth and make it a bless-ing and cause my Elect One(s) to dwell in her. In those days, mountains shall dance like rams; and the hills shall leap like kids satiated with milk.... And the earth shall rejoice.... (Enoch 45:4–5, 51:4–5)[8]

Paul speaks of creation as being under a bondage which corrupts, as having been subjected to futility or purposelessness (Rom. 8:20–21). It is not clear who did the subjecting. He could mean that by rejecting his role as ruler over creation on behalf of God, Adam brought creation under another dominion. He could mean that the rulers of this age ("the principalities and powers") have seized control. Or, he could mean that as punish-ment for human sin God has made creation inhospitable and thus has temporarily diverted it from its intended purpose of serving human needs. Regardless of the agent he intends, Paul's main point is clear: The subjection was "in hope," and now creation sees new promise that the hope will be fulfilled through human renewal.

Paul recalls the promise that all things will be renewed in the new age. He goes further and actually portrays creation as longing for it, using highly expressive terminology: creation "eagerly awaits" (or "strains forward," literally "awaits with outstretched head"); the word expresses "impatient straining for a glimmer of hope."[9] Creation is in labor pains!

Paul's gospel often sounds otherworldly and nonhistorical: salvation is placed beyond the historical order, freedom is the restoration of a glory possible now only on the other side of the fallen world. There is no doubt some real truth in this perception of Paul's gospel; certainly there are many passages that confirm it. This small section of Romans, however, is sufficient to remind us that sometimes Paul's letters give us only a glimpse of central convictions which lie like bedrock under surface appearances.

Unlike Jesus, Paul was a person of the city for whom motifs from rural and natural life did not come easy. Nevertheless, Paul's theology retains Hebraic anchoring in the concrete world of nature and history. That anchoring never allows salvation to become for him a spiritualistic enterprise offering escape from a world full of problems; salvation is restoration not only of the isolated spirit, but also of God's entire creation. Human renewal is connected with the renewal of all things, just as human degradation is connected with all things.

Modern readers might be in a better position than Paul was to appreciate that connection. They know in a scientific way not available to Paul the acute effects on nature of human alienation from the created world. But even without scientific accuracy, Paul makes a provocative connection between human salvation and the renewal of all things. Creation has been subjected to futility, to a frustration of its purpose. Its purpose and destiny had been tied to that of humankind from the beginning, so that it was to supply human needs and to enjoy human tending. Though the break from that purpose was from the human side, the effects were felt in the natural world as well as in the historical. Alienated humanity cannot develop God's creation according to God's purpose. Technological conquest cannot restore creation to its intended purpose; apart from reconciliation it can only continue to distort and subject creation to futility.[10] Human dominion over the world is demonic when it does not derive from right relations.

If Paul were the proponent of a "spiritual" salvation only, he would have no occasion to mention the problem of the universe subjected to futility, which yearns for freedom from the corrupting bondage to which it has been subjected. Human redemption for Paul involves a resurrection of the body; that symbol is directly connected to the symbol of a renewed creation. Humans are not now nor in the future disembodied beings, an image of spiritual nakedness which Paul finds very unappealing (2 Cor. 4:16—5:5). Even if flesh and blood cannot inherit the Kingdom (1 Cor. 15), neither is salvation equated with immortality of the soul. Resurrection of the body implies the renewal of the unitary life of humans, "body and soul"; resurrection of the body thus implies the renewal of the whole world within which human life is expressed. It naturally follows, then, that the whole universe will participate in the glory which is revealed through those who are becoming God's new children; creation looks forward eagerly and experiences labor pains as it awaits the birth of those children whose freedom from alienation will also bring about its freedom.

Paul's speaking of creation's groaning in this passage is not intended to create sympathy for creation, nor is its primary intent to exhort humans to be more responsible for the environment. Both those concerns may appear worthy applications of Paul's theology to the present ecological crisis, and persons concerned about the environment may welcome the assistance of the apostle in responding faithfully to that crisis. But Paul's intent was not to discuss the problems of creation as such; it was to focus upon the sufferings of the present time, and especially upon the question of whether those sufferings nullify the hope he has for the future. His answer is emphatic: the believing community is called in suffering, but that suffering, like the agony of creation, is in the context of hope.

Salvation and Hope

"We were saved in hope," Paul says of the believing community (see Rom. 8:24). Ordinarily Paul uses salvation in the future tense, but here he uses past tense; however, the past has a future connotation by being connected with "hope": "for who hopes for what [one already] sees?" (see Rom. 8:25). The community of faith is caught up in a movement, a process which it does not control and whose end it can see only as hope. The same sufferings could be seen as either the throes of death or the pangs of birth: we are being given up to death, "For thy sake we are being killed all the day long" (8:36). If that is true of the whole community it is even more true of the apostles: "God has exhibited us apostles . . ., like [people] sentenced to death" . . . (1 Cor. 4:9). But these same people are designated as "stewards of the mysteries of God" (1 Cor. 4:1), including the greatest mystery of all—that out of death comes life. Paul utilizes the apocalyptic idea that the sufferings of the present are paradoxically the signs of a new age whose dawn is as sure as are those sufferings themselves.

That assurance does not derive from the power of human perseverance; rather human perseverance can derive from that assurance. Paul's assurance is grounded in death, the death of Christ. The deliverer has come—and died—and thus deliverance is assured! Ordinarily death is not a sign of hope; thus the community of faith shares with Abraham a hope against hope (Rom. 4:18). It can hope because God has shown that he can bring into being things which do not exist (creation, Isaac, resurrection of Jesus). Hope is not fantasy, but trust in the power of God to renew what seemed hopelessly lost; further, it is based upon present experience of God's Spirit, which guarantees the community's final possession of its inheritance (2 Cor. 1:22; cf. Rom. 5:5 and Eph. 1:14).

In the context of assurance Paul includes a statement (Rom. 8:29–30) which is strongly predestinarian in tone, the purpose of which is not to distinguish between the elect and the non-elect, but to affirm the confidence which one may have that God will bring to completion ("glorify") what God has begun in the human community. The chain of verbs (foreknew, predestined, called, justified, glorified) expresses not a sequence of events so much as a certainty of conviction: because of what has already begun in the new community of faith comprising Jew and Gentile, one can have full confidence in the ultimate outcome.

The community was "foreknown" or "known in advance." God's knowledge is election. Amos describes Israel's relation to God in terms of knowledge: "You only have I known of all the families of the earth . . ." (3:2). Paul, in anticipating chapters 9—11, speaks of the community of faith as being the objects of God's election in order to give assurance that the future really does belong to them as God's children. God also "foreordained" them, or "set them apart." There is little or no distinction between the two verbs "foreknow" and "foreordain"; both are ways of identifying the community of faith as the objects of God's eternal concern. Their hope is not in what they have become, any more than their fear should be of what they might make of themselves. Their hope rests in the God who has been there for them even before they knew God's call.

God *has* called them, as they now know. If the purpose of God's predestination is to be fulfilled in their becoming "conformed to the image of his Son" (Rom. 8:29), then they must be called. Election is not derived from nor dependent upon experience, but it works itself out through the experience of the community. In their call to be God's people they know his electing grace. Thus, in being called, they were also justified or set in a right relationship with God so they could begin to live as God's people. In this relationship they find their lost glory restored. In being restored in the image of God's son, they are being glorified, or having restored to them the splendor (glory) which was missed in rebellion (Rom. 3:23).

Paul again departs from his usual reticence to bring the fulfillment of God's purposes into the present (cf. 8:24: "We

were saved"). He speaks as though the whole process is complete, and that final salvation has been realized: ". . . those
whom he justified he also glorified" (Rom. 8:30). In bringing
the future into the present he confirms their hope for that
which is not seen but toward which they are being impelled by
the power of God's grace.

Predestination is thus presented as a "comfortable" doctrine,
as John Calvin says. Not that it is intended to give false comfort, or that it is intended to express a limitation upon the
quantity of God's saving action by identifying the saved and
the damned. It comforts by giving the community of faith the
assurance for the future which it needs for living in the present.[11]

The final hymn (8:31–39) celebrates the certainty of hope:
grounded in God's electing grace, hope is confirmed in the resurrection of Jesus. Suffering, threats, powers, not even death
itself can separate God's community from God. Chapters 1—8
have been leading up to the climax of this triumphant hymn.
The church is God's beloved people, Gentile as well as Jew; the
faith of Abraham and God's promises to him are confirmed; the
old age is being done away with, a new age has dawned upon a
new community composed of Abraham's descendants among
both the Jews and Gentiles. Nothing can prevent the completion of that which God has already begun in history.

The letter might come to an end at this point, but there is
one large problem which has surfaced from time to time which
still insists on a fuller hearing: have God's promises to Israel
come to fulfillment, or have they failed? The final doxology
must wait until an answer is given to that question. Paul under-
takes an answer in chapters 9—11.

8

The New Covenant
Does Not Nullify
the Old

(Romans 9—11)

The resounding optimism at the end of Romans 8 suddenly gives way to an expression of anguish in chapters 9—11, as Paul struggles with a subject which profoundly distresses him: "my relatives by race," that is, those Jewish people related to Paul ethnically but who do not share his view that in Jesus God culminates his historical dealings with the covenant community. As it appeared to Paul at the time of writing, the gospel was working out to be not "to the Jew first and also to the [Gentile]" (Rom. 1:16) but to the Gentile instead of to the Jew! With Gentiles responding favorably in far greater numbers than Jews, the Church was apparently becoming largely Gentile.

It seemed incredible to Paul either that God could finally reject the chosen people or that those people could finally reject God. But there was no easy answer to his perplexity. Paul's internal torment is reflected in the agonizingly difficult and sometimes tortured course of his arguments in chapters 9—11, as he ponders the problem: have God's promises failed? Has Israel turned its back upon God, or has God rejected Israel?

Paul's earlier chapters (1—3) reflect prophetic themes of Israel's apostasy and God's abandonment; he has even used those themes to indicate the commonality of Gentile and Jew in covenant breaking and in the consequent experience of God's judgment. He used those themes in the context of the good news that God has not finally abandoned either Gentile or Jew but has renewed the presence of grace to both in Christ. Paul's intent in earlier chapters was to affirm that Gentiles are included in God's mercy on the same basis as Jews, that such an inclusion confirms God's promises to Abraham and fulfills God's purpose in dealing with Israel. Paul now questions whether that inclusion of Gentiles has been at the expense of the Jews.

Interpreters of Paul have expressed considerable disagreement over the place of Romans 9—11 in the overall structure of the letter. Typically, Protestant interpreters who have seen individual justification by personal faith to be the essence of Paul's theology have tended to discount the importance of this section or have seen in it confirmation that it is after all individual, personal faith and not belonging to particular human communities which is decisive for salvation. In recent years, largely under the influence of the Scandinavian scholar Johannes Munck, these chapters have been given considerably more weight in interpreting not only Romans but the whole of Paul's ministry and message.[1] Krister Stendahl highlights their importance by suggesting that chapters 9—11 constitute the real substance of the letter, while chapters 1—8 are essentially introductory.[2] Even if Stendahl's position is regarded as overstatement, it has served to counterbalance earlier understatements of the importance of this section.

Chapters 9—11 do contain a concentrated discussion of a single issue, with a clear beginning (Paul's anguish in 9:1) and a clear conclusion (the hymn of praise in 11:33—36) which serve to separate the section from what precedes and follows it. For that reason one may justifiably say that it is the most self-contained part of Romans.[3] But it also has many connections with the rest of the letter.

First, the issue itself is raised by the end of chapter 8, which celebratively anticipates the triumph of God's love over all that threatens to separate God's people from God's purposes. Nothing "will be able to separate us from the love of God ..." Paul triumphantly exclaims (Rom. 8:39). But one can imagine a challenger within Paul's own psyche: what about those people of God's covenant who even now are steadfastly resisting the gospel you proclaim? Will such lack of responsiveness ultimately thwart God's intention? The juxtaposition of this question with Paul's affirmations of chapter 8 reveals an aching tension within Paul that must have accompanied him wherever he preached the gospel. The ache was no doubt personal, but the tension was theological as well: if God's promises to Israel are failing to find fulfillment, how can one be so confident of his promises in Christ? This theological tension and his personal agony led Paul to address the issue.

Thematic connections between chapters 9—11 and chapters 1—8 are also seen in Paul's cataloguing of what belongs to Israel (9:4–5): theirs is the adoption as God's people which Paul sees the Spirit creating anew (8:14–16, 29); theirs is the glory which belongs to God's people (8:17), which once lost by all (3:23) is now being restored (8:17, 30); theirs are the covenants of the past (cf. 4:13), and by implication the new covenant as well; theirs is the Torah-giving, and although the Torah did not result in Israel's righteousness (3:20) and even led to greater sin (5:20), the Torah still expresses God's will and thus the possession of it is a terrible advantage (3:1–2); theirs is the worship (sacrificial cultus), the God-ordained means of removing sin (3:25) so that the covenant could continue; theirs are the promises of God and the ancestors to whom those promises were given, promises which are now bearing fruit (4:11–14); finally, from Israel (humanly speaking) came the Christ (cf. 1:3–6), in whom centers the whole gospel which has been the subject of the theological exposition so far (cf. 1:3–6). Such connections show that Paul is taking up an issue in chapters 9—11 which is no mere tangent, but which is integrally related to what has gone before.[4] There are also connections with chapters 12—15 which I will explore in chapter 9.

In anticipation of fuller discussion, let me state now that
although Paul never says precisely and explicitly what Israel's
failure is, there is no doubt in my mind that he considers the
rejection of the gospel by the majority of Jews to be the cause of
their temporary isolation from God's covenant and promises.
In his thoroughly Christological view, Paul believes that the
acceptance of Christ in faith is the key to inclusion within the
continuing people of God. But Paul holds his christological
conviction not as one who has ceased to be a Jew, but as one
who has always been, is now, and will always be a Jew.

First, the Conclusion

The course of Paul's argument through chapters 9—11 often
presents great difficulties to the interpreter. Paul seems first
to go in one direction and then to reverse his field and drive
hard in another direction. He apparently argues in 9:6–29
that due to God's sovereignty in election, not only does no one
have any claim upon God, but also anyone who is included
among God's people is included on the basis of God's arbitrary
election. Then in 9:30—10:21 he apparently argues on the opposite side, that the message of salvation is within the grasp of
all who will listen; they need only cease to be stubbornly disobedient. Then in chapter 11, apparently abandoning both lines
of argument, he asserts that ultimately God will see to it that
all events will lead to the salvation not only of the Gentiles,
but also of "all Israel" "for the sake of their ancestors," since
"the gifts and the call of God are irrevocable" (Rom. 11:29).

There may be logical ways to hold these apparently contradictory lines of thought together, but scholars cannot agree on
how to do so. One suspects that in this case, as in many others,
Paul's conclusions dictate his arguments more than his arguments lead with logical force to his conclusions. If so, we might
understand him better by beginning with the conclusion and
working backward.

The conclusion of this section (11:33–36) takes the form of a
doxology or hymn of praise. Echoing words of Scripture[5] and
Stoic philosophy,[6] Paul praises God who is the "Source, Guide,

and Goal of all that is" (Rom. 11:36, NEB), whose ways are beyond human comprehension, and who waits neither upon human wisdom nor upon human gifts for determining what to do.

This doxology could, then, be read to mean that humans will neither understand God's ways nor be able to influence God's arbitrary will; that after all attempts at understanding there remains a profound mystery which at best will be revealed only at the end. But for Paul the mystery of God's acting is not so much in *what* God is going to do, as in *why*. Just before the concluding doxology, Paul indicates that he does know what God is doing. Here as elsewhere for Paul, "mystery" is what God has revealed in the present which was not discoverable by ordinary human insight. The community of faith has the Spirit and the mind of Christ (1 Cor. 2:6–16). Thus Paul is not expressing uncertainty about the future ("only God knows") but rather responding "with astonished praise"[7] for what he knows through the Spirit.

To understand the reason for the doxology in 11:33–36 we are forced back to his earlier statements in 11:25–32 concerning God's working with Gentile and Jew. Paul says an insensitivity ("hardening" [RSV]) has come upon part of Israel. Statements in 11:15, 21 indicate that this insensitivity was God's doing and will last until the intended conversion of the Gentiles is complete, when God will banish sin and ungodliness from Israel, renew the covenant, and fulfill the irrevocable promise and call.[8] Then it will be clear that God has utilized the propensities and choices of Gentile and Jew, even their rebellion and unrighteousness, to accomplish the very purpose which both have seemingly thwarted: to bring both Gentile and Jew into one harmonious, newly covenanted community. "For God has consigned all . . . to disobedience, that he may have mercy upon all" (Rom.11:32).[9]

Peter Richardson correctly asserts that the conclusion of chapters 9—11 reveals the main points of the preceding verses and "the basic intention of Paul."[10] Having viewed the conclusion, one can comprehend more readily the course of the whole passage. After describing the major components of Paul's argument, I will discuss some of the key issues raised by the whole.

A Brief Analysis of Chapters 9—11

A. *9:1–5:* Paul laments Israel's present situation in which most Jews are not responding affirmatively to the apostolic proclamation. His anguish is such that he can pray to be accursed, have his "in Christ" relationship become "apart from Christ" if that would reverse the situation of those who are his brothers and sisters by biological descent. Paul intentionally or unintentionally recalls in the reader's mind the example of Moses' intercession for idolatrous Israel: ". . . if thou wilt forgive their sin—and if not, blot me . . . out of thy book . . ." (Exod. 32:32).

There is no obvious connection between the lament in verses 1–3 and the listing of what "belongs to" Israel in verses 4–5. Do the possessions of Israel increase the pathos of their present separation (cf. 11:17)? Do they point to the inconceivability that the separation could be final (cf. 11:28–29) and thus reduce the anguish? Do they serve to confirm that there really is no difference between the Gentile and Jew, that just as Gentiles did not sufficiently honor God in response to the knowledge they were given, neither did the Jews in response to their even greater gifts? Do they lead to the next question addressed in verse 6: has the word of God in promise and calling been so frustrated that not even God's word can be trusted to overcome human recalcitrance? The context suggests it is primarily this last question with which Paul wishes to deal, though not necessarily to the exclusion of other concerns.

B. *9:6–13:* Paul's lament is already leaping forward to the next question raised by the fact over which he laments: has God's word of promise failed? That question implies another: since the word of promise given to Abraham entails a people, what is the nature and quality of that people? Does election of Abraham's descendants mean that when any of his descendants fail to apprehend the word of promise, the word itself has failed? Beginning in verse 6 Paul reflects upon other "failures" (Ishmael, Esau) and what they mean. He affirms that an apparent connection with the promises is not necessarily a real connection, that God pursues the fulfillment of his word of promise in ways that confound human understanding and even natural human instincts. God acts that way, Paul argues, in order to make clear that election is not dependent upon nor determined by human response, nor subject to human manipulation or control; election is God's own inscrutable work. These verses already anticipate the doxology of 11:33–36, showing that Paul has his conclusion in mind from the beginning.

C. *9:14–29:* Affirming the inscrutability of God's call raises in Paul's mind the question it would raise in the mind of any of his sensitive readers: if God acts in such a seemingly arbitrary way, on what basis are humans judged? Is God unjust (vs. 14)? This question leads Paul deeper and deeper into issues of theodicy which he does not resolve by clear argument, but which he finally puts aside as inappropriate and then resolves by a theological affirmation: God's work is a work of mercy, and God's astounding mercy justifies all apparent arbitrariness. Paul does not deny the arbitrariness: God chooses as God wills and is no more answerable now than when Pharaoh's heart was hardened in order to achieve God's purpose of demonstrating mercy to Israel. Paul affirms, in a word, that God uses people, an affirmation that understandably offends—even outrages—some of his readers. Paul believes that behind apparent divine caprice, even apparent injustice, there stands the purpose of God to extend mercy to Gentile as well as to Jew. If there is any attempt to justify the ways of God here, it is by asserting that the end of mercy justifies the means by which God extends it.

The reader should keep in mind that Paul is not speaking here of the eternal destiny of "some men and angels,"[11] but of the course of history which anticipates the renewal of creation in the eschatological end. The end (11:32) reveals a purpose hidden from the beginning: God shut up all people in disobedience in order to have mercy upon *all,* not only upon those select ones whose hearts were not temporarily hardened. In 9:25–29 Paul affirms that God is always free to reverse the apparent situation of those through whom the divine will is carried out. He alludes to the past, when historical forces threatened the very existence of God's people, when there was no apparent hope, and when God saw to it that children were left to Israel, even if only a remnant was preserved at any given time. So also in Paul's present time, he warns that one should not judge the situation to be final: God's historical acts have been full of surprises, both negative and positive, but his purpose is clear: to make known his mercy and his saving power to those whom he has called, "not from the Jews only but also from the Gentiles" (Rom. 9:24).

D. *9:30–33:* These verses form a transition between the preceding emphasis on God's free act and the following emphasis upon the inadequacy of human zeal to maintain the covenant (10:1–21). Both points are made here, in reverse order: Israel pursued righteousness but in the wrong way (30–32a); that pursuit itself was brought about by God's action in laying in Zion a stone which causes stumbling and scandal.

The primary point in these verses is probably not Israel's "stumbling" so much as it is the surprising nature of God's action on two fronts: the inclusion of Gentiles, and the stumbling of Israel, both due to God's way of working. Both points anticipate the conclusion presented in chapter 11 and confirm the inscrutable nature of God's action. The stone which causes Israel's stumbling probably means Jesus as the messiah.[12] In any event, the stumbling is later said (Rom. 11:11) not to lead to a "fall" but to the fulfilling of God's purpose in causing it.

E. *10:1–21:* Considered the most difficult part of this whole section, these verses use many scriptural quotations, allusions, and interpretations, the purposes of which are often obscure and unconvincing to the modern reader. Substantially autobiographical in character, verses 1–4 generalize Paul's own experience, previous attitudes, and present convictions, and apply them to all who are related to him by ancestry.

As Paul describes them, the Jews have a "zeal for God" (10:2) just as he, too, was so "extremely zealous . . . for the traditions of [his] fathers" (Gal. 1:14) that he persecuted the church and misused the Torah (Phil. 3:5–6). Like the Jews who in Paul's description are "unenlightened" and "ignorant of the righteousness ... from God" (10:3), Paul, too, had required enlightenment by a revelation of Christ (Gal.1:12, 16) before he could give up confidence in his human capacity (Phil. 3:3). Paul criticizes those Jews who still seek to establish their own righteousness and consequently do not subordinate themselves to God's righteousness; like them, he had previously pursued a righteousness of his own based on the Torah, which he exchanged for a righteousness from God based on faith (Phil. 3:9; cf. Gal. 2:16, 19–20). Christ brings the righteousness sought under the Torah to fulfillment (10:4); therefore, just as Paul himself "died to the [Torah], that [he] might live to God" (Gal. 2:19–20; cf. Phil. 3:8), so should other Jews accept that right relations with God are not established by works derived from the Torah (Gal. 2:16; Phil. 3:9), but that "every one who has faith may be justified" (Rom. 10:4).

In his days as a zealous Pharisee, Paul would have expected loyal Jews to share his convictions; now Paul as a zealous follower of the Messiah Jesus expects other Jews to share his present ones. He also believes he has insight into the situation of Jews so that he can "bear witness" to what motivates them. To a real extent Paul considers himself "everyJew."

Verses 5–13 are an attempt to support from Scripture Paul's contrast between two approaches to righteousness. The modern reader is likely to be perplexed by the opaqueness of Paul's argument, and to be aghast at the way Paul takes liberties with the scriptural texts. As John Calvin says, Scripture "seems to be improperly applied by Paul," and to be "turned to a different meaning."[13] Paul uses the Torah against the Torah; he contrasts what *Moses writes* with what *righteousness says;* he contrasts righteousness derived from works and righteousness derived from faith, not recognizing, as Calvin says, that for Moses, too, "the keeping of the law should be traced from its own fountain, even the righteousness of faith";[14] he takes a passage (Deut. 30:1–14) in which Moses speaks of the word of the Torah being within the reach of the people, "in your mouth and in your heart," and reapplies it to show that the gospel is radically different from the Torah. Paul's purpose is obviously not that dispassionate search for the original meaning of the text to which a modern interpreter might aspire; rather, Paul uses texts in such a way as to support an innovative re-interpretation of the tradition by which he had lived. How could he hope to be convincing to a reader who knew Hebrew Scriptures? Perhaps because his methods of exegesis were not really different from the standard *pesher* style of interpretation generally employed in Jewish circles of Paul's day, and which he had learned in his Pharisaic training.[15] By that approach, then, Paul can confidently believe that when the promise is made that whoever calls upon the name of the Lord will be saved, the reference is to confessing that Jesus is Messiah and Lord.[16]

In verses 14–21, Paul applies the message derived from Scripture to the proclamation now being made by the messianic community, affirming (again through quoting Scripture) that not to receive the proclamation is to be "disobedient and contrary" to God's call (10–21).

F. *11:1–32:* This section is much easier to understand than chapters 9 and 10. Since I have already looked at its conclusion, which is also the conclusion of the whole section, I need now only to indicate the course of his argument: one cannot say God has rejected the chosen people, in spite of the fact that it now appears that most Jews are rejecting the gospel; only God knows how large the remnant really is who respond to God's grace with faith (11:1–6). God's purpose is at work even in the insensitivity of the Jews, that purpose being to include the Gentiles among his people, and to include "all Israel" and "the full number of Gentiles" in the one people of the renewed covenant (11:7–32). Paul stresses the idea that if Jews are now excluded it is not because God has rejected them but because of their own unbelief; this point is intended to counter the arrogance of those Gentiles who wanted to believe that God had rejected the Jews in favor of them.

THEOLOGICAL QUESTIONS RAISED

This brief analysis of chapters 9—11 reveals several theological questions raised by the way Paul deals with the "problem" of Jewish rejection of the gospel. Many of Paul's theological and pastoral concerns converge in Romans 9—11: his insistence that God's righteousness is being manifested in the renewal of Gentile and Jew, both of whom stand in need of grace due to their rejection of past covenants; his emphasis both upon the continuity of the gospel with God's promises in the past and upon the radical newness of God's present action; his concern that grace be seen *as* grace, and not as human achievement; the removal of barriers between Gentile and Jew; the eschatological nature of the present time. There is truth in Stendahl's overstatement that earlier chapters are prologue, and that 9—11 form the heart of the letter—these chapters form a culmination of all that has gone before and an anguished attempt to harmonize present reality with Paul's vision of the future.

Three issues raised in the letter as a whole become acute in these chapters: (1) Was Paul anti-Judaic? (2) Must Jews become Christians? (3) Did Paul teach that all persons—whether Gentile or Jew, whether presently believing in Jesus as the Christ or not—will ultimately be saved?

Is Paul Anti-Judaic?

Recent New Testament interpreters have expressed urgent concern about the degree to which modern anti-Semitism has its roots not only in the post–New Testament history of the Christian church, but even in the New Testament itself.[17] The question is two-fold: First, is the New Testament anti-Semitic, or at least anti-Judaic? Second, has an intellectual (as perhaps opposed to a subjective) anti-Semitism infected New Testament scholarship and influenced scholarly interpretation of the New Testament?

Markus Barth illustrates the later problem by quoting an eminent scholar who maintains that Paul's "essential adversary is the pious Jew."[18] According to Barth, he asked in correspondence whether the scholar was using "Jew" symbolically (to stand for the religious person in any age); the scholar "flatly refused this suggestion. Thus, for him, the 'essential adversary' is also the 'real' enemy, even the devoted Jew of every generation."[19]

Although the scholar reportedly declined the suggestion, undoubtedly a major motive for attributing anti-Judaism to Paul is to affirm a prophetic (Protestant) critique of religion in favor of genuine faith; "religion" in this sense means a human effort to secure God's favor and to gain life for oneself, an enterprise which is assumed to be characteristic of Judaism in Paul's day. Paul is correctly seen as an exponent of radical faith, of utter reliance upon God's grace in salvation. But even if Paul's radical statement of faith is over against an understanding of the relationship with God which in retrospect he sees himself to have had as a zealous Jew, one is not warranted in seeing Paul as the implacable enemy of Judaism.

Paul's radical change in his own perspective, however, does show clearly that he did abandon a previous way of thinking and being, did repudiate something which he now counts as "refuse," and he was liberated from something. We cannot exclude the possibility that Paul was dissatisfied with his life under the Torah, or that he chafed under Jewish exclusivism which seemed to him to ignore Gentiles or to give them an inferior place,[20] nor can we exclude the possibilities that Paul at least subconsciously had already begun to perceive his own attitude (and that of some other Jews) as being self-righteous, or was increasingly troubled by his own maltreatment of those whom he regarded as enemies of the Torah. His "volcanic internal crisis" then might not have been the sudden thing it seemed to him to be.[21] It certainly is not difficult to believe that the appearance of Christ to Paul "lit up and answered a hidden quest in his soul."[22] There is some reason, probably deeper than either his polemic or pastoral admonitions reveal, why Paul speaks of "slavery" under the Torah, of the Torah of sin and death, of the joyful spirit of adoption as opposed to the fearful spirit of slavery.

However we conceive of the psychological and/or supernatural reasons for it, Paul made a decisive change in his theological and religious convictions. It is, however, a gross historical anachronism to label this change a conversion from Judaism to Christianity. Regardless of how one finally judges Paul's attitude toward the Torah (see below), Paul did not in his own understanding consider himself abandoning his Jewish heritage or citizenship in the commonwealth of Israel. He changed Jewish sects, but he did not leave Judaism.[23]

Paul probably did not give up his own observance of the Torah entirely; in working among Gentiles he may have lived like a Gentile, but when among Jews he would have been more circumspect out of consideration for their consciences. When pushed by circumstances to choose between observing the Torah or affirming the freedom of Gentiles by fully identifying with them, Paul almost certainly would have opted for the latter, as the situation at Antioch attests (Gal. 2:11–14). Such a practice could easily have led to the charge of inconsistency and vacillation. Paul preferred to think of it as going to the maximum possible extent, without compromising the gospel, to meet Jew and Gentile within their particular circumstances. But he did not thereby intend to abandon his Jewish traditions, or to separate himself from the synagogue. "He kept showing up," even when to do so led to harsh discipline.[24] Among the sufferings he recalls in 2 Corinthians 11:23–29, several might have been formally imposed by Jewish authorities: thirty-nine lashes (five times!), stoning, beating with rods, "danger from my own people."

Paul's harshest criticisms of the Torah and of those who followed it were made in the context of heated debate as he sought to carry out his call as apostle to the Gentiles. Paul did not begin that mission; it was already under way, possibly without the requirement of circumcision, when he came into the messianic community. Paul carried it forward and provided some of the rationale for it. Krister Stendahl argues persuasively that Paul's teaching of justification by faith originates not in abstract thinking or in his own personal religious experience but in his concern for the equality of Gentile and Jew within the context of that mission.[25] Thus, Paul's advocacy of the principle of faith was not a theoretical attack on the Torah, but a practical matter of enhancing the Gentile mission.[26] Paul's views were strongly opposed by some who could support their position with convincing arguments from Scripture and tradition. Paul posed counter arguments; he reflected upon his own experience and that of early Gentile believers, searched Scripture for texts to support his arguments. As the intensity of the battle increased, so too did Paul's negative statements about the Torah, until finally he went so far as to attribute an increase of sinfulness to the Torah, and to associate with Torah not righteousness and life but sin and death. But this was too far, even for Paul, and in Romans 7 he backs away from this position, recoiling from the logic which had been driving him.[27] In Romans 7 he attributes the whole problem not to the Torah but to human weakness in being overpowered by sin, raising questions of theodicy concerning God the Creator which he never answers.[28]

Even in his most vehement arguments against the Torah, however, Paul does not consciously argue against his Jewish heritage, nor does he renounce it. It is as a Jew that he understands the relationship between the Torah and Christ, and if he does not inherit a tradition that the Torah ceases in the messianic age,[29] he invents one: "Christ is the end of the Torah." A new age and a new way are open to God's people so that they might complete the promise given to Abraham and renewed in Deutero-Isaiah "to be a light [and a covenant] to the Gentiles."

Even though Paul's real enemy was not the Jews, there was a severe tension between Paul and contemporary Judaism. While he saw in Christ the fulfillment of God's promises to Israel, he also saw Christ as the abrogation of something within the current Jewish religious scene. He did not, in other words, believe that faith in the crucified and resurrected Messiah would come easily for Jews: it is a "scandal" to the Jew.[30] What did Paul see within Judaism which had to be abrogated? Was it Jewish exclusivism, which treated Gentiles as inferior even when it accepted them as proselytes? Was it circumcision as a requirement for membership in the messianic community? Was it the assumption that "works of the Torah" would produce righteousness? Was it the "Jewish way of life"? Was it the Torah—its ritual or ethical dimension, or both? Was it the old covenant, established through Moses and centering on Torah? Was it Israel itself as the true people of God?

The issue of whether Paul was anti-Judaic or anti-Semitic revolves around these questions. Paul's distance from his Judaic heritage obviously depended both upon what he abrogated and upon the relative importance for Judaism of that which he abrogated. For instance, if Paul thought the Torah should be abolished, and if the Torah was the very essence of Judaism, then one would conclude that Paul struck at the very nerve center of Judaism.[31] On the other hand, if it should be determined that the only quarrel Paul had with his Jewish heritage was its exclusivism in attitude and practice toward Gentiles, and if such exclusivism was not vital to Judaism, then Paul would be anti-Judaic neither in intent nor in effect. The discussion of Paul's relation to Judaism will accordingly be advanced by looking at each of these questions in turn; some will demand fuller treatment than others.

1. *Exclusivism?* Paul certainly wished to do away with any exclusivism which denied Gentiles full access to the messianic community or full acceptance of them by the community: "There is no distinction" between Gentile and Jew in terms of need for God's grace or of its availability to them. "To the Jew first and also to the Gentile" expresses the historical mode of God's operation but no final partiality on God's part. The impartial, inclusive nature of God's dealing with all humanity is fundamental and unalterable. In fact, almost all of Paul's other attitudes toward the Jewish heritage are determined by this conviction. How seriously Paul disagrees with fellow Jews on this point is debatable. Josephus suggests that many wanted to abolish the wall of exclusivism.[32] Perhaps because of his messianic and eschatological perspective Paul did not believe that removing impediments to the inclusion of Gentiles violated

any fundamental principle of Judaism.[33]

2. *Circumcision for Gentiles?* Paul is adamant in rejecting the requirement that Gentiles be circumcised to become members of the messianic community.[34] His debate in Galatians centers around this issue. The Torah expresses the matter unambiguously: "Every male among you shall be circumcised.... Any uncircumcised male who is not circumcised in the flesh of his foreskin shall be cut off from his people; he has broken my covenant" (Gen. 17:10, 14). In Paul's time, however, there was debate as to whether this law applied to proselytes.[35] Within the messianic community itself there was debate and disagreement about the requirement (see Acts 15, Gal. 1—2), with Paul supporting the more radical position of nonrequirement and evidently believing that his position had been agreed to by the Jewish apostles in Jerusalem. Paul went further than most and argued strenuously not only that one did not have to be circumcised, but also that to do so nullified one's relation to Christ: "...if you receive circumcision, Christ will be of no advantage to you.... [You would be] bound to keep the whole [Torah]. You are severed from Christ, you who would be justified by the [Torah]; you have fallen away from grace" (Gal. 5:2–4). Here Paul ties together circumcision, obligation to keep the whole Torah, and justification by the Torah into one package to be negated, at least for Gentiles.[36]

It is quite possible that Paul's opponents (whether Jewish Christian missionaries or Gentile converts is arguable) hold the view that while the whole Torah is not necessary, at least a minimum of observance is, including circumcision and possibly other cultic activities (Gal. 4:10). To uphold his principle that circumcision is not required, Paul responds by a fierce polemic that drives a radical wedge between the Torah itself and Christ, so that for Gentiles to opt for both is an impossibility.

Beker's admonition that we interpret Paul's letters contextually serves us well here; applying it we see that Paul is less intent on announcing universal and eternal truths than he is on guarding and defending a principle. The principle is that one enters into God's covenant community through faith in

Christ, not by way of circumcision. Circumcision or lack there-
of is of no consequence; what matters is faith becoming effective through love (Gal. 5:6). To guard the simplicity of that
principle and the creative freedom it generates, Paul makes an
assault on the opposing position which seems out of proportion.
His arguments to support his position might well be different
from the reasons for which he maintains that position.[37] One
reason is surely to be found in his concern for the Gentile
mission, which is a corollary of his conviction that in Christ
God has acted decisively for the salvation of the whole world;
for God's grace to triumph, Gentile and Jew must be brought
together "without distinction" into one covenant community.
His advocacy of a Torah-free gospel for Gentiles probably originates in his missionary tactics more than in his theoretical
thought; it is possible that he had learned from an earlier
engagement in Gentile mission (as a Pharisaic Jew) the difficulty posed by circumcision and other practices.[38] His removal
of circumcision as a requirement would surely aid his gospel's
acceptance by Gentiles.

3. *Works of Torah as the way to righteousness?* Paul, then,
rejects circumcision for Gentiles out of concern for his principle
of a universal, inclusive salvation through faith in Jesus as
Christ. Did he have other reasons for rejecting circumcision as
well? Was he also in principle rejecting a kind of righteousness
promoted by the Torah? In Philippians 3:9 he describes himself
as previously having "a righteousness of my own, based on [the
Torah]."[39] The phrase is almost identical to his accusation
against the fellow Jews who are "ignorant of the righteousness
that comes from God" and thus seek "to establish their own"
righteousness (Rom. 10:3; cf. also 9:31–32).

Protestant interpretation has typically taken these statements to be a characterization of Judaism in Paul's day: the
Jews were legalists who sought to save themselves by doing
works of the Torah; to them faith was unimportant, they were
self-righteous, proud, self-idolatrous. In attempting to break
through the Jewish religion of works, Paul posed as its antithesis his gospel of salvation by grace through faith. Since

Judaism was essentially a religion of works, Paul necessarily rejected Judaism and became a Christian.

Jewish interpreters have understandably reacted negatively to that characterization—or caricature—of Judaism. It is argued by some that Paul is grossly unfair to Judaism in positing such an antithesis and in putting Judaism on the negative side of it. Paul's setting of Jewish observance of the Torah in antithesis to the gospel of God's grace thus creates a false dichotomy. Jewish piety, it is claimed, was thoroughly grounded in recognition of God's gift of the covenant to the elect people; Hebrew Scripture and Jewish writings show that neither election nor covenant were based on human achievement. Gaston, Gager, and (somewhat differently) Sanders deny that the antithesis is really present.[40] "My own righteousness" or "a righteousness of their own" means, they believe, a hoarding of righteousness and a denial of Gentile inclusion. The problem with Judaism, then, as stated above, is its exclusiveness, not its attempt at self-salvation by works of the Torah.[41] There is an element of truth in this position: the type of righteousness referred to is peculiarly possible only for those whose pursuit of it is through the Torah; thus, it is not a righteousness available equally to Gentile and Jew.[42]

Gaston's arguments that Paul does not set Torah and faith in antithesis as two rival means of salvation remain unconvincing, however. His rejection of the antithesis necessitates giving *nomos* (principle, law, Torah) the two radically different meanings of "Torah" and "law" within the same context and even within the same sentence.[43] His major criterion appears to be that if *nomos* has a primarily positive connotation it is translated "Torah" and if it has a basically negative connotation it is rendered "law." Although Gaston's procedure makes Paul less open to the charge of being anti-Jewish, its arbitrariness creates a problem of credibility.

Gaston's approach fails also to take into account the prophetic critique of Judaism inherent in the movement begun by Jesus. As a sectarian movement it had by definition set itself over against other sectarian movements. While there are some good reasons for arguing that Jesus was a "rabbi" or even a "Pharisee," still he was sufficiently different from others to create threat and strife. That tension was increased by what was probably at least complicity in Jesus' death on the part of the dominant Pharisees and Sadducees. It did not diminish in the early days after Jesus' death when Paul and others were violently opposing at least some of Jesus' followers. To suppose that there was not a strong antithetical drive within this sectarian movement is to ignore historical reality.

Paul entered a community which was already engaged in implicit and probably explicit criticism of the currently dominant Jewish faith and practice and which was offering itself as a corrective force from within the Jewish community. The appearance of Christ to him, as he describes it in Galatians 1, was quite similar to a prophetic call. While it is not inconceivable that Paul regarded Jewish exclusivism as the only really serious problem within Judaism, it is unlikely. In light of his new perspective he did evaluate his former attitude and approach to relations with God as at best inadequate.[44] For him, God's act in Christ decisively put the whole world in a new situation. Now, Gentile and Jew alike are to be brought to faith in the Christ whom God has given for the renewal of Israel and also for the salvation of the nations. Just as the Torah has been replaced with Christ as the center of his life, so for Paul, as "everyJew," it seemed natural for the same to happen to all God's people.

Paul does contrast two kinds of righteousness: "A righteousness of my own, based on the Torah," and "that which is through faith." The same contrast is applied to all Jews in Romans 9:30–32: they did not attain righteousness because pursuing "the righteousness which is based on [the Torah] . . . they did not pursue it through faith, but as if it were based on works" (Rom. 9:31–32). Paul seems to set two rival principles of salvation over against each other: works of the Torah and faith.[45] The former principle he declares invalid; the latter he declares to be valid not only because it has been inaugurated by the Christ event but also because it has been there from the beginning, unrecognized and unaccepted by the very ones who should have seen and welcomed it.

Gaston's reasoning is unconvincing, finally, because it does not sufficiently take into account the problem Paul saw with his opponents. Even if Munck's thesis is accepted, that Paul's opponents were neither Jews nor Jewish-Christians but Gentiles who had become enamored with the Torah, still his opponents wanted to Judaize; they wanted to perfect themselves by doing at least a part of what the Torah required by way of ritual performance. Their way of putting the question might have forced Paul to state a more antithetical opposition between the Torah and Christ than he would have asserted merely on the basis of calm theological reflection. Nevertheless, he did state that antithesis. He did it, not because he was anti-Jewish but, as I have already argued, because he wanted to affirm emphatically the principle of inclusiveness and because in his own religious life Christ, no longer Torah, was at the center.

4. *The Jewish way of life?* Little evidence suggests the degree to which Paul himself continued to live as a Jew. His principle of "being all things to all people" in order to advance the gospel would have been difficult to apply when with Gentiles and Jews at the same time. His stated principle suggests there is no intrinsic value in living like a Jew or in ceasing to live like a Jew. This squares uneasily with some of his statements in Galatians, in which Paul strongly suggests that for Gentiles to adopt certain Jewish practices endangers their relationship to Christ. For a Jew to renounce Jewish practices which were not of a hindrance to faith or for a Gentile to affirm Jewish practices which did not grow out of the messianic community and its convictions could indicate that too much emphasis was being put on the negative or positive value of the practice in question. What finally matters, Paul asserts, is neither circumcision nor lack of it, but faith and its resultant love (Gal. 5:6). Circumcision became an issue only when it was insisted upon by those who did not share Paul's view concerning its irrelevance. The same would probably be true in general—when a ritual is required by others, it is forbidden by Paul. Paul can

even imply negative things about baptism and speaking in
tongues when such practices are utilized by their proponents
to erect barriers within the covenant community (see 1 Cor. 1:
12–14).

Paul's Christology, soteriology, and eschatology all led him
to regard as "indifferent" patterns of living which did not injure
neighbor, violate conscience, or disrupt community. Christ lib-
erates from patterns and norms which oppress, imprison, or
pervert; for his followers to form new patterns of slavery is
inconsistent with his purpose. Moreover, Paul believed the end
of things was at hand: "I think that in view of the [impending]
distress it is well for [persons] to remain as [they are] . . ."—circumcised or uncircumcised, slave or free, married or unmarri-
ed; changing one's worldly circumstance has no real value in a
world whose "form . . . is passing away" (1 Cor. 7:26–31). In the
case of marriage and divorce, if there are compelling reasons
for it, change can be made, but to remain as one is, is the preferred course. In the same way, Paul is not against the Jewish
way of life, but he is not an advocate of it either, for Jews or for
Greeks, any more than he is either an opponent or a proponent
of Gentile ways for either.

5. *The Torah and the Mosaic covenant?* I have noted above
that if Paul *did* abrogate the Mosaic tradition and the notion of
Israel's election, then he has in effect rejected all that makes
Israel Israel and has stuck a knife in the heart of Judaism. Did
he do so? My brief summary of Romans 9—11 has anticipated
my general conclusion: Paul does not consider the people of
Israel to be rejected by God; such a notion is to him simply inconceivable. Even now their ultimate, eschatological salvation
is assured, regardless of the present condition of their faith or
faithlessness, for it is finally God's faithfulness and not their own
which assures it. That conviction provides Paul with the freedom to deal radically with the issue of the Torah, for the Torah
neither originated that election nor in itself maintained it. The
Torah, for Paul, came centuries after the election, and therefore can cease without abrogating election; Israel's election is
contained in God's promises to Abraham, witnessed to by the

Torah; Israel continues to be beloved for the sake of their ancestors (11:28).[46]

Moses is mentioned by name only eight times in Paul's letters. Four of the eight references simply identify Moses as the maker of scriptural statements, and show no negative or positive attitude toward Moses himself.[47] The remaining four references are negative in their connotations about the effect of Moses' work.[48] Paul's negative attitude toward Moses is tied up with his attitude toward the Torah.[49] The inefficacious nature of Moses' covenant is due to the nature of the Torah which stipulates conduct under that covenant. It is a dispensation of condemnation because the Torah can only condemn wrong action—it cannot empower one to do right. It is a dispensation of death in consequence of disobedience.

Paul does not mean that the Torah is itself wrong, or that it commands the wrong things: "The [Torah] is holy, and the commandment is holy and just and good" (Rom. 7:12). Because human nature is weak, however, human response to the Torah prevents it from bringing about the good it commands. Paul's understanding of human psychology therefore causes him to see the Torah as inadequate.

Paul's radical attack upon the way of the Torah as the way of righteousness is just that —radical—striking at the very root of Jewish identity. But it is not wholly without antecedents. He makes use of the prophetic tradition in which God reacts to Israelite disobedience by threatening to destroy the covenant and to cast off the chosen people. He also makes use of the idea of the "new covenant" from Jeremiah 31,[50] a covenant that is radically inward, not written on tablets of stone but upon the heart; with this, one must compare Paul's statement in 2 Corinthians 3:6, where he claims to be a minister of a new covenant which is "not in a written code but in the Spirit; for the written code kills, but the Spirit gives life." Jeremiah's new covenant is based not upon the people's performance, but upon God's forgiveness; Paul almost never uses the term forgiveness, probably because it can suggest a pardon without transformation; rather he speaks of redemption, setting free from the power of sin. But in spite of this change in terminology, Paul derives from Jeremiah the notion that the new covenant deals effectively with the human problem that led to the breaking of the old covenant.

In his radical dealing with the Mosaic covenant, therefore, Paul does not do what the gnostic Marcion did in the second century: reject the old covenant and the old covenant God as demonic. Paul agrees with the truth of what Moses says; he agrees with the validity of the Torah as at least a limited expression of God's will. He wishes to show that the Torah and the prophets "bear witness" to the "righteousness of God [which] has [now] been manifested apart from [the Torah]" (Rom. 3:21). Within the Torah itself he finds Abraham with whom God formed a covenant which, unlike the Mosaic covenant, ultimately included Gentile and Jew alike. The Mosaic Torah, Paul says, came 430 years after Abraham was declared right with God through his faith in God's promises, and the Torah could not change the terms of that covenant. The Torah thus is dependent upon the promises, not vice versa. The promise to Abraham was not fulfilled in the Torah; indeed, that part that appertains to Gentiles could not be.[51]

Paul's use of Abraham and Moses, then, expresses his desire to denationalize faith in the one God, and to harmonize two divisions of humankind into one community of faith. He uses positively those elements of covenant traditions which lend themselves to the universalizing of the gospel (those associated with Abraham); he evaluates negatively those covenantal traditions which are most closely tied to Jewish particularism and exclusivism (those associated with Moses). He does both to emphasize his conviction that in Jesus Christ there is neither Jew nor Gentile, but one new humanity.

6. *The Jews as the people of Israel?* The answer to our final question has already been given. Regardless of how severe one judges Paul's assessment of the Torah and the Mosaic covenant to have been—even if he rejected them entirely—Paul did not regard Israel's election as null and void; the new covenant of Jew and Gentile does not nullify the original covenant. The

election preceded the Torah and survives it. The Torah was temporary, election is not.

Some modern interpreters believe that such a position is inadequate and unrealistic. Since Torah is of the essence of Judaism, they argue, to reject one is to reject the other; if Paul was against the Torah, then Pauline Christianity is anti-Judaic or anti-Semitic. Such a position contains an anachronistic view of both "Judaism" and "Christianity" in Paul's time. Neither entity as we know it yet existed. Paul did not choose Christianity and reject Judaism. As a Jew he affirmed Jesus as Jewish Messiah, and in keeping with Jewish messianic thought he concluded that Gentiles were to be incorporated within the one chosen people of God.

Jacob Neusner maintains that *Torah* as Judaism now knows it did not come into being until around 70 C.E. The "definitive characteristics of Judaism as we know it, and as the world has known it from late antiquity" include:

> the rabbi as model and authority, Torah as the principle and organizing symbol, study of Torah as the capital religious deed, the life of the religious discipline as the prime expression of what it means to be Israel, the Jewish people.[52]

If Neusner is correct, as I believe he is, Paul could not have rejected this Judaism; it is much more accurate to say that out of the varieties of Judaism struggling for the soul of Israel in Paul's time, two have survived to become Judaism and Christianity. Each claims to be heir to the traditions of Israel. Both were in their own formative stages in Paul's day. Paul left one sectarian movement (the Pharisees) which regarded the observance of the Torah (as then constituted) as the essence of Israel's heritage, to join another which saw Jesus the Messiah as the fulfillment of Israel's traditions and hope for the future. Paul's own personal experience convinced him that Jesus had been raised from the dead; thus God had inaugurated a new creation in the new age. With that as his central conviction, Paul thought the Torah could no longer have the place it had had before. Its age had come to an end not in defeat and rejection but in fulfillment and supersession. Its purpose having been accomplished, the Torah had been replaced by Messiah Jesus as the fullest revelation of God, the guide to conduct, the source of community, and the hope of the world for the future.

There is no doubt that much anti-Semitism can point to Pauline statements for support; there is no doubt that some modern Christians do use Paul as a weapon against modern Jews. Both facts are greatly to be abhorred, and both require serious struggle within both communities of faith. Whether Paul would, if present, think that either modern Judaism or modern Christianity is in close continuity with God's promises to Abraham remains an open question. Whether one can find statements within Paul's letters which can be used in bridge-building between the two communities that presently go by varietal names within Judaism and Christianity is a question worth pursuing, but a first and essential step is an accurate historical reading of Paul, both by those who see him as anti-Semitic and by those intent in defending him against the charge. A second step might be to imbibe Paul's determination to engage in critical dialogue with his tradition in light of ongoing experiences, not letting tradition be a weight around his neck but a float under his body. Paul was innovative, he was daring, he was provocative, he was exasperating, he was inconsistent—and he was committed to his conviction that God was acting in Christ to reconcile, re-create, liberate, and unite Gentile and Jew in one newly covenanted humanity, in which "there is no distinction."

Must Jews Become Christian?

Eventually one must address the question of whether Paul's Christology necessitates the rejection of the Jews and the consignment of them to the category of faithless or reprobate. If Christ is the end of the Torah does that render invalid the continuation of the Jewish religion? Gaston and Gager wrestle vigorously with that issue which obviously has serious impact upon contemporary Jewish-Christian relations and upon Christian self-understanding. One does not wish to diminish the importance of the questions nor belittle serious attempts to resolve them. Even so, one must ask critical historical and theological questions about solutions proposed by Gaston and Gager.

According to Gager, the traditional and still dominant understanding is that

> . . . the Torah and Christ are mutually exclusive categories for
> Paul, that with the coming of Christ the Torah no longer represents God's path of salvation, and that Israel thus stands condemned and rejected by God for its refusal to have faith in
> Christ.

Gager believes that traditional view not only strikes at the heart of Judaism, but also is incorrect. Along with Gaston he claims that Paul did not fault the Jews for not believing in Christ. To support his claim Gager cites Romans 2—3, in which Paul discusses what Jews ought to do but have failed to do adequately: They ought to *do* rather than merely *hear* the Torah; they ought not to boast of an exclusive relation to God; they ought to trust in the righteousness God showed Abraham. The implication is, Gager maintains, that if they did these things their failings would be cured. There is no suggestion that they have failed because they have not believed in Jesus as Christ.[53]

Gager further cites Paul's use of Abraham, which he takes as indicative of Paul's conviction of the parity of Jew and Gentile. The example of Abraham

> enables Paul to buttress his claim . . . that the principle of faith
> applies not just to Gentile, whose justification is through Christ
> but to Jews whose justification is through the Torah. In this
> sense, the use of Abraham also confirms Paul's affirmation that
> he does not overthrow the Torah by faith![54]

Gager is correct in observing that Jewish sinfulness as described in Romans 2—3 has nothing at all to do with their rejection of Christ. However, one might note that the Gentile failing in chapters 1 and 2 is not expressed christologically either. Should one take this absence to mean that Paul doesn't really care whether Gentiles become believers in Christ? Regardless of the many problems of Romans 1—3, some of which I discussed in chapter 3 above, it is generally agreed and almost beyond doubt that Paul is in some sense expressing the situation "before Christ" to which God's act in Christ is the solution, to the Jew first and also to the Greek. Thus, Romans 2 cannot convincingly be used to demonstrate that Paul is unconcerned with the lack of acceptance of Christ as God's agent of universal salvation.[55]

The use Gager makes of Abraham is highly tendentious. No doubt Paul raises a christological problem by having Abraham exhibit saving faith that is not explicitly faith in Jesus as the Christ: if non-christologically expressed faith was adequate for Abraham before Jesus, why can it not also be adequate for others after Jesus? Perhaps Paul has proved more than he wanted to prove, for in demonstrating that since Abraham's saving faith and God's pronouncement of his consequent justification were prior to the Torah, he has also proved that they were prior to God's act in Christ. Has he not thereby proved, as Gager wants to argue, that faith in Christ is not necessary? Paul himself does not recognize this problem. But even if the logic of his statement argues for the validity of nonexplicitly christological faith, Gager surely is off the mark when he suggests the example confirms Paul's recognition of the validity of justification through the Torah. Paul's polemic against Judaizing (especially in Galatians) makes such a statement entirely incredible. There is no real textual evidence to support such an interpretation: Paul nowhere connects faith or justification with the Torah in a positive sense.[56]

Gager utilizes Romans 15:8–9 to argue that for Paul "Christ was not the climax of God's dealings with Israel but rather the fulfillment of his promise to Abraham concerning the redemption of the Gentiles." Gager (perhaps correctly) takes 15:9 to be in apposition to rather than in conjunction with 15:8: the Gentiles' glorifying God for his mercy is an expression of the truthfulness of God's promise to Abraham. Gager's application of this insight is less convincing. The context opposes that interpretation; Paul is exhorting "weak" and "strong" (Jew and Gentile in the church at Rome?) to accept and welcome one another. To solidify his exhortation Paul speaks of servanthood and mercy, traits which he admonishes them to exhibit toward one another, so that God may fill the praising community with joy and peace in believing (15:13). The admonition and the prayer following it neither intentionally nor unintentionally make the point that Christ is not the climax of God's dealings with Israel. Quite the contrary is implied: God's promise to Abraham to bless the Gentiles through him has not and can not come to fulfillment through the Torah, but it has now become a new possibility through Christ. In him Gentile and Jew alike have new access to God, and as a consequence "welcome one another" (Rom. 15:7) and so "with one voice glorify the God and Father of our Lord Jesus Christ" (Rom. 15:6). Only by arbitrarily shutting verse 6 off from verses 7–9 can one discover a non-christological basis for the commonality in salvation of Gentile and Jew.

The christological character of Paul's understanding of God's concern for Israel is clear in Romans 9–11. It is in this section that Paul explicitly addresses the problem of the Jewish situation of unbelief. The christological character of that unbelief, and the contrast of faith in Christ and works of Torah, are unmistakable in this passage. In 9:33, after saying Israel did not pursue righteousness through faith but "as if it were based on works," he asserts by scriptural quotation that God placed in Israel a "stone of stumbling," "a stone of scandal," but that the one who has faith in it [him] will not be put to shame. The stone of scandal is the same as the "scandal to the Jews" in 1 Corinthians 1:23, which is the crucified messiah upon whom Paul's kerygma centers.

Paul's agony throughout chapters 9–11 is occasioned not primarily by the fact that Jews who do not regard Jesus as the messiah are resisting inclusion of Gentiles within messianic communities—that is an argument which Paul has with members of the communities themselves. It is occasioned by the Jews' refusal to accept Jesus as Messiah. And while the inclusion of Gentiles in the church might have been one obstacle to their acceptance, it was not the only or primary one. The "scandal" to the Jew as Paul sees it is the proclamation of the *crucified* Jesus as Messiah.

If Gaston is correct, it is of no great moment to Paul whether

Jews accept Jesus as Messiah.[57] One suspects that this reading of Paul is determined by modern concerns more than by historical accuracy. While it is true that explicitly christological language is absent from chapter 11,[58] chapter 11 does not spell out what Israel is to do or to believe, or what the "failing" of Israel is. Chapter 11 envisages what God is doing, calls for Gentile humility and not arrogance, and anticipates the final salvation of Israel. It is in Chapter 10 that Paul expresses the current problem of Israel's unbelief, and that chapter is thoroughly christological.[59] Here Paul emphasizes that Christ is the end of the Torah; he calls for the central confession, "Jesus is Lord," as the believing response of those who read the Torah correctly. He affirms that faith comes from hearing the word about Christ which is available to all, even to those who in disobedience and contrariness refuse to hear.

Gaston finds attractive a suggestion attributed to J. Parkes that there may be two chosen people with separate, legitimate traditions. Paul "probably hoped that all Jews would come to share his faith. But he does not explicitly say so, and the absence of Jesus from Romans 11 (cf. also 1 Cor. 15:28) may give a hint in another direction."[60] Gaston finds further support for this view in Galatians 3:28: "Just as women do not need to become men nor men women to attain their full humanity, so Jews do not need to become gentiles nor gentiles to become Jews."[61]

Gaston surely is correct in his last point: Paul does not advocate the change of one's ethnic identity in order to be in the one people of God. That is the real issue in the controversy over circumcision of Gentiles; Paul asserts the appropriateness of each person remaining "as is." However, that does not mean that for Paul the appropriate faith for the Jew has no connection with Jesus as the messiah sent by God for the salvation of Gentile and Jew. But as I have argued above, Paul's advocating faith in Jesus does not mean that Jews should become "Christians" in the modern sense of those terms.

Gaston and Gager argue that Paul did not preach to Jews but only to Gentiles. In this view, Paul thought God would save Israel through God's own eschatological act, not through the mission of the church.[62] While that view has support in Romans 9—11, and while Paul certainly looks beyond the present and hopes for God's future resolution of the problem, he does not advocate abandoning the proclamation of the kerygma to Jew as well as to Gentile. Even if Paul never preached to Jews calling for their faith in Jesus as risen Lord,[63] still he believed it appropriate that others *were* preaching to Jews. What was Peter preaching as apostle to the circumcised? That now is the time for admitting Gentiles? Was not the center of Peter's preaching the messiahship of the crucified Jesus? There were varieties of christological viewpoint among the messianic communities, but almost certainly they all regarded Jesus as Messiah. There is no evidence for a kerygma of the early church which would assume that it was acceptable for Israel not to see Jesus as messiah. So far as one can tell from the evidence available, "Jesus is Lord" is among the earliest and most universal confessions of faith of the messianic communities.

Thus, while the final belief or unbelief of Israel is in God's hands, and while the *present* acceptance of Jesus as messiah is not ultimately determinative of their salvation, the mission of the apostles as Paul understood it included the preaching of God's act in Jesus as the key to the salvation of both Gentile and Jew.

Gager is correct in rejecting the second half of what he describes as the "traditional view": Israel stands condemned and rejected by God for its failure to have faith in Christ. That notion is not true to Paul; he does not believe God has rejected his people; he explicitly denies it in Romans 11:1, 28, 29. A particularly telling passage for discerning Paul's attitude toward his fellow Jews is Romans 11:8–10. Here Paul attributes to God the "hardening" of Israel, quoting from Psalm 69 an imprecation upon the enemies of God's righteous one:

> And David says,
> "Let their table become a snare and a trap,
> a pitfall and a retribution for them;
> let their eyes be darkened so that they cannot see,
> and bend their backs for ever."

That prayer expresses harsh judgment, no doubt. Quite likely some in Paul's day connected its sentiments with the story of Jesus' crucifixion, for Psalm 69 is used by all four Gospel writers to describe the suffering of Jesus. It is quite likely that the Psalm's imprecatory prayer for retribution against the persecutors of God's righteous one was already being used against "the Jews." Paul quotes it, also, and thus could be accused of the same sentiment. But Paul's interpretation takes a surprising turn: he breaks off the quotation before the Psalmist says, "Let them be blotted out of the book of the living." Perhaps he had heard that curse applied to the Jews, too. But Paul does not use the curse; instead, his next statement is, "Have they stumbled so as to fall? Hell no!" The hardening of the Jews did not lead to their destruction, but to the mission to the Gentiles! How much greater riches will come to the world when they are fully included with the Gentiles in the one people of God. However, Paul does believe that those who reject the gospel are shutting themselves off from God's promises at the very time God is bringing those promises to fulfillment for both Gentile and Jew. His hope centers in God's grace, which will "graft them in again" (Rom. 11:23, author's translation), overcoming their unbelief.

The reality of anti-Semitism and its horrors in the holocaust should have a sobering effect upon the way the Christian community interprets and enters into dialogue with its own tradition. That experience necessitates a critical awareness of the historical conditionedness of the anti-Judaic elements within the New Testament; it calls for the discovery of hermeneutical methods by which the tradition can be applied today in ways that avoid the evils of the past. But it does not necessitate a rewriting of the history of that strife between brothers and sisters or the denial that the theological as well as the sociological basis of that strife really existed. Honesty requires admitting when our forebears as well as ourselves have fallen short. In the end, better relationships between Jews and Christians today will be established not by bypassing that honesty but by repenting of that in the tradition which is unworthy of a faithful God whose intent is to unite both Gentile and Jew as one people of God.

Paul had the courage to pursue his missionary work and his theological quest in dangerous new directions; his example is for those "who pursue our theological quest in unorthodox directions...there simply *are* in Paul's work fascinating elements which justify the claim that it is a blueprint for radical if responsible Christian and theological freedom."[64]

Did Paul Teach Universal Salvation?

Paul's concern about his "relatives by race" leads him to make sweeping affirmations about the final outcome of God's historical working:

> [When] the full number of Gentiles come in...all Israel will be saved. (Rom. 11:25–26)
>
> God has consigned all [people] to disobedience, that he may have mercy upon all. (Rom. 11:32)

I have argued above that the pressure of debate and argument might sometimes have led Paul to overstate his case. On the matter of the Torah, the heated debate *almost* led him to say the Torah has only a negative purpose, that it was not from God, that it has no positive role to play in God's salvation of humankind. Again, in his arguing that saving faith existed before the Torah and thus has no necessary connection with it, Paul has also implicitly argued that it is prior to the Christ event, too. Paul does not always explicitly draw the logical inferences one could make from his assertions. Thus, in the present case a plausible argument is that Paul does not mean that all Gentiles and all Israelites will be saved.[65] Has his anxiety over the fate of Israel pushed Paul to assert a universal salvation which is inconsistent with his position as stated in other contexts? If one takes Paul's words literally at face value they would seem to imply universal salvation.

Paul's optimism about the ultimate triumph of God's grace over human sin and rebellion is not expressed only here; nor is it expressed only in contexts in which Paul specifically connects it with the fate of Israel. One can, indeed, make a strong case that such optimism is very near the center of Paul's theological perspective. Whoever is justified is justified by God's grace; Gentile and Jew alike are the recipients of God's saving grace; the ungodly are the ones who are justified; when human sin increased God's grace increased all the more. These ideas find fullest expression in Romans 5 and in 1 Corinthians 15:

> Then as one man's trespass led to condemnation for all so one man's act of righteousness leads to acquittal and life for all....(Rom. 5:18)
>
> For as in Adam all die, so also in Christ shall all be made alive. (1 Cor. 15:22) [66]

Paul's optimism of grace is closely tied to the resurrection of Jesus; that event forms the paradigm for God's dealing with the world of sin and death to which the gospel is addressed. The resurrection originates entirely from God, and its power is given to humans. Human sin did not prevent it—indeed, at one level, human sin provoked it; but human goodness did not produce it, either. "All this is from God..." (2 Cor. 5:18). Neither the old creation nor the new is the work of human beings, even though they are called to participate faithfully in God's work of reconciliation. Followed to its logical conclusion, this optimism of grace could easily mean that God will see to it that all will reach that condition in which they are renewed and made whole.

There is, however, another element which runs counter to Paul's optimism of grace and which has kept most interpreters from drawing that conclusion. That contrary element is the reality of God's "wrath," or God's judgment against human sinfulness. In Romans we read:

> For the wrath of God is revealed from heaven against all ungodliness and wickedness of [those] who by their wickedness suppress the truth. (1:18)
>
> By your hard and impenitent heart you are storing up wrath for yourself on the day of wrath when God's righteous judgment will be revealed....[F]or those who are factious and do not obey the truth, but obey wickedness, there will be wrath and fury. There will be tribulation and distress for every human being who does evil, the Jew first and also the Greek. All who have sinned under the law will be judged by the law. (2:5–12)

Persons of faith as well as those who reject faith confront the necessity of eschatological judgment (1 Cor. 3:13–15) and can even lose the standing within God's covenant people to which in faith they have gained access (Rom. 11:22). Paul uses such warnings as exhortations to continued faithful obedience more than as explanations of what will happen at the end-time. In keeping with prophetic tradition, such eschatological warning is given to prevent arrogance and presumption as well as to promote right living in the present. Paul spends very little time discussing what lies beyond the eschatological consummation, a fact which reflects Paul's intense concentration upon the here and now as the arena of faithful living. Eschatological judgment functions in Paul's language to invest the present with intensified value.

The emphasis upon judgment, therefore, does not necessarily preclude universal salvation. In general both the threat of judgment and its application have corrective discipline as their primary function. Retributive punishment is not entirely lacking, especially if 2 Thessalonians 1:5–10 was written by Paul; but it is decidedly secondary to Paul's positive interest. He actually speaks very little about what will happen to those who do not believe when Christ returns, or even whether there will be any. In Romans 11:26–27 he puts forward the notion that the return of Christ will be an occasion for the renewal of those who in the present have been rendered "insensitive" to the gospel:

"The Deliverer will come from Zion,
he will banish ungodliness from Jacob";
"and this will be my covenant with them
when I take away their sins."

(quoting Ps. 14:7; Isa. 59:20–21; 27:9)[67]

Whether punishment will be meted out is not stated, but if punishment is part of the scenario, it logically occurs between the return of Christ and the renewal of disbelieving Israel. Whether that scenario includes those of the past as well as those then present is not said; Paul seems in 1 Thessalonians 4:13–18 to expect a general resurrection at the return of Christ, though he specifically applies it only to those "in Christ."

Conclusion

Throughout Romans Paul emphasizes God's justification of the ungodly to show that there is no distinction between Gentile and Jew: alike in covenant-breaking, they are also alike in being included among God's covenanted people. The pious do not enter God's covenant by their piety, the moral by their morality, or the chosen by their pride. Neither are the impious, the immoral, and those who have nothing about which to boast ultimately excluded because of their human qualities or condition. It is God's grace that sets right those who are wrong.

Paul's theology is grounded upon that grace, and that grounding enables Paul to anticipate the future with optimism. Anguished as he is about the world, and especially about the rupture between himself as apostle of Christ to the Gentiles and his "relatives by race," his anguish turns into doxology as he reflects upon the amazing grace of God. That grace, the most powerful reality in the world, is able to conquer human sin and overcome alienation. The future will be a manifestation of the Lordship of the gracious God. Sin and death destroyed, God will be "everything to every one" (1 Cor. 15:28); for he is "Source, Guide, and Goal of all that is" (Rom. 11:36, NEB).

9

Admonitions to the New Covenant Community

(Romans 12:1—15:13)

In Romans 12—15 Paul's primary concern is with "ethics," that is, with behavior in the new covenant community. Many commentaries have distinguished between the dogmatic or doctrinal teaching of chapters 1—11 and the ethical teaching of 12—15. Such a distinction is misleading not only because it tends to separate doctrine and practice in an unpauline way, but also because it overlooks the communal and ethical concerns of earlier chapters.

Ethical concerns are in the forefront of questions about how human life can be renewed so that God's righteousness will be realized in human experience. I have claimed that covenantal relationships have been central throughout this letter: that sin is a break in human relations as well as in relation with God; that salvation involves the healing of those relationships within the covenant community; that new life "in the spirit" is life together in the body of Christ; that future hope is not merely for individual salvation but for the renewal of the whole human community. This perspective implies that ethical concerns are present in every "doctrinal" issue.

Paul's theology is grounded in God's initiative toward the world; it ends not in pious speculation about dream worlds yet to be, but in admonitions to let the new world of the future transform present human community. The earthly conduct of the believing community is to proclaim the message of God's salvation. Faith is proclaimed through the community of faith not as abstract truth stated in propositional terms but as lived truth expressed through the active life of the community. As personal response to God, faith must be the constant determinant of a person's life within community; that concretizing of faith presupposes the inward transformation which has begun in the initial act of faith symbolized by baptism.[1] But faith as the personal opening of the self to God is not a once-for-all event. Faith is not an act which takes place and then belongs to the past; neither is it a quality which automatically attaches to the person from the moment of its inception. Rather, obedient faith must be realized in each particular moment of a person's life—taking concrete form in decisions regarding one's relation to others—or one is not living by faith.

Paul considers admonition to be an appropriate way for one person to strengthen the faith of another or of the whole community (see 1:11; 15:14–15). Romans 12—15 represents his personal admonitions to the community of believers in Rome.

Theology and Ethics

Some interpreters deny any direct connection between Paul's theology and his ethics, pointing to the general admonitions Paul gives in 12:3–21. These instructions as well as those regarding the relations with the state in 13:1–7 seem rather tame and ordinary compared to the radical reorientation of life called for in Paul's theology.

The admonitions in these verses are quite diverse, with many abrupt transitions and few overt references to such theological themes as justification, grace, "in the spirit." Chapter 12, verses 3–13 apply mostly to relations within the community of faith.

Believers are admonished to be humble (verse 3), to recognize their mutual needs, and to put community interests ahead of personal interests; their attitudes are to be positive no matter what circumstances they face, and they are to love and care for one another. Chapter 12, verses 14–21, comprise a series of injunctions concerning relations with outsiders. Reflecting some of the same attitudes as the Sermon on the Mount, the injunctions involve nonretaliation, humility, a concern for the impact one has upon others, the need to live at peace with all people. Chapter 12 in its entirety has a lyrical and appealing quality. It is deceptively simple and surprisingly tame. In 13:1–7 Paul admonishes members of the community to conduct themselves as good citizens, accepting the power of the state and recognizing that it has a positive function to perform in the promotion of good order. The critical reader is inclined to ask, What is so special about Paul's admonitions? What does he advocate which cannot be found in other good moralists of any age?

One can point to several emphases in the chapter which might not find widespread endorsement in Paul's day: humility was not prized by Greco-Roman society, even though overweening pride was considered dangerous; although some Greek philosophers, including Plato, upheld the value of community over one's individual interests, this doctrine was by no means universal; Paul's emphasis upon nonretaliation for wrongs or insults would not appeal to those imbued with the heroic tradition. But even if these emphases taken together form a distinctive communal ethic, they are by no means unique. Is it possible, then, that Paul has overstated—or we have misunderstood— the radical change which the gospel is to make? Is it really true for Paul that one's foundational commitment to God's revelation in Christ transforms human existence and makes all things new, and that that newness is to be expressed in one's conduct? If the ethic turns out to be only a modified version of other available ethics, does that mean that Paul's real concern after all is for salvation in a strictly otherworldly sense—have we been deceived by Paul's earlier rhetoric? Or does Paul mean to suggest that the difference between the person of faith and other persons is that the person of faith can more successfully do what everyone already knows is right because of access to the power of God that others do not have—everyone can know what is good, but only the one assisted by God can do it?

There is certainly an otherworldly element in Paul's thinking which renders all earthly acts temporary; the believer lives in this world "as if not" a part of it (1 Cor. 7:29–31). There is no doubt, further, that Paul thinks the believer has access to the power of God's presence through the reality of a committed relationship and is consequently enabled to act differently, free from the compulsive power of sin. But it is a misconception to suggest that for these reasons alone Paul can utilize a fairly standard ethical system.

A better explanation is that the radical ethic of Paul does not mean the rejection of all the values of the present social order. As I shall show, there is an element of "rationality" in Paul's ethics. He affirms much of what is affirmed by Greco-Roman philosophers; unbelieving alienation from God is thus seen as not so complete that the good is *always* rejected and the evil is *always* done. In chapter 1 Paul has recognized that Gentiles apart from the Torah often did what was right because they were "a law unto themselves." Thus, he can glean ethical admonitions from Greco-Roman traditions as well as from the Torah.

But for Paul, all values are to be judged neither by the Torah nor by traditions of the Greco-Roman world, but by the revelation of God in Jesus Christ. Not all within the church is good; not all outside it is evil. Not all claims to be in the spirit are valid, and not all living "according to the flesh" is outside the church. But by what standards are goodness and badness to be judged? Paul's answer is, according to whether any action or attitude leads to the realization of the new humanity which has been revealed in Jesus Christ. When Paul echoes teachings of the Torah and of Greco-Roman moralists, it is not to affirm their validity as such, but because those teachings have value for community-building. His covenantal theology, centering inevitably in communal relationship, is the filter through which all traditions pass.

The gospel enters the world of broken community and offers the body of Christ for the healing of the nations. The community of faith is to function internally so as to overcome divisions among insiders, divisions which they brought with them but which they are now to put aside. Within the community there is no Jew or Greek, no insider or outsider, no first-class or second-class, no superior or inferior members. Function is divided; people are not. Gifts are graces, not achievements; graces are for the community, not for the individual; all things are held in common, and the ministry of one is the ministry of all.

In its external relations the community is to mirror its internal values. Hatred of the human race outside the church is no effective way of overcoming the division between insider and outsider. Even those who treat members of the community with contempt are not to be hated in return, nor to be dealt with as enemies. One should note here the partial parallel between God's way of dealing with the world of unbelief and the church's way. Extending grace to the alienated leads to conquest of evil, just as God has acted to overcome human opposition by approaching in grace. But even if God's approach to humanity involves the revealing of his judgment (1:18), the community of faith is not to engage in that judgment, but to leave it entirely to God (12:21).

Paul puts proverbial wisdom to the service of the gospel. The question is not whether his admonitions are unique, nor whether he has grounded each particular one in a particular aspect of his theology. What *is* grounded in his theology is the concept of the church as the new covenant community, the body of Christ; particular admonitions derived from traditions find new significance in that context. Jesus in the Sermon on the Mount related aphoristic wisdom to the Kingdom of God; Paul relates it to the life of the church in the world.

Connections between Paul's theology and ethics, then, will not be found primarily by looking at each particular admonition to see what logical connection it has with particular theological tenets. The same admonitions might possibly be paralleled by other writers. The connection will be seen in the radical shift of perspective from which each particular bit of wisdom is regarded and within Paul's concern to build a new human community. In these chapters (12—15), Paul displays two themes which dominate that perspective: radical transformation (12:1–2) and the centrality of love (13:8–10).

Radical Transformation

Chapter 11 ended with a doxology praising God who is the Source, Guide, and Goal of all that is. That conviction is the basis for Paul's optimism that ultimately God's salvation will incorporate the whole of humanity, Gentile as well as Jew. That action will express God's mercy, but as always Paul couples affirmations of God's grace with admonitions for the reciprocal human movement: "I appeal to you, therefore, [brothers and sisters], by the mercies of God, to present your bodies as a living sacrifice, holy and acceptable to God..." (Rom. 12:1). Interpreters debate whether the "therefore" in this instance is a casual transitional particle or an attempt to make a logical connection with what has gone before. Regardless of the answer, Paul does connect his admonitions thematically with his earlier theological affirmations.

The first connection with the theological statements may be seen in Paul's speaking of the response as a sacrifice. Paul does not often speak of Christ's death in sacrificial terms, and even less frequently does he speak of the human response in those terms. But in 3:25 and 8:32 he did use sacrificial terminology and here he reflects that earlier use. A gift which is a new relationship can be accepted only by entering into the relationship. Begun through a sacrifice offered by God, the new covenant can be established only by a reciprocal sacrifice of the believing self. In both cases what is really offered to the other is the self; apart from that offering no community can be established. Paul's admonition is akin to the prophetic theme that the sacrifice which is pleasing to God is not the outward rite, but the gift of the inner self:

> What [sacrifice] does the LORD require of you
> but to do justice, and to love [covenant loyalty],
> and to walk humbly with your God? (Mic. 6:8)

Paul uses cultic language even as he seeks to replace cultic thinking.[2] The sacrifice is to be *living*—that is, expressed not in rite but in daily conduct. Paul makes the same point in other words: neither circumcision nor lack of it is anything, but faith working through love captures God's will and best expresses the right relationship with God (Gal. 5:6).

Paul claims that such a living sacrifice is a *logikē* worship. The adjective *logikē* provides the translator with a dilemma. It can be given its more philosophic meaning of "logical" or "rational" or its more religious meaning of "spiritual." The difficulty with the first is that it suggests too rationalistic an understanding for Paul. The problem with the second is that it too easily moves into the kind of "spiritualism" which plagued the Corinthian church. The New English Bible attempts to render one Greek adjective with two English nouns: "The worship which accords with *mind* and *heart*" (my italics), suggesting appropriately that Paul is speaking of the response which engages the whole inner life. *Logikē* here refers to what is appropriate given the nature of the case: since God has given so much, the total response of the person is the only reasonable response; that response accords with the nature of the human being who has the capacity of knowing and affirming God's will, and who denies human nature when failing to acknowledge God's.

Paul implicitly contrasts the interior self with animal or other material sacrifices. But by using "bodies" to refer to that sacrifice, he also shows that he does not promote a spirituality of inward piety which is devoid of concrete obedience. The use of "proving" the will of God, "what is good and acceptable and perfect" (Rom. 12:2) suggests further a rational component of human obedience. Claims to spirituality are to be tested in terms of the concrete results in the community of faith. Do actions build or destroy the community? Do they enhance or detract from its effectiveness in being a beach-head for the new age?

Such questions are answered for Paul not merely by appeal to revelation but also by critical examination: one should consider (*dokimazō* = put to the test, examine, prove by testing) what is the will of God. In Paul's view it is only through giving the whole self—mind, will, spirit, heart, or whatever pertains to human life—that one can hope to know God's will. The mind must be sacrificed, in the sense not of giving it up as mind, but of offering its intelligent service to God. So also with other inner faculties with which a person is endowed. Everything is sacrificed, but paradoxically nothing is given up, for everything is fulfilled in living. There is an analogy here with Paul's earlier claim to be "crucified with Christ," which is not death at all but a more complete life. Paul's covenantal understanding of human existence includes the idea that life is gained only through renewed relationships.

The Hebraic notion of "two ways" is reflected again in Paul's admonition not to be "conformed" but to be "transformed" (Rom. 12:2). One can be one or the other, but not both. Conformity to the world is participation in its alienation from God, reflection of its values, adoption of its outlook. That conformity would include adopting the world's way of treating people according to their classifications: Gentile, Jew, male, female, slave, free. Perpetuating within the church a social order which has had divisive and corrosive effects in the larger social order is to miss the church's reason for being, and to miss the transformation offered in the new community.

Opposed to conformity is transformation: the believing community should be transformed by the renewing of its mind. "Probably only a Hebrew could think of a mind being renewed,"[3] because for a Hebrew "mind" is not "intellect" as much as it is "will." To renew the mind is equivalent to repentance, involving a change in thought, attitude, and outlook so that conduct may correspondingly change. To renew the mind is to adopt a new point of view concerning God's will for humankind and in regard to what is good and what leads to the renewal of human community. Paul thus calls for a radical life reorientation in the believer and in the believing community. The nature of that radical orientation may be summed up as love.

"Let Love Be Genuine"

There are good reasons for claiming that love dominates Paul's ethical teaching, even though the term does not dominate his vocabulary.[4] (1) Love ties together his theology and ethics more closely than any other concept. Love expresses God's gracious act in setting the world right, not out of the merit of those set right, but out of God's own free choice: "God shows his love for us in that while we were yet sinners Christ died for us" (Rom. 5:8). That understanding of love as deriving from the will and purpose of the one who loves rather than from a calculation of the deserving recipient is very close to the model of love that Paul utilizes in his ethical teaching. (2) Love is the primary criterion by which to measure the rightness or wrongness of an action: "If your brother or sister is distressed by your eating, you are no longer living by the standard of love" (Rom. 14:15, my translation). (3) Love is the fulfillment of God's will expressed in the Torah: "love is the fulfilling of the [Torah]" (Rom. 13:10). (4) Thus, love demonstrates the reality and the power of faith: "faith [expressing itself] through love" (Gal. 5:6).[5] (5) Love is the sum of the never-ending obligation that humans have for each other, just as it is the expression of God's never-ending grace: "Nothing can separate us from the love of God"...(8:39); similarly, "Owe no one anything, except to love one another" (13:8).

As usual, Paul does not define or systematically describe his key word (though he gives a moving lyrical description in 1 Cor. 13), and as usual, the word is subject to misunderstanding. The most serious and most frequent misunderstanding is to take love to be a sentiment, an emotion which one person feels for another. As a counter to the tendency to sentimentalize love, it is often asserted that love is more of an action word than a feeling word. That statement is generally accurate, but it too may easily distort what Paul intends. For him love is not a cold action based merely upon a rationalistic understanding of what is good, any more than it is a mechanical obedience to an external commandment. Love is a caring concern for the other, expressed in action; it is

> energetic and beneficent good will which stops at nothing to secure the good of the beloved object. It is not primarily an emotion or an affection, but an active determination of the will.[6]

If one understands "stops at nothing" to mean "without consideration of cost to oneself," and if one understands "good will" and "beloved object" to include caring concern, Dodd's definition is quite adequate.

Dodd's stress on "will" captures an essential dimension of love: *love* is a covenant word which expresses the key element of election. God's love for Israel is manifest in the election of Israel. While God's sentiment for Israel is not excluded, Israel was not elected out of sentiment. Rather, God's sentiment for Israel derives from the fact of election. This perspective perhaps grows out of the metaphor of Israel as God's bride; God wooed that bride in the wilderness, reflecting the ancient practice of having emotional bonding follow marriage rather than precede it. In a similar way, love for neighbor is choosing the neighbor as neighbor, even as family member, prior to good feelings for the person and commiting oneself (active determination of the will) to procure the profoundest well-being of the neighbor. In that choice and its subsequent expression in action, one's sentiments might also change, but sentiment is not the key element in loving.

If this correctly describes Paul's understanding of love, he shows himself to be in harmony with his Hebraic heritage. He derives images from Israel's past and makes them even more powerful by applying them to the love which God and Christ express through the death of Jesus: "[God] did not spare his own Son but gave him up for us all" (Rom. 8:32); "Christ did not please himself" by giving himself up to death on the cross (15:3). This superb understatement has the effect of holding up a mirror in which the strong can see the pettiness of their own actions toward the weak. The life of faith is not to be a life of self-gratification, but a life modeled on Christ's self-giving.

Love modeled after God and Christ is to be the criterion for evaluating actions by those participating in the community of faith. If one's acts injure a brother or sister, one is not walking according to love (14:15), for "love does no wrong to a neighbor" (Rom. 13:10). By love one can see what is in the commandments; love will not do the injurious acts prohibited by the Torah, even though it does not need the external compulsion of commandment to avoid them. Love fulfills the Torah, not only by refraining from what the Torah prohibits, but also by establishing the community of concern toward which the Torah also aimed.

But now that community of concern is expanded to include Gentile as well as Jew, and neighbor is expanded to include not only those within the inclusive community but also those outside it. Love's purpose in the world is to overcome evil with good; thus, it expresses itself in nonretaliation, in pursuit of peace and harmony, in its refusal to treat enemies as enemies and its decision that enemies are to be treated with a hospitality calculated to make them as friend and family (12:14–21).

By defining faith as a life which expresses itself in love (Gal. 5:6), Paul shows the dominance of ethical living over theological knowledge or religious piety. That dominance is lyrically expressed in 1 Corinthians 13, where Paul makes emphatically clear that it is not theology or piety which constitutes the expression of faith, but rather the quality of love manifested in relationships. Although the occasion of Paul's address to the Romans does not trigger the concentrated presentation of love which the Corinthian situation did, still the primacy of love underlies the whole of Romans 12—15.

Attitude Toward the State

The idea of a radical ethic deriving from human transformation is severely tested in Paul's admonitions regarding the community's responsibility to the state. On first reading, this passage sounds as though it could have been written by the emperor himself! During the history of "Christian" empires and kingdoms it has provided comfort for many autocrats. At least on the surface Paul says that God is the source of all authority, including that of the governing authorities. They are appointed by God to promote the good, and anyone who resists the governing authorities resists what God has appointed, and thus can expect not only their wrath but also God's.

One could argue that this surface meaning is Paul's real intent. Paul's actual situation probably inclined him to say good things about the state. The Roman government inaugurated by Augustus made the roads and seas of the Mediterranean world safe for the kind of travel Paul's missionary journeys required and provided a measure of unity among formerly disparate nations, enhancing the appeal of the universal gospel Paul preached. The Romans had brought an unusual degree of tolerance of religious and cultural diversity, which made the proclamation of a Judaic-based gospel an acceptable option. The Roman government provided a measure of personal safety to Paul in his travels (this would be especially true if Acts is correct in naming Paul a Roman citizen). Because of such benefits it is certainly plausible that Paul believed that God had ordained this government specifically for the "fullness of time."

Paul's eschatological beliefs might well have contributed to his evident acceptance of the Roman government. A new age is replacing the old. As part of the old order, the state does not need to be replaced by a "Christian" state, since all human institutions are passing away, and all authorities will be subjected to Christ. In the meantime, the Roman state, with its positive benefits, is to remain in place to give order and a measure of stability in an otherwise insecure world. The community of faith is to approve and cooperate with those legitimate endeavors, living peaceful and respectful lives. Such an admonition does not sum up Christian ethics, but it is a consistent part of it.

Paul's statements also might reflect the position of powerlessness, which a minority and suspected religious movement always occupies. There was no possibility that the powers of the state could be significantly influenced by that small community. There was no point in addressing admonitions to the state or of offering moral guidance for its officials. There was certainly nothing to be gained in provoking the wrath of the state needlessly.

In this and in other issues, Paul reflects unquestioningly the accepted wisdom of his day that "subordination" within social ordering is legitimate and good. In 1 Corinthians 11, he offers a ranking of authority: God, Christ, man, woman. Given this hierarchical principle, Paul could well have accepted the legitimacy of even authoritarian government as consistent with God's general ordering principle.

While this position has a certain amount of plausibility about it, however, it raises certain questions. As a practical way of adapting to the current situation, it seems sensible enough. But it would suggest that Paul makes no connection between the life of citizenship and the christological basis of all Christian action; nor does it make love the dominant principle for action. Most seriously, it ignores the question as to whether there is any limit to the believer's obedience to the state: would Paul agree with those who maintain that "We must obey God rather than [humans]" (Acts 5:29)? What if the state should begin to treat as criminals members of the community of faith, as it did within a few years of this writing? Would Paul have spoken differently then? If so, are his absolute-sounding admonitions here really to be understood so absolutely? In fact, the word Paul uses is not "obedience" but submission; submission could imply recognizing subject status, without necessarily saying that believers should obey every particular command of the state.

There may be implicit within this statement a further limit on obedience to the state: "Pay all of them their dues, taxes... revenue...respect...honor..."(13:7). This statement is close to one found in 1 Peter 2:13–17, where "Fear God" is given alongside "Honor the Emperor." Implied is a limitation upon what is due the state and a recognition that the payment of what the state demands is held within limits of consistency with what God demands. This implicit limitation is less clearly expressed in Paul, but the basis for it is there. If there is no implicit limitation, then Paul contradicts a fundamental principle of his own theology, which is that anytime one acts contrary to faith one acts wrongly. Faith is for him one's absolute commitment to God; that precludes giving absolute allegiance to any other. The state, even ordained by God as it is, has a secondary claim upon the person of faith. When the state performs its proper function of maintaining order and promoting the good as seen from the perspective of faith, it is to be obeyed. The basis for that limitation might be more obvious if one translates the participial adverbially: "when they attend" or "insofar as they attend" to God's will.[7] One should note that Paul himself resisted the constituted authorities by escaping form King Aretas (2 Cor. 11:32–33).

Paul does not intend here to be offering a complete theoretical position regarding the nature and purpose of government, and certainly not regarding the type of government intended by God. But in admonishing decent and quiet citizenship on the part of the community of faith in Rome, he suggests that no one government has exclusive claim to be chosen by God, as many of his contemporaries within Judaism might have asserted.[8] The Roman state, too, can perform God-given functions. It is not to be despised, nor is it to be left to be the instrument of those gods whose support it claims. It belongs to the God who is making covenant with the people of the world, Gentile as well as Jew. It has no more power than God allows it to have. Just as the Israelites in time past adopted kingship from the Canaanites and placed kingship under the authority and judgment of God, so Paul acknowledges that the Roman empire is under the authority and judgment of the same God, thus providing a basis for a critical evaluation of particular persons or acts.

The Weak and the Strong

In chapters 12—13 Paul's admonitions are general, applicable anywhere. With the possible exception of the relationship with the state, these admonitions do not reveal a knowledge of specific issues or problems facing the church at Rome. Chapters 14—15 are different: they address a particular problem which threatens to divide the church. We are not told how Paul has learned of this problem, but he speaks as though he knows the specific issues at least in a general way; his discussion shows that the problem in Rome contains manifestations slightly different from those of the similar problem which he knew firsthand in Corinth (see 1 Cor. 8—10).

From his admonitions we can learn that there were at least two dominant viewpoints in Rome which might be related to the predominant Gentile and the minority Jewish members.[9] One group, whom Paul calls the "weak," thinks that faith requires them to eat only vegetables (Rom. 14:2) and to observe certain holy days (Rom. 14:5). The other group, whom Paul calls the "strong," thinks dietary habits and observance of holy days have nothing to do with faith (Rom. 14:2, 5). The weak judge the strong harshly for their lack of religiously motivated observance, while the strong despise the weak for their useless observances, pious legalisms, and lack of freedom.

Paul identifies himself with the viewpoint of the strong: "I know and am persuaded in the Lord Jesus that nothing is unclean in itself" (Rom. 14:14). But he does not try to persuade the weak to agree with him. In fact, most of his admonitions are addressed to the strong rather than to the weak. Paul has celebrated the grace of God whose saving help was extended to those who were weak; in response to such grace the relatively strong have a greater burden than the relatively weak members of the community. Just as Paul appealed to the Corinthians to be generous to those who had less by appealing to the example of Christ who "though he was rich, yet for your sake... became poor" (2 Cor. 8:9), so he now appeals to the strong to exhibit a caring attitude toward the weak. The strong have the advantage that they are free to eat or not to eat, for their conscience does not dictate a course of action; the weak, on the other hand, are not free to eat without violating their consciences.

The particular admonitions which Paul addresses to each group are simple and few. To the weak he says, Don't judge

your neighbors who do not follow your taboos and requirements; they are God's servants, and they express gratitude to
God for what they eat. Their loyalty and service are given to
God, and it is God who will judge the sincerity of their faith
and the effectiveness of their service. To the strong he says, Do
not be arrogant because your conscience is not so weak; the one
whom you are inclined to despise intends to render faithful
service to God. You should be more concerned not to offend the
conscience or to outrage the standards of the weak than to
express your freedom flagrantly. Food is not going to make you
right with God, as you already know, but neither is it so important that you should cause others to stumble in faith and violate their consciences because of your eating. Just as Christ did
not seek his own pleasure, neither should you (Rom. 15:3). To
both groups Paul appeals for mutual concern and tolerance
rather than assertion of the rightness of their respective positions.

There are indications that underlying the issues of diet and
observance of holy days is a conflict between Jewish and Gentile members of the community. While the vegetarianism of
the weak is not part of orthodox Judaism, mourning for the
national condition as relations within Judea worsened could
have led to special kinds of fasting.[10] Perhaps more likely, in a
pagan city one could not be sure what kind of meat one was
eating, and it might seem prudent simply to avoid meat altogether. The strongest evidence that Gentile-Jewish conflicts
are involved comes from the emphasis upon Gentile-Jewish
relations beginning at 15:7. The final admonition to "welcome
one another...as Christ has welcomed you," leads to a series of
scriptural quotations which affirm the appropriateness of Gentile joining Jew in glorifying God. Here Gentile and Jew take
the place of the weak and the strong.[11] If I have been correct in
claiming that the relation between Jew and Gentile has dominated Paul's concern throughout the letter, the case is stronger
that weak and strong factions may be related in some way to
that larger issue. The impartiality that God manifests in calling both together into one new covenant community is to be
reflected in the impartiality of their acceptance of each other.[12]

This passage reveals a great deal about the way Paul's theology is expressed in pastoral admonitions. Often accused of being a dogmatist in theological matters, Paul actually manifests a great deal of latitude. It is true that in writing to the Galatians he excoriates those who present a different gospel, but the context of the argument more than a general trait of intolerance may account for the tone of that letter. His own intolerance of those who required the submission to the Torah was elicited by what he regarded as a divisive intolerance by the Judaizers who would not accept all people on the same basis of faith. He does not display the same theological intolerance in dealing with disputes within the community at Corinth (1 Cor. 1—4); there he does not assert the correctness of his doctrine over against that of Apollos or Cephas as a way of settling the dispute; rather, he focuses upon the cross of Christ and not upon human wisdom as offering the way to unity in the church. Here in Romans he does not take sides in the dispute, although he lets his position be known. Rather, he calls for tolerance and acceptance of diverse viewpoints.

Conclusion

Although Paul manifests a tolerance for diversity, there is an absolute value for him: the maintenance of the one new covenant community. For the unity of the community, rather than for theoretical opinions, he is a tenacious advocate. He warns against dividing the church by disputes over opinions as vigorously as he calls for keeping strong the bonds of love.

The principles of relationship within the community for which he argues include the following: (1) Freedom is held within the context of responsibility. Paul often had to argue for responsibility because he asserted freedom so strenuously; people tended to take his advocacy of freedom too far in wrong directions. In his view freedom is freedom from internal compulsion; it does not need to be proven to others in a display of disregard for convention and consideration of others. (2) Concern for the other takes precedence over concern for the self and for the exercise of one's own freedom. Genuine freedom is expressed through the lack of necessity to prove oneself a free person; when one is free from the necessity of proving oneself, one is free for positive relationships with others. (3) Diversity within the covenant community is to be accepted as a manifestation of the Spirit, who gives various gifts for the benefit of the whole; to condemn others who are different or differently endowed is to deny the Spirit's action within the whole body. (4) The unity of the church as the body of Christ is not to be destroyed by jealousy or disputation. The creation of one new humanity of Gentile and Jew is such an astounding achievement of God's grace that the mutual acceptance within that community ought now to be axiomatic. (5) The mutual upbuilding of that one new covenant community ought to be the primary motivation and desire of all as they relate to each other. (6) Love should be the binding instrument within the community. (7) The example of Christ "who did not please himself" is the image all should hold before their eyes.

Paul does not set these out as new "rules" for the community, but he places them before those to whose conscience he apppeals. He would have such concerns "written on the hearts" rather than laid down as external legislation. Faith does not provide a set of ready-made answers to ethical questions about how person relates to person within the community of faith or how the community relates to the larger world. But faith does provide resources and perspective which enable those answers to be discovered. Faith provides, first, freedom from the world so that the community can be free for the world. Freedom from the world releases the community of faith from the compulsion to act in ways dictated by the culture around it. Knowing that its life is not given by the culture but by God's grace which comes from beyond the observable, the community of faith is free from fear that the culture can threaten its well-being; it is free to gain its life independently, in reliance upon God alone. That freedom enables the church to engage in critical appraisal of the standards and values it confronts within the secular order: it is free to accept as well as to reject, to sort out the good from the bad on the grounds which faith provides. Faith commits the community and the person of faith to doing God's will as that will is discovered by the discerning mind committed to the transforming power of a new creation. That commitment means living in the spirit, living oriented to God and God's will. The committed life is the empowered life, so that faith does give access to increased power for doing the good. Free from fear, free to be critical of all claims to righteousness, free within commitment, the community of faith is a powerful community because it is an empowered community.

10

Future Plans and Final Greetings

(Romans 15:14—16:27)

Future Plans to Relate to Gentile and Jew

Concern for unity of the weak and strong leads into Paul's discussion of his own plans for the future, for those plans have direct bearing upon the issue of the unity of the church. As often in Paul, the one theme leads into another without clear transition. Chapter 15, verses 1–6 seem to be leading to the close of the weak/strong issue, as he cites the example of Christ as the clinching argument about their mutual care for one another; then follows a benediction which one would expect to mark a major transition. He then calls for harmonious accord so that "with one voice" they may glorify God (15:6).

But 15:7–13 still stays with the theme of weak and strong, urging both to "accept one another," repeating the admonition which opened the issue in 14:1. Their mutual acceptance is to be grounded in their common acceptance by Christ and is therefore necessitated by their faith-response to the good news that they have been included within the new covenant community. That response is part of their evangelical proclamation, for it will lead others to praise God ("for the glory of God," RSV) who has united Jew and Gentile into one.

Paul quotes from Scriptures—from the Torah, the prophets, and the Psalms—sounding the theme of the inclusion of the Gentiles and the joint worship of Gentile and Jew. Again, in verse 13, he pronounces a blessing upon them.

The inclusion of the Gentiles in the praise of God leads into Paul's account of his own missionary work and his plans for future work among the Gentiles. His call and his gift are especially to be a "minister to the Gentiles." That ministry has by God's grace been successful in winning the obedience of the Gentiles to God. He has reason to be proud of his work, for his accomplishment is by no means small. Following his policy of preaching only in new places where Christ has not yet been named as Lord, he has "fully preached" the gospel "from Jerusalem as far round as Illyricum."

This strange statement makes an astounding claim. What could Paul possibly mean by saying that he no longer has room to preach in the northeastern Mediterranean? In various ways this statement has been interpreted in light of Paul's eschatological expectation. Perhaps he believes that "every land" is to receive the gospel before the return of Christ, which he thinks is not far off; thus he symbolically establishes churches among "nations" and "peoples," not expecting to convert them all, but at least to have a representative group of Gentile believers to welcome Christ upon his return. Then, with Jew and Gentile praising him, Christ himself will be revealed to all, and all will believe. Whether this scenario is exactly what was in Paul's mind we cannot say, for *he* does not; but it must be something similar. At any rate, he says that his next evangelical step is to go on to new territory, to Spain, in keeping with his policy of preaching only in new territory. Does he intend to follow that principle in Rome, where others have preached? He does not say exactly what he will do there, but it is likely that his main interest was not missionary preaching. It is difficult, however, to imagine that Paul would not engage in evangelical activity wherever he was.

He apparently envisages leaving the eastern part of the Mediterranean completely; he wants to be sped on his way by the encouragement and support of the Roman community. His evangelical work no longer detains him from his long-intended visit to Rome, but something else does, something which is for him of overwhelming importance. If, as we have suggested, he does not anticipate returning to "these regions" any more, this is his final opportunity to resolve the largest hindrance to his vision of one new covenant community embracing Gentile and Jew. From early in his ministry, and probably even before he entered the new community of believers in Jesus, a serious rift had developed within the church between those who insisted that Gentiles included in the new covenant community should be circumcised and keep a minimal Torah, and those who believed that they should not. Paul's ministry had carried the central thrust of the second, more radical position, and he had held his convictions with a vigorous and uncompromising stance. His vitriolic outbursts against his opponents in Galatia show the intensity of the struggle and Paul's uncompromising attitude.

Whether the changing situation enabled him to be more tolerant by the time he wrote Romans, or whether he himself had mellowed, he maintains his theological convictions here in a more conciliatory spirit. Whether or not his decision to go to Jerusalem to try to heal the breach is tacit admission that his earlier stance has been unnecessarily harsh, he evidently knows that he is the strongest symbol of the mission to the Gentiles and that it is he who must symbolically bring them to Jerusalem. To go farther west without resolving the tension would contradict his theology of the one new covenant community, and his agony over the alienation of Israel (Rom. 9—11) would remain unrelieved.

Paul plans to deliver a monetary gift to the Jerusalem church. He describes it as a voluntary offering from the churches in Macedonia and Achaia which is intended to aid the poor among the saints in Jerusalem. But for Paul (and perhaps for the contributors), it is more than monetary aid: it is a symbol of indebtedness and gratitude, and as such it can be an instrument of healing. In effect it is a thank offering which Paul, acting as "priest" for the Gentiles (Rom. 15:16), brings to the "altar" in Jerusalem. The cultic language Paul uses, which is not characteristic of him, shows the theological investment which he has in this effort. If it were only aid for the poor, others could deliver it; but if it symbolizes the Gentiles' recognition of their participation in the heritage of Israel, and Israel's acceptance of them and their offering, then who besides Paul should serve as priest in this endeavor?

Paul does not face the journey lightly, for he knows that it is fraught with dangers. He does not dramatize the foreboding dangers the way the author of Acts does (Acts 20:17—21:14); he merely requests the readers to take up the struggle with him by praying to God on his behalf. The three petitions which their prayers are to include reveal the chief concerns Paul has about the trip. First, that he may be delivered from the unbelievers in Judea. Evidently Paul knows, for his missionary experience has taught him well, that his preaching is perceived by many Jews to be a threat to the Torah—i.e., to the whole Jewish way of life. Although Paul does not consider himself to have abandoned Judaism, both his teaching and his actions are deemed unacceptable by orthodox standards. Whether he anticipates mob action or official action is not clear, and is finally irrelevant. Second, he asks for prayers that his service will be acceptable to the saints. Paul knows he is *persona non grata* not only to orthodox Jews but also to many of those who belong to the new covenant community. He does not say he feels endangered by the latter, but if they reject his priestly ministry on behalf of the Gentiles, the whole purpose of the trip will be lost. The rift between Gentile and Jew will not only fail to be resolved, but will probably have been exacerbated. The third petition will be fulfilled if the first two are: That "I may come to you with joy and be refreshed in your company" (Rom. 15:32).

Theology in the Apostolic Greeting

There is some question as to whether chapter 16 was an original part of Paul's letter to the Romans. Some manuscript variations suggest that the letter could have ended with the benediction in 15:33. One wonders how Paul would have known so many people in the church he had never visited. The language of 16:25–27 sounds less like Paul than like the unconvincing imitator of Paul who wrote the Pastoral Epistles. On the other hand the textual evidence is not decisive; given the large flow of traffic between Rome and the provinces it is not unlikely that Paul knew many people who had made their way to Rome, and that he would want to mention as many connections with the church there as possible. Even if the closing doxology is not by Paul, that does not necessarily rule out the rest of the chapter; the last verses might have been written by Tertius, the scribe who added his personal greetings in verse 21.

In some ways it matters little whether one regards chapter 16 as part of the letter. It is taken up mostly with personal greetings and offers very little distinctive theological content to the letter. Even if it was not part of this letter, it is still likely written by Paul (with the possible exception of doxology). The main advantage that would be gained by the certainty of its inclusion would be the demonstration that Paul knew the situation of the church to which he is writing, and that his admonitions to the weak and the strong are not merely general, idealized instruction about how to deal with this sort of conflict. If the admonitions relate specifically to Jewish-Gentile strife in the church, my thesis that this issue forms the context of the whole letter would be strengthened. But I cannot change my preferences into "facts," and thus must leave the issue open as to whether chapter 16 belongs to this letter.

When the reader encounters the long list of names beginning in 16:1 the inclination is to close the book and consider it finished, regardless of who wrote it to whom. However, there are some intriguing statements and implications in these verses which help one to see the nature of the covenant community in Paul's day and provide insight into the character and concerns of the apostle.

These verses show that Paul's community is inclusive, that social distinctions based on sex, class, and condition are irrelevant. Phoebe is described not only as a sister ("fellow believer") but also as a deacon (*diakonon*) in the church in Cenchreae near Corinth. Paul commends her to the church at Rome, asking that she be accepted as a fellow believer and given any necessary assistance as she completes her task, for she herself has assisted many, including Paul. We do not know exactly what "deacons" were in Paul's church, but it was either an elected or appointed office in the local congregation. Deacons are mentioned along with "overseers" (bishops) as part of the congregation in Phil. 1:1. They served in some capacity including but not limited to ministry to the practical needs of the community. Exactly what functions in liturgy, preaching, and teaching the deacons had is not certain, but it is not at all improbable that they had many. Paul might well have sent Phoebe on the sensitive and vital mission of communicating for him with the Roman believers. He clearly wants the church to accord her the same high respect he has for her—a clear indication that Paul is not the despiser of women he is often portrayed as being.

Paul's positive attitude toward women is confirmed in the next greeting: to Prisca and Aquila, a couple who worked with Paul in Corinth, and who had a church in their house in Asia (1 Cor. 16:19), presumably in Ephesus. According to Acts 18:1-4, 18-26 they had lived in Rome until they were expelled when Claudius ordered all Jews to leave Rome; they made their way to Corinth, where they plied their tent-making trade. Paul worked with them there, and then they went with him from Corinth to Ephesus, where they stayed while Paul went on to Syria. There in Ephesus they encountered Apollos, an eloquent Alexandrian Jew, and taught him "the way of God more accurately," even though he was already a believer. Paul refers to an incident in which Prisca and Aquila "risked their necks" for him. If chapter 16 is indeed part of the Roman letter, they are now back in Rome, with a "church in their house" again. Paul puts the two on a completely equal footing, not distinguishing between them either in their devotion to him or their commitment to the community of faith, or the work which they do. They are both "fellow workers in Christ." Evidently they shared fully in preaching the gospel, in teaching, and in hosting the church.

Paul greets another couple: Andronicus and Junia,[1] who either with Paul or like Paul had been imprisoned for their faith.

Again Paul does not make any distinctions between the two persons on the basis of sex. Astoundingly he places them both among the group called apostles and says that they were outstanding. The RSV translators find all this so incredible that they make both to be men who were "well-known to the apostles." In this case, it is more honest to change the perception of what an apostle was than to translate according to one's preconceptions. The "apostles" were evidently not the numerically and sexually restricted group which church tradition has made them to be;[2] "'the apostles' must be given a wider sense as denoting those itinerant missionaries who were recognized by the churches as constituting a distinct group among the participants in the work of spreading the gospel."[3] That group evidently included women, a fact which Paul accepts as a matter of course.[4]

These greetings also reveal the class and racial inclusiveness of Paul's church. Some of the names are Jewish: Aquila and probably Prisca were Jewish according to Acts; possibly Mary (Rom. 16:6) is from Hebrew Miriam, though it could be from Latin Marian. Some are obviously Gentiles: Phoebe's name derives from the Greek god Apollo, Epaenetus and Andronicus are Greek names, while Junia is Roman. It does not take the personal names to tell us that the Roman church was mixed, but the names fit that perception.

Perhaps even more importantly, the names suggest that members were from various social classes. Some have names which are common slave names: Ampliatus, Urbanus, Philologus, Julia. Urbanus, Stachys, and Ampliatus are common slave names in the imperial household. It is possible that this is the Aurelius Ampliatus found in the tomb of Domitilla; if so, he was a highly esteemed person and it is possible that through him "the gospel first penetrated into the noble household to which Flavia Domitilla, the Emperor Domitian's niece and wife of Flavius Clemens, belonged."[5]

But not all were from the slave class. Paul sends greetings to "the household of Aristobulos." It is quite possible that this household included nobility—the grandson of Herod the Great named Aristobulos lived in Rome as a friend of Emperor Claudius. His household might well have included Jews who had become members of the new covenant community. Paul's compatriot Herodian might also have been of that household or have had some connection with the family of Herod. Some members might have been of the household of that Narcissus (16:11) who was a "notorious freedman of the Emperor Claudius, whose wealth was proverbial" and who was forced to commit suicide by Agrippina a year or two before Paul's writing.[6]

Paul makes no social or class distinctions among these various people. In the church there is, as he tells the Galatians, "neither Jew nor Greek, there is neither slave nor free, there is neither male nor female; for you are all one in Christ Jesus" (Gal. 3:28).

These greetings thus form an appropriate ending to a letter which has emphasized the lack of partiality which God has shown. That same impartiality is to be characteristic of the church as one body in Christ, the new covenant community. In it divisions are overcome, enmities healed through the reconciling act of God which makes all things new.

Those who create dissensions (16:17–20) are guilty not of minor disturbances. Rather they deny by their actions the central element of faith itself: the believing acceptance of the good news of one's inclusion in the one new covenant community. Faith stands in direct opposition to petty selfishness and to all attempts to assert one's own desires over the well-being of the covenant community. Through covenant living the community can know the peace of God which overcomes the satanic power of divisiveness.

Epilogue

The modern reader who knows the story of Paul's arrival in Jerusalem as told in the book of Acts inevitably reads this letter with a note of sadness. Paul's ministry was dominated by his conviction that he was a "[minister] of a new covenant" (2 Cor. 3:6). He believed that the time was fulfilled, that God's power was at work, that the renewal of humanity had begun, and that it would all come to completion with the full inclusion of Gentiles and Jews in one people of God, as Christ returns in glory. His impending trip to Jerusalem would be undertaken in that expectation.

Very little of what Paul hoped for came to pass historically. Not only did his final attempt in Jerusalem fail, but for the most part Jews opted against his covenant community. Following the tragic destruction of Jerusalem in 70 C.E., they solidified their Torah-religion in ways that would make Paul's inclusive covenant community impossible for them to realize. Jewish members of the new covenant community gradually died out, and the church became Gentilized and increasingly Hellenized, with little interest in healing the breach with Judaism. Increasingly the Gentile church looked upon Jews as the rejected people of God, as a synagogue of Satan, as murderers of Christ. The Jews who read Paul saw in him an apostate who rejected all they stood for, a hater of his own race. The Christians, as the Gentile church came to be known, read Paul in a similar fashion: they saw in him a rejection of Judaism and an excuse to hate and persecute Jews. Paul's perspective was no longer acceptable to either group.

Paul did not live to see the consummation of salvation at the return of Christ. History continued, and human alienation, self-seeking, and greed did not come to an end. The human race did not become a community; it remained "in Adam" more than "in Christ."

Must Paul, then, be classed with other visionaries who failed? Certainly, if success means that one's dreams of a new world come to direct fulfillment in history.

But Paul's vision stretches beyond human history. He has created a vision of human community which even in its elusiveness continues to draw us with power. It is my hope that this volume has helped make that vision more compellingly real for the reader, as the writing of it has made it more compellingly real for the author.

Notes

Chapter 1: Paul's Covenant Convictions

1. The lens metaphor is suggested by Max Delbrück's study of the evolution of human knowledge. Delbrück maintains that we see the world through multiple lenses, some physiological and some socially acquired. Knowledge involves recognizing those lenses, even taking them off so that we may perceive what is there apart from them; but we could never remove all the lenses through which we perceive things. Max Delbrück, *Mind From Matter? An Essay on Evolutionary Epistemology*, ed. by Gunther S. Stent, *et al.* (Palo Alto: Blackwell Scientific Publications, Inc., 1986), 118.

2. A.C. Purdy, "Paul the Apostle," *The Interpreter's Dictionary of the Bible,* volume K-Q, ed. by G.A. Buttrick *et al.* (New York: Abingdon Press, 1962), 684–85.

3. Paul refers to his experience of transformation in terms of encounter with or vision of Christ: 1 Corinthians 15:8: Christ "appeared to me"; Galatians 1:12: Paul's gospel "came through a revelation of Jesus Christ"; Galatians 1:16: God "revealed his son to me"; 1 Corinthians 9:1: "Have I not seen Jesus our Lord?" 2 Corinthians 4:6: God "has shone in our hearts to give the light of the knowledge of the glory of God in the face of Christ." He also refers to a transformation of his self without indicating the visionary aspects connected with it: Galatians 2:20: "I have been crucified with Christ"; Philippians 3:8: "I have suffered the loss of all things...in order that I may gain Christ." The Acts of the Apostles gives three separate narrative accounts of Paul's "Damascus Road" experience in 9:1–19; 22:3–16; 26:12–18; these accounts concentrate upon the external quality of the event and say little about Paul's subjective experience.

4. See W.D. Davies, *Paul and Rabbinic Judaism: Some Rabbinic Elements in Pauline Theology,* 4th edition (Philadelphia: Fortress Press, 1980), as an example of this approach.

5. H.J. Schoeps, *Paul: The Theology of the Apostle in the Light of Jewish Religious History,* trans. by Harold Knight (Philadelphia: The Westminster Press, 1961), 29, 35.

6. Martin Hengel, *The Atonement: The Origins of the Doctrine in the New Testament,* trans. by John Bowden (Philadelphia: Fortress Press, 1981).

7. For a discussion of various possibilities, see Karl P. Donfried, (ed.), *The Romans Debate* (Minneapolis: Augsburg Publishing House, 1977).

Chapter 2: Paul Introduces Himself and His Gospel

1. Cf. Jeremiah, who uses the corresponding Hebrew term to refer to the covenant community. The context in Jeremiah is similar to that in Romans 11:28. Jeremiah questions whether the "beloved" has any right in YHWH's house, "because they have broken my covenant which I made with their [ancestors] (Jeremiah 11:1–17). "Beloved" there is a reference to the covenant community.

2. Ernst Käsemann, *Commentary on Romans,* trans. and ed. by G.W. Bromiley (Grand Rapids: Wm. B. Eerdmans Publishing Co., 1980), 15, correctly says that "beloved" "can hardly be differentiated from" "called." He incorrectly says that the call has been transferred from "the Old Testament people of God to Christianity" (15–16). More accurately one would say that the notion of a people called to be dedicated to God now includes both Gentile and Jew.

3. Paul Minear, *The Obedience of Faith: The Purposes of Paul in the Epistle to the Romans,* (London: SCM Press, Ltd., 1971), 7, 41ff explains the absence of *ekklesia* on the basis that as long as the church was feuding and lacked genuine community, Paul could not call it a church. That view is not plausible when one notices that Paul does use *ekklesia* to address the badly divided Corinthians. Robert Banks, *Paul's Idea of Community: The Early House Churches in Their Historical Setting* (Grand Rapids: B. Eerdmans Publishing Co., 1980), 40, aruges that the reason is that the term *ekklesia* applies only to the gathered church, and since there were several such gatherings in Rome, Paul could not have addressed them as "church." This view is not plausible when one notices that Paul addresses one letter to "the churches...in Galatia." He could have addressed the churches of Rome similarly. Käsemann, *Romans,* 15, thinks no explanation is available.

4. Banks, *Paul's Idea of Community,* 10–11. The following paragraphs are indebted to Banks' treatment of the search for community in the Roman world; 13–22.

5. Ibid, 33.

6. Banks' argument, *Paul's Idea of Community,* 36–37, that Paul does not think of the universal church ignores the dependency of

the concept upon the notions of the solidarity of Israel no matter where particular individuals or groups resided.

7. J. Christiaan Beker, *Paul the Apostle: The Triumph of God in Life and Thought* (Philadelphia: Fortress Press, 1980), 313.

8. Ernst Käsemann, *Essays on New Testament Themes,* trans. by W.J. Montague, "Studies in Biblical Theology" No. 41 (Napierville, Illinois: Alec R. Allenson, 1964), 63–65.

9. Ernst Käsemann, *New Testament Questions of Today,* trans. by W.J. Montague (Philadelphia: Fortress Press, 1969), 245–46.

10. The "overseers" (or "bishops") and "servants" (or "deacons") mentioned in Philippians 1:1 are not "ordained" ministers in the modern sense but members of the community to whom certain tasks within the community were entrusted.

11. John Gager and Lloyd Gaston maintain, wrongly, I think, that Paul was apostle *only* to Gentiles. See John G. Gager, *The Origins of Anti-Semitism: Attitudes toward Judaism in Pagan and Christian Antiquity* (New York: Oxford University Press, 1983) and Lloyd Gaston, "Abraham and the Righteousness of God," *Horizons in Biblical Theology,* volume 2, 1980, 39–68; also Gaston's article, "Paul and the Torah" in Alan Davies (ed.), *Antisemitism and the Foundations of Christianity* (New York: Paulist Press, 1979).

12. One can plausibly argue, of course, that the Jewish expectation that the Messiah would rule the whole world from Mt. Zion has been taken up by Paul as a basis for his assertion of the universal sovereignty of Jesus Christ (see Rom. 15: 9–12, for example).

13. The translation of this word is disputed. The options usually argued for are either "designated" or "appointed." "Designated" frequently is understood as pointing out a preceding fact: "shown to be the son of God he always was." "Appointed" would suggest that Jesus "became" Son of God only at the resurrection, a view generally held to be inconsistent with the christological orthodoxy defined later by church councils. A strong case is made by Leslie C. Allen for the translation "decreed" ("The Old Testament Background of [PRO-]'ORIZEIN in the New Testament" *New Testament Studies,* volume 17, 1970–71, 104–108). Allen argues that Psalm 2:7 is the origin of this expression: Through the resurrection Jesus has been decreed to be Son of God. As Psalm 2 has its setting in the enthronement ceremony, at which the prince actually becomes king and as such is acclaimed God's Son: "Today I have begotten you," similarly Jesus was enthroned at the resurrection and proclaimed God's Son. Allen's interpretation, like that of "appointed," is "adoptionistic" by later christological standards.

14. Regardless of what Paul thought, this formula almost certainly originated in a context in which adoptionistic rather than metaphysical modes of thought prevailed.

15. F. Blass and A. Debrunner, *A Greek Grammar of the New Testament and Other Early Christian Literature,* trans by Robert W. Funk (Chicago: The University of Chicago Press, 1961), 174–75.

16. Hans Dieter Betz, *Galatians: A Commentary on Paul's Letter to the Churches in Galatia* (Philadelphia: Fortress Press, 1979), 207, thinks Paul is quoting a formula here, especially since "born of woman" receives no application at all.

17. See Reginald H. Fuller, *Foundations of New Testament Christology* (New York, Charles Scribner's Sons, 1965), 203 ff.

18. Betz, *Galatians,* 206, note 47, asserts that 1 Corinthians 8:6, 2 Corinthians 8:9, Romans 8:3, and Philippians 2:6–11 demonstrate that "Paul does have a pre-existence Christology."

19. If Paul wrote Colossians, it would be an exception.

20. *Pistis* can be either "faith" or "faithfulness"; my translation elects the latter, since that was the meaning of the word in the text Paul quotes from Habakkuk and by which he meant "God's faithfulness." "To" faith is *eis,* which can indicate direction or purpose; the translation above elects the latter. Thus, righteousness is revealed through God's acting faithfully to his promises in order to bring about the human response of faith.

Chapter 3: Gentile and Jew: Alike in Covenant Breaking

1. Ernst Käsemann, *Commentary on Romans,* trans. and ed. by G.W. Bromiley (Grand Rapids: Wm. B. Eerdmans Publishing Co., 1980), 34.

2. Robin Scroggs maintains that two sermons may be found in Romans, one comprising chapters 1–4, 9–11 and a second comprising 5–8. "Paul as Rhetorician: Two Homilies in Romans 1–11," *Jews, Greeks and Christians: Religious Cultures in Late Antiquity: Essays in Honor of William David Davies,* ed. by Robert Hamerton-Kelly and Robin Scroggs (Leiden: E.J. Brill, 1976), 271–298.

3. W.D. Davies, *Paul and Rabbinic Judaism: Some Rabbinic Elements in Pauline Theology,* Fourth Edition (Philadelphia: Fortress Press, 1980), 63–64.

4. Isaiah 3:1–4. For notions of eschatological salvation of the "peoples" see Isaiah 2:2–4; Micah 4:1–3; Isaiah 25:6–8; 51:4; Jeremiah 16: 19–21. Georg Bertram, *"ethnos," Theological Dictionary of the New Testament,* vol II, edited by Gerhard Kittel (Grand Rapids: Wm. B. Eerdmans Publishing Co., 1964), 368.

5. A similar description of the nation of Israel is given in II Kings 17:14–17 as a justification for God's putting Israel out of sight (cf. "God gave them up," Rom. 1:24, 26, 28).

6. Even if Käsemann, *Romans,* 54, is correct that 2:1 is an interpolation, the same point is made in 2:3.

7. Some interpreters think Paul unfairly attributes such boasting to the Jews of his day. E.P. Sanders, *Paul, the Law and the Jews* (Philadelphia: Fortress Press, 1983), 32–33, thinks Paul accused the Jews of boasting of privilege or status as opposed to Gentiles but not of boasting in their meritorious achievement. Similarly Gaston, Gager, Räisänen think Paul did not accuse the Jews of self-deification (it would have been an unfair accusation) but only of pride in relation to Gentiles.

8. It is true that Hosea attributes this lack of knowledge to the failure of the priests, but that is only a rhetorical way of saying that even the priests are guilty, or that they are especially guilty; Hosea does not, any more than any other prophet, excuse the people when he blames their leaders.

9. Paul thus shares the Hellenistic Jewish perspective reflected in Wisdom of Solomon 14:27: "For the worship of idols...is the beginning and cause and end of every evil"; the author thus concludes a listing of the results of the error of knowledge of God as that error is manifested in strife, adultery, sexual perversity, etc.

10. Compare Paul's list with that given in Wisdom of Solomon 14:24–26: "They no longer keep either their lives or their marriages pure, but they treacherously kill one another, or grieve one another by adultery, and all is a raging riot of blood and murder, theft and deceit, corruption, faithlessness, tumult, perjury, confusion over what is good, forgetfulness of favors, pollution of souls, sex perversion, disorder in marriage, adultery and debauchery."

11. Käsemann, *Romans,* 50.

12. C.K. Barrett, *A Commentary on the Epistle to the Romans* (New York: Harper and Brothers, 1957), 40, says the list has parallels in Hellenistic-Jewish or Hellenistic lists. Käsemann, *Romans,* 49–50, demonstrates the difficulty of solving the problem of the origin of such lists, which he says were not unusual in popular philosophy.

13. Käsemann, *Romans,* 50.

14. Käsemann, *Romans,* 63, discusses the possibility that Paul's statement might be related to the Greek notion of "unwritten Law." Markus Barth, "Speaking of Sin: Some Interpretative Notes on Romans 1.18—3.20," *Scottish Journal of Theology,* vol. 8, 292, thinks the Gentiles in question here are Gentile children of the new covenant; for that view there are no strong arguments. The passage surely applies to non-believing Jews.

15. C.H. Dodd, *The Epistle of Paul to the Romans, The Moffatt New Testament Commentary* (London: Hodder and Staughton, 1932), 19, 30.

Chapter 4: One New Covenant for Gentile and Jew

1. In quoting the Greek version of Genesis 15:6, Paul used a word (*elogisthe*) which refers to commercial dealings, with the meaning of "charging up a debt" or "evaluating"; in earlier, classical literature, it meant "logically deliberating" or "considering" as a result of logical reasoning. In both cases, it has to do with analyzing facts and coming to an evaluation based on them. H.W. Heidland, *"logizomai," Theological Dictionary of the New Testament,* vol. IV, ed. by Gerhard Kittel (Grand Rapids: Wm. B. Eerdmans Publishing Co., 1967), 284.

2. C.K. Barrett, *A Commentary on the Epistle to the Romans* (New York: Harper and Brothers, 1957), 89.

3. Robert A. Spivey and D. Moody Smith, *Anatomy of the New Testament,* 3rd edition (New York: Macmillan Publishing Co., Inc., 1982), 372.

4. Ernst Käsemann, *Commentary on Romans,* trans. and ed. by G.W. Bromiley (Grand Rapids: Wm. B. Eerdmans Publishing Co., 1980), 96, who argues that *dikaioo* is "incontestably forensic," and that Dodd's and others' attempts to maintain that the legal term is inadequate for expressing that relation are based on "discredited liberalism."

5. Hermann Ridderbos, *Paul: An Outline of His Theology,* trans. by John Richard de Witt (Grand Rapids: Wm. B. Eerdmans Publishing Co., 1975), 260 and n. 13.

6. E.R. Achtemeier, "Righteousness in the OT," *The Interpreter's Dictionary of the Bible,* R-Z, ed. by George A. Buttrick (New York: Abingdon Press, 1962), 81.

7. Walter Bauer, *A Greek-English Lexicon of the New Testament and Other Early Christian Literature,* trans. by William F. Arndt and F. Wilbur Gingrich (Chicago: University of Chicago Press, 1979), 899.

8. Hans Dieter Betz, *Galatians: A Commentary on Paul's Letter to the Churches in Galatia* (Philadelphia: Fortress Press, 1979), 262, argues that Galatians 5:5 demonstrates the eschatological nature of justification. Paul speaks of "the hope of righteousness" (*dikaiosynē*). However, one should note that this passage is addressed to those who wish (future) justification on the basis of Torah. In other words, they wish to improve on their faith-relationship to God by adding to it the performance of the requirements of the Torah: to them Paul says "through the Spirit, by faith, we wait for (*apekdechometa*—an eschatological term, 'wait eagerly,' 'reach for') the hope of righteousness." In other words, he maintains that future righteousness is based on the same thing as present righteousness— grace through faith—and that nothing more needs to be added. This

unusual expression of "hope of righteousness" should not therefore be taken as normative.

9. Käsemann, *Romans,* 102; Nils A. Dahl, *Studies In Paul* (Minneapolis: Augsburg Publishing House, 1977), 10.

10. Krister Stendahl, *Paul Among Jews and Gentiles* (Philadelphia: Fortress Press, 1976), 26.

11. Ibid, 29, 26.

12. Betz, *Galatians,* 255.

13. Ibid, 42; see 2 Maccabees 7:32, 37; 4 Maccabees 6:27–29; 17:21–22; see also Isaiah 52:13—53:12. See also the sacrifice of Isaac.

14. Bauer, *Lexicon,* 776.

15. Romans 8:21, Barrett's translation in *Romans,* 166.

16. Ibid, 148ff.

17. Even though Ephesians was probably not written by Paul, its author correctly perceived one of Paul's major concerns: that in Christ the "dividing wall of hostility" between Jew and Gentile should be removed.

18. Such terms may derive from apocalyptic theology, in which this world (or this age) is believed to be under the power of forces alien to God and hostile to his covenant people. The origin of apocalyptic thought is much controverted, but almost certainly one ingredient in its complex origins was a frustration over the course of historical, political events. That frustration causes apocalyptic thought to appear very apolitical at times, but that appearance might be deceptive: far from being disinterested in political affairs, the apocalyptist might be desperately longing for a new political day; in some cases, might even be preparing for it not only spiritually but also militarily. That political frustration is not directly reflected in Paul's writings, as it is in the Qumran scrolls.

19. J. Christiaan Beker, *Paul's Apocalyptic Gospel: The Coming Triumph of God* (Philadelphia: Fortress Press, 1982), 40.

20. Many translators (including those of the RSV) read "the wrath of God," although "of God" is not found in the Greek text, to indicate (correctly) that Paul is thinking of God's judgment at the end-time.

21. Heinrich Schlier, *"eleutheros," Theological Dictionary of the New Testament,* Volume II, ed. by Gerhard Kittel (Grand Rapids: Wm. B. Eerdmans Publishing Co., 1964), 493.

22. Ch. Duquoc, "Liberation and Salvation in Jesus Christ," *Liberation Theology and the Message of Salvation,* ed. by Rene Metz and Jean Schlick, translated by David G. Gelzer (Pittsburgh: The Pickwick Press, 1978), 52, argues that... "it is precisely the anti-messianism of Jesus which defines the political meaning of his struggle." Jesus' rejection of messianism was a political act, not a non-political one. See also Jose Severino Croatto, *Exodus: A*

Hermeneutic of Freedom, trans. by Salvator Attanasio (Maryknoll: Orbis Books, 1981), 62.

23. For an account of Jewish and Gentile strife, see Bo Reicke, *The New Testament Era,* trans. by David E. Green (Philadelphia: Fortress Press, 1968), and John G. Gager, *The Origins of Anti-Semitism: Attitudes toward Judaism in Pagan and Christian Antiquity* (New York: Oxford University Press, 1983).

24. The translation "put forward" is uncertain. In all other uses by Paul, the Greek word means "to plan," "to intend," "to purpose." Many scholars, perhaps most, think the context here argues for the meaning "publicly display," or "offer" (as a sacrifice). In either case, Christ's death is seen as a sacrifice which deals with sins. My translation suggests that God offers Christ as the sufficient means of dealing with sin. This interpretation is supported by Romans 8:32: "God did not spare his son, but gave him up for us all." This language reflects Genesis 22, where Abraham did not "spare" Isaac (vs. 16), but offered him as a sacrifice. Paul might have had that instance in mind as a model, and thus have thought of God's offering Christ as a sacrifice. In Galatians 2:20, Christ offers himself (as a sacrifice). Cf. Jewish lore about Isaac's willingness to be sacrificed. Alternately one could understand "put forward" as "appoint" or "plan"; in this case, just as God had established the sacrifices of the Torah as the means of atonement, so also God established Christ; but just as God did not personally offer the sacrifices, so God does not personally sacrifice Christ.

25. See also 10:21, where "cup" precedes "table."

26. The two elements are symbolically the same in the longer text of Luke, as "given for you" indicates (Luke 22:17–20); the longer text of 1 Corinthians 11:24, "broken," also makes the identification.

27. For the twin notions of purification and consecration, see Leon Morris, *The Apostolic Preaching of the Cross* (Grand Rapids: Wm. B. Eerdmans Publishing Co., 1956), 71; see also Edward Gordon Selwyn, *The First Epistle of Peter* (London: Macmillan and Co., 1955), 120–121.

28. Hans Conzelmann, *A Commentary on the First Epistle to the Corinthians,* trans. by James W. Leitch, ed. by George W. MacRae (Philadelphia: Fortress Press, 1975), 172.

29. William F. Orr and James Arthur Walther, *1 Corinthians* (Garden City: Doubleday and Co., Inc., 1976), 269.

30. In 2 Corinthians 7:1 Paul admonishes the readers to "let us cleanse (*katharisomen*) ourselves of every defilement of flesh and spirit," i.e., inwardly and outwardly. Here he is using cultic language, and here and in the following verse he uses Hebraic conceptions of holiness as a way of reminding the Corinthians that the whole of life is to be lived in holiness to God. Being "mismated with unbe-

lievers" (6:14) is thus not an acceptable mode of life to express one's belonging to Christ. In Romans 14:2 Paul discounts the ritual rules of cleanliness: "Everything is pure (*kathara*)." He goes on to emphasize concern for others rather than such rules. In 2 Corinthians 11:2 Paul says he presented the Corinthians to Christ as a pure (*hagnen*) bride; *hagnos* is a cultic term, "originally an attribute of divinity and everything belonging to it." (Bauer, *Lexicon*, 11). Paul seems to think of *hagnos* as innocence as the following verse shows, and probably thinks of the innocence of the new-found faith or the innocence of the newly baptized, or both. In 2 Corinthians 6:6 Paul has acted in *hagnotete*, probably understood as in 2 Corinthians 11:2, "in innocence," without guile. In 1 Corinthians 6:11 the language of purity is associated with baptism and contrasts the appropriately purified state of believer with the prior state of unbeliever.

31. See E. P. Sanders, *Paul and Palestinian Judaism: A Comparison of Patterns of Religion* (Philadelphia: Fortress Press, 1977), 500–501, for other explanations of Paul's lack of use of forgiveness. Sanders' own position is that Paul prefers "lordship" to "forgiveness," since sin is an enslaving power more than a transgressive act.

32. Paul may have sacrificial ideas in mind when he reminds the Corinthians that "God made him who knew no sin to be sin for us" (2 Cor. 5:21, my translation). Many translate "to be sin" in sacrificial terms, "to be a sin-offering." W. G. Kümmel sees sacrificial imagery in Romans 6:10, which he translates, "He died for sin" (cf. RSV: "He died to sin"). W. G. Kümmel, *The Theology of the New Testament,* trans. by John E. Steely (Nashville: Abingdon Press, 1973), 192.

33. See the treatment of propitiation in Morris, *Apostolic Preaching of the Cross,* chapters 4 and 5.

34. Ibid.

35. Harald Riesenfeld, *"huper," Theological Dictionary of the New Testament,* VIII, trans. and ed. By G. W. Bromiley (Grand Rapids: Wm. B. Eerdmans Publishing Company, 1972), 512.

36. In light of the fact that the most substitutionary language comes later—e.g., in Hebrews, the Pastorals—it seems more likely that Paul's language should not be pressed unnaturally to derive that point from it.

37. Orr, *1 Corinthians,* 184.

38. Conzelmann, *1 Corinthians,* 99, n. 54, suggests that the early Christians celebrated their own version of Passover.

39. One might note that in presenting Christ's death as a sacrifice, nothing is said about the historical *human* agents of that death; except in 1 Thessalonians 2:15 Paul does not blame the Jews for the death of Jesus; he rather concentrates on the theological cause,

i.e., God's will, which is not related to the historical cause as such.

40. Though Paul uses two different expressions here, "on the ground of faith" and "through faith," they are different only for rhetorical reasons, not to present a difference between Jew and Gentile; the latter would be contrary to the whole force of his argument.

41. Beker, *Paul the Apostle*, 95.

42. Note the reverse of Paul's order, suggesting that the covenant was given in response to Abraham's keeping the Torah.

43. Note that the promise comes as a consequence of Abraham's faithfulness.

44. Betz, *Galatians*, 139.

45. MeKilta Beshallah 3; quoted by Sanders, *Paul and Palestinian Judaism*, 91.

46. Ibid.

47. Mek. Pisha 16; quoted by Sanders, *Paul and Palestinian Judaism*, 90.

48. In Galatians 4 he does mention Isaac, but goes on to interpret Isaac allegorically as representing those presently children through faith, in contrast to those who are children of slavery, born of the one from Mt. Sinai (Gal. 4:21–28). In Romans 9:6–9 he uses Isaac again to symbolize those who are children of promise (i.e., by God's action) in contrast to children by flesh (i.e., by human action alone). In all the preceding instances, Paul's treatment of Isaac is symbolic and represents Paul's movement away from the ethnic and nationalistic understanding which could be given to that promise.

Chapter 5: The New Covenant as Grace and Peace for All

1. Ralph P. Martin, *Reconciliation: A Study of Paul's Theology* (Atlanta: John Knox Press, 1980), makes reconciliation the theme by which to organize Paul's theology. That approach correctly suggests a great deal of terminological overlap in Paul's writings. Some regard "justification by faith" as Paul's most distinctive contribution; see John H. Reumann, *Righteousness in the New Testament: Justification in the Lutheran-Catholic Dialogue* (Philadelphia: Fortress Press; New York: Paulist Press, 1982) who finds antecedents of Paul's use of justification in earlier New Testament writings.

2. Or, if one still regards justification in forensic terms, it is a metaphor from the law courts, which proclaims that those deserving the sentence of condemnation and death are graciously and mercifully acquitted and released from guilt to live as God's people.

3. Karl Barth, *Christ and Adam: Man and Humanity in Romans 5*, trans. by T. A. Smail (New York: Harper and Brothers Publishers, 1957) 29, 30.

4. Jouette Bassler, *Divine Impartiality: Paul and a Theological Axiom*, ed. by William Baird, "Dissertation Series" (Chico, CA: Scholars

Press, 1982), 160.

5. J. Christiaan Beker, *Paul the Apostle: The Triumph of God in Life and Thought* (Philadelphia: Fortress Press, 1980), 86–87.

6. Ibid, 83,85.

7. Ibid, 87.

8. "Christian" might well have been applied to the Jesus sect during Paul's time, even though the earliest documentation probably comes from some decades after Paul (Acts, 1 Peter, correspondence between Pliny and Trajan). The term was probably derogatory at first; when Christians accepted it as a self-designation is uncertain. See E. J. Bickermann, "The Name of Christians," *Harvard Theological Review*, vol. 42, 1949, 108–124; Harold B. Mattingly, "The Origin of the Name *Christiani*," *Journal of Theological Studies,* New Series, Vol. 9, 1958, 26–37.

9. There are alternate ways of understanding the parenthesis: (1) It could begin with verse 13; that reading would include within the main sentence the explanation of how death spread to all ("because all sinned"), an explanation that probably shows Paul's engaging in a Jewish theological debate about individual responsibility for sin. (2) The parenthesis could end with verse 16; verse 17 and 18 are really parallel, and either could be taken as the return to the main point. My choice rejects (1) because it seems that Paul's real interest here is not in giving an explanation for universal sinfulness, but in affirming its reversal. I reject (2) because verse 18 begins with a phrase equivalent to the beginning of verse 12 ("therefore"). True, the Greek expressions are different (*dia touto* in vs. 12, *ara oun* in vs. 18), but they can have the same meaning either as transition particles or as expressing the consequence of something (one could argue for either of these meanings here). *Ara oun* further can indicate a return to the main theme after parenthetical remarks, strongly suggesting that verse 17 is part of the parenthesis.

10. Robin Scroggs, *The Last Adam, A Study in Pauline Anthropology* (Philadelphia: Fortress Press, 1966), 32.

11. Although most interpreters understand Christ to be the one to come whose type Adam was, the context seems to me to argue for Moses. Christ fills the role in that he is a universal figure; Moses fills it in that, like Adam, he symbolizes a relation to God fulfilled through obedience to commandments. The antithesis Paul posits between Adam and Christ in the rest of this chapter is not dependent on this point.

12. Scroggs, *Last Adam*, 98.

13. Quoted by W. D. Davies, *Paul and Rabbinic Judaism* (Philadelphia: Fortress Press, 1980), 32–33.

14. Ibid.
15. D.E.H. Whiteley, *The Theology of St. Paul* (Philadelphia: Fortress Press, 1966), 15.
16. That fact is admitted by many who want to maintain Augustine's anthropology: e.g., F.F. Bruce says "'in whom'...may be a mistranslation...[but] it is a true interpretation" (*The Epistle of Paul to the Romans: An Introduction and Commentary* (Grand Rapids: Wm. B. Eerdmans Publishing Co., 1963), 130.
17. Scroggs, *Last Adam*, 78, cites Oepke in TWNT III, 48. See also Rudolf Bultmann. "Adam and Christ According to Romans 5," *Current Issues in New Testament Interpretation: Essays in Honor of Otto Piper*, ed. by Wm. Klassen and Graydon F. Snyder (New York: Harper and Brothers, 1962), 151.
18. Ernst Käsemann, *Commentary on Romans,* trans. by G. W. Bromiley (Grand Rapids: Wm. B. Eerdmans Publishing Co., 1980), 149.
19. Ibid.
20. Scroggs, *Last Adam,* 36.
21. It is not likely that the Rabbis thought of Torah as restoring what had been lost by Adam, except in the general sense of offering a corrective; most rabbis thought of Israel also as sinning in this world, and thus the Torah is significant more in preparing Israel for the world to come than in undoing Adam's fall in the here and now. See Scroggs, *Last Adam,* 53.

Chapter 6: Answers to Opponents' Objections

1. Jouette Bassler, *Divine Impartiality: Paul and a Theological Axiom,* 160.
2. Paul's most emphatic denial. Literally, "let it not be (so)." RSV translates, nonliterally and tamely, "By no means"; the expletive chosen above, while certainly not literal, carries the force intended.
3. David M. Stanley, *Christ's Resurrection in Pauline Soteriology,* "Analecta Biblica," Volume 13 (Romae; E Pontifico Instituto Biblico, 1961), 189, believes 7:7–24 "must be considered a digression."
4. Paul does not explicitly distinguish between what we might call ethical and ritual commands, though he seems to make some such distinction at the level of practice. At any rate, the "moral" commandments are upheld in his ethical teaching, though he scarcely could have followed the ceremonial and dietary rules when among the Gentiles. See Heikki Räisänen, *Paul and the Law* (Tübigen: J.C.B. Mohr, 1983) and E.P. Sanders, *Paul, the Law, and the Jews* (Philadelphia: Fortress Press, 1983).
5. Jesus himself might have practiced baptism after he was baptized by John the Baptizer, though there is no clear evidence that he did. See John 3:22; 4:1–2.
6. "With thee I am well pleased" echoes Isaiah 42:1, "my chosen in

whom my soul delights." Jesus' baptism, then, designates him as the Servant whose suffering is redemptive.

7. Acts 19:1–8 portrays Paul as connecting belief, baptism, and Spirit, but no mention is made of Jesus' death. Some think Romans 8:15 reflects the idea of receiving the Spirit at baptism; if so, the lack of explicit mention even more strongly supports the idea that Paul is playing down the ecstatic element in baptism. See D.E.H. Whiteley, *The Theology of St. Paul* (Philadelphia: Fortress Press, 1966), 169. In 1 Corinthians 12:13 he does associate Spirit with baptism in a passage in which he seeks to move the Corinthians away from emphasis upon charismatic gifts. "For by (*en*) one Spirit all of us were baptized into one body, whether Jews or Greeks, whether slave or free, and all were made to drink of one Spirit." Baptism, Spirit, and incorporation into the body of Christ (1 Cor. 12:27) are tied together as a way of reminding the Corinthians that the first gift of the Spirit was *unity* and *incorporation,* not ecstatic experience. Whatever validity charismatic experience might have had (and Paul does not deny that it can be useful to individual faith), it is subordinated to unity in the one body. Galatians 3:2 could suggest that the Spirit is not directly linked to baptism, but may precede it. Cf. the story in Acts 10:1—11:18: Baptism could not be denied those who had received the Spirit in conjunction with a believing reception of the preached word.

8. This is a disputed interpretation. Some interpreters think Paul's addressees in 1 Corinthians 15 are those who *deny* the resurrection altogether in favor of a spiritual existence in this life and of spiritual immortality in the life to come. In either case, they believed that they had already moved spiritually beyond ordinary people. The interpretation adopted here suggests that they used the symbol of (spiritual) resurrection which they believed put them beyond ordinary ethical and mortal concerns.

9. Walter Bauer, *A Greek-English Lexicon of the New Testament,* trans. by Wm. F. Arndt and F. Wilbur Gingrich (Chicago: University of Chicago Press, 1979), 633.

10. Ernst Käsemann, *Commentary on Romans,* 172. The usual break according to this scheme is chapters 1—4 (justification), 5—8 (sanctification), with the rest of the letter being a sort of unimportant appendix.

11. Whiteley, *The Theology of St. Paul,* 178. See Romans 10:5–13, where Paul speaks of hearing, believing, and confessing as the process by which salvation comes. However, it is likely that Romans 10:9 contains a typical baptismal confession, so that confession is closely tied to baptism. As a formal act confession may thus occur at baptism, but as a personal decision, it is prior to it. The question as to whether baptism of infants is permissible in this

understanding of baptism is one on which Paul gives little direct help. One can make a case on other grounds for the appropriateness of a ceremony which symbolizes the biblical notion of the solidarity of the family within the covenant community: baptism may be an acceptable act to symbolize that inclusion. Any notion that such an act for infants or adults is sufficent for wholeness of relationship, regardless of faith, would go counter to the basic thrust of Paul's theology. Apart from faith there is no wholeness of human existence in relation to God or others.

12. Ibid., 45: "...many of St. Paul's fundamental doctrines can be properly understood only if we realize that he took for granted the presupposition of human solidarity." A frequently cited example of such solidarity is that of Achan, whose whole family was punished because they were deemed to be guilty along with him for his sin, even though he alone committed the act (see Josh. 7:1ff). Many regard this primitive notion of solidarity as persisting throughout Israel's history; even the growth of individual freedom and responsibility did not obliterate a strong current of corporate identity and life.

13. L. Cerfaux, *The Church in the Theology of St. Paul*, trans. by Geoffrey Webb and Adrian Walker (New York: Herder and Herder, 1959), 213. *Kata Christon* is found in Romans 15:5, applying to behavior in accord with one who belongs to Christ; cf. Colossians 2:8, where the term applies more to having an outlook which accords with Christ instead of with human philosophy.

14. C.K. Barrett, *A Commentary on the Epistle of Paul to the Romans* (New York: Harper and Brothers, 1957), 130.

15. Günther Bornkamm, *Early Christian Experience*, trans. by P.L. Hammer (New York: Harper and Row, 1969), 80.

16. Ibid, 82, Bornkamm calls this imperative a "summoning comfort and comforting summons."

17. The *paidagogos* was not the teacher but the attendant, usually a slave who led the son to the teacher for instruction. When the young man came of age, the role of the *paidagogos* ended. The application to the Torah suggests that it is inferior and temporary, though important. Bauer, *Lexicon*, 603.

18. E.P. Sanders, *Paul, the Law, and the Jews* (Philadelphia: Fortress Press, 1983), 76, says Paul "recoiled" at his own negative words about the Torah; Romans 7 is an attempt to restate the problem, blaming sin rather than Torah.

19. Käsemann, *Romans*, 194.

20. Räisänen, *Paul and the Law*, 245, confidently asserts, "Paul did *not* derive his theology of the law from the promise of the new covenant in Jeremiah 31." While it is true Paul does not quote Jeremiah in support of his view, there are many resemblances

between Paul's thought and Jeremiah's. U. Wilckens, "Statements on the Development of Paul's View of the Law," *Paul and Paulinism: Essays in Honour of C.K. Barrett,* ed. by M.D. Hooker and S.G. Wilson (London: SPCK, 1982), 20, believes Paul did make use of Jeremiah 31:31.

21. John Calvin, *Commentaries on the Epistle of Paul the Apostle to the Romans,* trans. and ed. by John Owen (Grand Rapids: Wm. B. Eerdmans Publishing Co., 1948), 388–91.

22. Whether the "coming one" refers to Moses, as taken here, is not decisive in this interpretation. Even if the coming one refers to Christ (as most interpreters think), the situation between Moses and Adam is analogous.

23. Note the lack of commandment in Paul's ethics. However, the ethical commandments are very much in the background of Paul's thinking about what constitutes the will of God. The summary of the Torah in one commandment (Rom. 13:8–10) is not an exception to Paul's general disinclination to offer commandments. Rather, it shows that Paul does take the commandments seriously as expressing God's will; it is not presented as a command brought by Christ.

24. Bornkamm, *Early Christian Experience,* 93.

25. Ibid.

26. Krister Stendahl, *Paul Among Jews and Gentiles* (Philadelphia: Fortress Press, 1976), 78–96. Most interpreters regard W.G. Kümmel, *Man in the New Testament,* translated by John J. Vincent (Philadelphia: Westminster Press, 1963), to have decisively demonstrated that Paul does not refer to his own personal experience; the "I" refers to the person under the Torah, not as that person experiences it, but as perceived by one who has been freed from it. J.D.G. Dunn has made a vigorous argument for a Christian autobiographical interpretation in "Rom. 7:14–25 in the Theology of Paul," *Theologische Zeitschrift,* Vol. 31, 1975, 257–273. Although one can affirm almost everything Dunn says about Paul's concept of the life of faith (as being torn by frustration, incompleteness, and imperfection), one still may be unconvinced that that is Paul's reference in 7:14–25.

Chapter 7: New Covenant, New Life, and the Spirit

1. The same meaning is found in 2 Corinthians 7:13: Titus' spirit "has been set at rest" by the Corinthians; cf. Romans 1:9, "serving God with my spirit," and 1 Corinthians 14:15, "pray with the spirit."

2. C.K. Barrett, *A Commentary on the Epistle to the Romans* (New York: Harper and Brothers, 1957), 157. The term translated "the Torah's requirement of righteousness" gives interpreters difficulty.

Paul probably intends one to understand the right relationship and the right conduct flowing from it.

3. Rudolf Bultmann, *Theology of the New Testament,* vol. 1, trans. by Kendrick Grobel (New York: Charles Scribner's Sons, 1951), 209.

4. See G.R. Driver, *The Judean Scrolls: the Problem and a Solution* (Oxford: Basil Blackwell, 1965, 535–36.

5. Some manuscripts have Paul shift first to the second person singular in 8:2: "...has set you free...", but whether the reading "me" or "you" is correct in 8:2, the shift is not complete until verse 4: "the righteousness which the Torah requires might be completed in us who live...according to the Spirit."

6. Knowledge of sin and its consequences is implied in Romans 1:32 and 7:7–24 as well as in 8:19–22.

7. Quoted by Ernst Käsemann, *Commentary on Romans,* trans. and ed. by G.W. Bromiley (Grand Rapids: Wm.B. Eerdmans Publishing Co., 1980), 233.

8. Translation by F.I. Anderson in James H. Charlesworth (ed.), *The Old Testament Pseudepigrapha,* Volume I: *Apocalyptic Literature and Testaments* (Garden City: Doubleday and Company, Inc., 1983), 34, 37.

9. Käsemann, *Romans,* 235.

10. G.W.H. Lampe, "The New Testament doctrine of *Ktisis,*" *Scottish Journal of Theology,* volume 17, 1964, 457.

11. Barrett, *Romans, 171.*

Chapter 8: The New Covenant Does Not Nullify the Old

1. Johannes Munck, *Christ and Israel: In Interpretation of Romans 9—11,* trans. by Ingeborg Nixon (Philadelphia; Fortress Press, 1967); *Paul and the Salvation of Mankind* (Richmond: John Knox Press, 1959).

2. Krister Stendahl expresses his indebtedness to Munck in the preface to his collection of articles, *Paul Among Jews and Gentiles* (Philadelphia: Fortress Press, 1976), vi, even though he has since adopted a "different model" from Munck's. He believes that chapters 9—11 constitute the "climax" of Romans (4, 85), and that chapters 1—8 are a "preface" (29).

3. Ernst Käsemann, *Commentary on Romans,* trans. and ed. by G.W. Bromiley (Grand Rapids: Wm.B. Eerdmans Publishing Co., 1980), 253.

4. It is instructive also to notice what Paul does *not* list among the privileges of Israel: the gift of land. See W.D. Davies, *The Gospel and the Land* (Berkeley: University of California Press, 1974), 167. Land could be included among the promises, but still one must ask why it is not explicit, when adoption is. The answer is that in universalizing the covenant, Paul separates it from the

nationalism which land most strongly suggests.

5. Isaiah 40:13, Job 15:8; Jeremiah 23:18; 1 Kings 2:16.

6. Marcus Aurelius, *To Himself,* iv. 23: "From thee are all things, in thee are all things, unto thee are all things." Quoted by C.K. Barrett, *A Commentary on the Epistle to the Romans* (New York: Harper and Brothers, 1957), 229, n. 2, who prefers to think of Paul's statement as being parallel to but not dependent upon Stoic thought; the ideas in the quotation "are axioms of biblical theology." Cf. Käsemann, *Romans,* 318–319.

7. Käsemann, *Romans,* 320. Contra Peter Richardson (*Israel in the Apostolic Church,* "Society for New Testament Studies Monograph Series," Matthew Black, (ed.) [Cambridge: At the University Press, 1969], 126–27), who thinks Paul ends in uncertainty after this "trial run" at a solution to the problem of Israel.

8. Cf. Psalms of Solomon 9:18: "Thou madest a covenant with our fathers concerning us; and we hope in thee" (Charles' translation). Cf. also Assumption of Moses 4:3–6: "God will remember them on account of the covenant which he made with their fathers…" (R.H. Charles, *The Apocrypha and Pseudepigrapha of the Old Testament* [Oxford: Clarenden Press, 1913], vol. II, 417).

9. Cf. Galatians 3:22: "But Scripture has shut up everything together under sin in order that by the faithfulness of Christ the promise may be given to all who have faith" (my translation). Richardson, *Israel,* 127, maintains that 11:28–32 is "very carefully structured" and that it "directs the reader away from election and retribution towards gospel and mercy."

10. *Israel,* 127.

11. *Westminster Confession of Faith,* III.3: "Some men and angels are predestinated to everlasting life, and others foreordained to everlasting death."

12. John G. Gager, *The Origins of Anti-Semitism: Attitudes toward Judaism in Pagan and Christian Antiquity* (New York: Oxford University Press, 1983), 250, interprets the stone of stumbling as the inclusion of the Gentiles, in keeping with the notion that Paul's emphasis is entirely upon that and not upon the belief in Jesus as the Christ. In my opinion this view does not stand up to close scrutiny, especially because in 1 Corinthians Paul speaks of the crucified messiah as the stumbling block. C.K. Barrett, "Romans 9:30—10:21: Fall and Responsibility of Israel," *Die Israelfrage nach Rom 9—11,* herausgegeben von Lorenzo De Lorenzi (Rom: Abteil von St. Paul vor den Mauern), 111, maintains that the meaning adopted above derives from 1 Peter; Barrett thinks that in the context the stone is more likely the Torah, which in its own way can cause Israel to stumble, depending on how it is received.

13. John Calvin, *Commentaries on the Epistle of the Apostle Paul to*

the Romans, trans. and ed. by John Owen (Grand Rapids: Wm. B. Eerdmans Publishing Co., 1959), 388.

14. Calvin, Romans, 389.

15. Käsemann, Romans, 285.

16. Richardson, Israel, 130, says Romans 10:12–13 contains two propositions which are basic for all Paul's work: "no distinction" and "all who call."

17. The following are among many recent works that challenge New Testament interpreters to examine long-held attitudes about Jews reflected in Christian scripture and interpretation; their provocative questions demand consideration in any responsible treatment of such a crucial passage as Romans 9—11: Rosemary Radford Ruether, Faith and Fratricide: The Theological Roots of Anti-Semitism (New York: Seabury Press, 1974); Gager, The Origins of Anti-Semitism; Alan Davies (ed.), AntiSemitism and the Foundations of Christianity (New York: Paulist Press, 1979); Markus Barth, "St. Paul—A Good Jew,"Horizons in Biblical Theology, volume 1, 1979, 7–45; Lloyd Gaston, "Abraham and the Righteousness of God," Horizons in Biblical Theology and "Paul and the Torah."

18. Quoted by Markus Barth, "St. Paul—A Good Jew," Horizons in Biblical Theology: An International Dialogue, Volume 1, 1979, 7.

19. Ibid, n. 2, 38.

20. E.P. Sanders, Paul, the Law and the Jews (Philadelphia: Fortress Press, 1983), 152.

21. Heikki Räisänen, Paul and the Law (Tübigen: J.C.B. Mohr, 1983), 231–232.

22. This quotation as well as suggestions for a responsible psychological approach to Paul's "conversion" may be found in Räisänen, 229–236.

23. Hans Dieter Betz, Galatians (Philadelphia: Fortress Press, 1979), 64, says Paul changed Jewish parties "from Pharisaism to Jewish Christianity." What Betz argues for is correct, but his use of "Christianity" is anachronistic and highly misleading, though he shares that fault with a broad range of interpreters. W.D. Davies, Paul and Rabbinic Judaism (Philadelphia: Fortress Press, 1980), 71, argues that Paul did not even change sects, but remained a Pharisee.

24. Sanders, Paul, the Law, 192.

25. Stendahl, Paul Among Jews and Gentiles, 26–27.

26. Sanders, Paul, the Law, 131, cites Philo, Migr. 92, Quest. ex. II.2 as evidence that some Jews believed that circumcision had been accomplished when ethical aspects of the Torah had been carried out. This idea is not found in the Rabbis, Sanders affirms, and is in Paul only in Romans 2. The notion is in some ways similar to Paul's statement that belief in Christ fulfills the Torah for Gentiles.

27. Ibid, 76.
28. Ibid, 75.
29. There is very little evidence that this view was held by Jews in Paul's day, though some interpreters think it was. See Davies, *Paul and Rabbinic Judaism,* 72, who says the new law in Rabbinic usage means "new not in the sense that it would be contrary to the Law of Moses but that it would explain it more fully." Davies admits the evidence is late.
30. 1 Corinthians 1:23; cf. "new wine in old wineskins," Mark 2:23. Paul also asserts that faith in the crucified messiah does not come easily for Gentiles, either; for them it is foolishness. Mark's statement suggests the incompatibility of the gospel and Judaism, whereas Paul suggests that faith in Jesus cannot come without wrenching adjustment to Judaism as it stood. Cf. his own being "crucified with Jesus."
31. Markus Barth, "St. Paul...," 13–14, maintains that to speak of temporary validity of the Torah is to relegate Israel to the position of fossil; repeal or abolition of the Torah could only mean to the Jew the "cutting of the vital nerve of Jewish people...." Sanders maintains that Paul had two criticisms of Judaism: lack of faith in Christ, lack of equality for Gentiles, and that "both strike at Judaism as such." On the other hand, the "finding that Paul criticized his kinsmen for zeal for good works is simply bewildering"; "...the supposed objection to Jewish self-righteousness is as absent from Paul's letters as self-righteousness is from Jewish literature" (*Paul, the Law,* 155–156).
32. Räisänen, *Paul and the Law,* 72, cites Josephus, *Antiquities* IV, 145–47.
33. J. Christiaan Beker believes that inclusion of Gentiles was a dividing line between Paul and other Jews, and that Romans is both an apology for Israel and a polemic against the Jewish doctrine of election. "For the Jew, God's faithfulness and election mean the segregation of the Jew from the Gentile, because the covenant, the Torah and circumcision constitute the essential privileges of Israel." Integration of Jew and Gentile would contradict "covenantal nomism" (*Paul the Apostle: A Triumph of God in Life and Thought* (Philadelphia, Fortress Press, 1980) 87.
34. Sanders makes a useful distinction between entrance requirements and requirements for behavior of members; he puts the issue of circumcision in the first category. At Galatia, however, the question arose in relation to those who were already in the community: should they be circumcised to be *fully* in?
35. Betz, *Galatians,* 89.
36. There is no solid evidence to conclude that Paul advocated the Torah-free gospel for Jews as well as for Gentiles. From his

arguments that the Torah alone is inadequate to provide salvation, and that faith in God's act in Christ is both necessary and sufficient, one could conclude the Torah should be abandoned by Jews; but Paul probably did not advocate that position.

37. For this distinction, see Sanders, *Paul, the Law,* 4.

38. Ibid., 102.

39. Sanders says Paul explicitly contrasts two righteousnesses here: by law, by faith, and that his passage is "extremely revealing for Paul's overall view of the law" (Ibid., 43). I agree.

40. Lloyd Gaston, "Paul and the Torah" in Davies, 66; Gager, *Origins,* 224. Sanders, *Paul, the Law,* 155, says Paul blames Jews not for salvation by works but for neglecting Gentiles and for rejecting Christ.

41. Gaston, "Paul and the Torah," 66. "Though zealous, Jews were 'ignorant of the righteousness of God and sought to establish their own' (10:3), which, of course, does not mean that individual Jews attempted to justify themselves by their own actions in defiance of the God of the covenant, but that Israel as a whole interpreted the righteousness of God as establishing the status of righteousness for Israel alone, excluding gentiles from election." Gager thinks "boasting" is "the only disagreement between Paul and other Jews (*Origins,* 214); see also 247. Sanders, *Paul, the Law,* 38, agrees with the emphasis upon exclusivism, but thinks Paul faults the Jews primarily on their lack of reception of Christ as messiah.

42. Räisänen, *Paul and the Law,* 177.

43. "When Paul is most negative about the law, he opposes it to—the law, i.e., the Torah! Opposed to 'the other law, the law of sin' is 'the Torah of God' (7:22f). The condemnation which lay on the children of Adam (5:16, 18) is overcome in Christ (8:1), because opposed to the 'law of sin and death' is 'the Torah of the Spirit of life in Christ Jesus' (8:2). Opposed to 'the law of works' is 'the Torah of (God's) faithfulness' (3:27). Paul even said paradoxically that "I through the Torah died to the law' (Gal. 2:19). For Jewish Christians, and presumably for Paul himself, Christ was seen as the fulfillment of the Sinai covenant, and the word *nomos* in the passages just cited has the connotation of election" ("Paul and the Torah," 65).

44. Gager, *Origins,* 204, agrees with Gaston that Paul did not offer any critique of Judaism, but only of Christian Judaizers. But see Romans 2—3; see also Sanders, *Paul and Palestinian Judaism,* 551.

45. Räisänen, *Paul and the Law,* 162. It is true that Paul in Galatians 5:4 and 2:16 is arguing against Judaizers, not Jews, but he clearly sees in Christ the end of an old order and the beginning of a new. See also Sanders, *Paul, the Law,* 43.

46. Käsemann (*Romans,* 90) agrees with this emphasis upon the prom-

ise to Abraham as being decisive for Paul. The promise is an "anticipation or complement of the gospel, is substantially identical with it." Promise is the gospel pre-given; gospel is the promise eschatologically revealed. The gospel replaces the law, but not the promise.

47. Romans 9:14; 10:19; 1 Corinthians 9:9; 2 Corinthians 3:15.

48. (1) In Romans 5:14 Paul says "Death reigned from Adam to Moses," even though the law had not been given to condemn certain kinds of behavior. As Paul shows in Romans 7, sin finds opportunity in the Torah, and through the Torah brings death. The time of the Torah is thus the time of sin and death. (2) In Romans 10:5 Moses is identified by name as the one who says those who would be righteous under the Torah must live by it, which he shows elsewhere no one does; thus Moses condemns all. (3) In 1 Corinthians 10:2 Paul argues that being "baptized into Moses in the cloud and in the sea" did not prevent the people's apostasy and consequent punishment; thus Moses is ineffectual. (4) Most telling of all is Corinthians 3:13, where Moses veils his face while presenting what Paul refers to (sarcastically) as the "dispensation (*diakonia*) of condemnation" and "dispensation of death" (vss.7,9). The reference here is to the story in Exodus 34:29–35, according to which Moses' face glowed so brightly after being in the presence of God while receiving the Torah that the people were afraid of him. The story goes on to say that Moses alleviated their fears, and delivered God's word to them, and then veiled his face; whenever he talked with the people or with God he would remove the veil, but otherwise he wore it. Paul interprets this to mean that Moses veiled his face "so that the Israelites might not see the end of the fading splendor," i.e., to keep them from understanding the transiency, the limitedness, and the ultimately inefficacious nature of the covenant delivered through him. Richardson, *Israel,* describes the opposition to Paul in Corinthians as "Jewish in origin," 118, and interprets the new covenant to be in direct opposition to the Mosaic; thus "Paul is saying: 'Christ is the end of the Law,'" 121.

49. C.E.B. Cranfield, *A Critical and Exegetical Commentary on the Epistle to the Romans,* volume II (Edinburgh: T. & T. Clark, 1979), 853, thinks Paul did not abrogate the law, but legalism, or the misuse of the law; his negative-sounding statements about the law are due to the fact that there was no word for "legalism." As Räisänen points out, however, it is hard to reconcile Cranfield's view with what Paul says in 2 Corinthians 3 and Galatians 2: "Paul speaks quite clearly of the inferior, transient and temporary character of the law given at Sinai" (*Paul and the Law,* 45–46).

50. Räisänen, *Paul and the Law,* 240 ff., maintains that Paul does not utilize the "new covenant" of Jeremiah in his arguments about the

Torah; Jeremiah thinks in terms of a new inner attitude, not of abolition of Torah, and Paul never cites Jeremiah 31 in his discussion of the Torah. However, a good case can be made that Paul, too, does not get rid of the Torah, but that in actuality he upholds the moral commands of the Torah and believes that the Spirit enables their fulfillment.

51. Nils Alstrup Dahl, *Studies in Paul: Theology for the Early Christian Mission* (Minneapolis: Augsburg Publishing House, 1977), 122, points out that Paul does not speak of the promises being fulfilled; fulfillment is in the future. In Romans 15:8–9 the promises are confirmed, but they remain promises. One could argue that in the Torah, too, there is confirmation of the promises, even though through Torah they will not (for Paul) come to fulfillment, whereas through Christ they will be, since in Christ all God's promises find their "yes" (2 Cor. 1:20).

52. Jacob Neusner, *Formative Judaism* (Second Series): *Religious, Historical and Literary Studies* (Chico, CA: Scholars Press, 1983), 59.

53. Gager, *Origins,* 251.

54. Ibid, 218. Sanders, *Paul, the Law,* 39, is in agreement with the position taken above: the word of faith for Paul includes the confession "Jesus is Lord." I agree with Sanders that modern Christian theology in dialogue with Jewish theology might wish to distinguish between the two in a way that would not have occurred to Paul.

55. On the problem of Romans 2, see Sanders, *Paul, the Law,* pp. 128f. Sanders thinks Paul might have used a synagogue sermon which called Jews to greater faithfulness.

56. Gaston's appeal to a different reading of "faith" ("Abraham," *Horizons*) is more convincing, but it applies to a different point. He argues that in Romans 3:20 "faith" means God's "faithfulness," not human faith; thus, both the circumcised and the uncircumcised are justified on the basis of *God's faithfulness* to his promises to Abraham. The point that Gaston makes is that in his faithfulness to Abraham God will fulfill his promise relating to both Jews and Gentiles. Such an interpretation of faith has much to commend it in certain contexts, and Gaston's point has support in Romans 11:28. But Gaston's interpretation does not argue against the christological nature of faith for Gentile and Jew.

57. Gaston, "Paul...," 67.

58. As Stendahl also notes in *Paul Among Jews and Gentiles,* 4.

59. The "current" problem to some extent is the fact that Israel has not recognized God's solution to the past problem described in chapters 2—3.

60. Gaston, "Paul...," 67.

61. Ibid.

62. Beker, *Paul*, 335, also holds this view. See also Stendahl, 4.
63. This seems almost impossible, and is at least highly unlikely, even if Acts is wrong in describing Paul's preaching to synagogues; Paul's continuing relationship to synagogue is shown by the treatment he received from synagogue authorities: what was he doing at the synagogues, unless preaching? And what did he preach except his christological faith? See Galatians 2:7–9. Paul speaks of "winning Jews" in 1 Corinthians 9:20. The term "win" (*kerdaino*) is a missionary term for gaining believers, according to Bauer, *Lexicon,* 429. In 1 Corinthians 9:19 and 22, "win" and "save" (*sozo*) are synonymous. See further, Heinrich Schlier, *"kerdos," Theological Dictionary of the New Testament,* ed. by Gerhard Kittel (Grand Rapids, Mich: Wm. B. Eerdmans Publishing Co., 1965) volume III, 673.
64. Räisänen, *Paul and the Law,* 269.
65. *Pleroma* ("full number") can mean the "sum total" as well as "full number" (Bauer, *Lexicon,* 678); *pas* ("all") Israel can mean every Israelite.
66. Sanders, *Paul and Palestinian Judaism* (Philadelphia: Fortress Press, 1977), 472ff, argues that Paul got carried away by his Adam/Christ analogy and asserted more than he meant; he did not believe in universal salvation.
67. There is very little interest in this passage, or throughout Romans 9—11, upon the *time*—whether short or long—before the return of Christ. In chapter 13 he does indicate a shortness of time. Perhaps when he thinks of the situation of Israel he tends to shift any emphasis away from imminence.

Chapter 9: Admonitions to the New Covenant Community

1. Rudolf Bultmann, *Theology of the New Testament* volume 1, trans. by Kendrick Grobel (New York: Charles Scribner's Sons, 1951), 324; and *Theological Dictionary of the New Testament,* vol. II, 868ff. Cf. Hermann Ridderbos, *Paul: An Outline of His Theology,* trans. by J.R. de Witt (Grand Rapids: Wm. B. Eerdmans Publishing Co., 1975), 257: The indicative represents the already, the imperative, the not-yet of the present historical situation of the believer.
2. Ernst Käsemann, *Commentary on Romans,* trans. and ed. by G. W. Bromiley (Grand Rapids: Wm. B. Eerdmans Publishing Co., 1980), 327.
3. E.C. Blackman, "Mind," *Theological Wordbook of the Bible,* ed. by Alan Richardson (New York: The Macmillan Company, 1951), 146. See also J. Behm, "Noeō," *Theological Dictionary of the New Testament,* Vol. IV, 958: "...the inner direction of...thought and will and the orientation of...moral consciousness."
4. The word love is less prevalent in Romans 12—15 than elsewhere

in Paul but the reality is present throughout the passage.

5. Walter Bauer, *A Greek-English Lexicon of the New Testament,* trans. by Wm. F. Arndt and F. Wilbur Gingrich (Chicago: University of Chicago Press, 1979), 265.

6. C.H. Dodd, *Gospel and Law: The Relation of Faith and Ethics in Early Christianity* (New York: Columbia University Press, 1951), 42.

7. John Howard Yoder, *The Politics of Jesus* (Grand Rapids: Wm. B. Eerdmans Publishing Company, 1972), 208.

8. It is quite possible that Paul's admonitions reflect his knowledge of the revolt which Zealots were encouraging against Roman rule of Judea. Paul's statement is thus political in that it does not endorse anti-Roman activity; it does not endorse the Zealot understanding that only self-government under the Torah would be in accord with God's will. Paul might well have seen such a prospect to be more repressive than liberating, and opted for quiet citizenship under Rome.

9. Minear, *Obedience of Faith,* 43, refers to five groups in Rome.

10. Käsemann, *Romans,* 367, cites Billerbeck as offering evidence that some adopted abstention from meat and wine after the Fall of Jerusalem. It is at least possible that the impending crisis might have led some to unusual fasting before that event, though this is admittedly speculative.

11. Ibid, 384.

12. Jouette Bassler, *Divine Impartiality: Paul and a Theological Axiom,* ed. by William Baird, "Dissertation Series," (Chico, CA: Scholars Press, 1982), 162.

Chapter 10: Future Plans and Final Greetings

1. The RSV translates the second name *Junius,* masculine; but C.E.B. Cranfield, *A Critical and Exegetical Commentary on the Epistle to the Romans* (Edinburgh: T. & T. Clark, 1979), 788, says Junian is probably a feminine accusative. Junius as a man's name is "not found elsewhere....Ancient commentators took Andr. and Junia as a married couple" (Bauer, *Lexicon*), 380.

2. See 1 Corinthians 9:5, where Barnabas is called an apostle, and 2 Corinthians 8:23, where additional apostles are mentioned, although the RSV translates apostles there as "messengers."

3. Cranfield, *Romans,* 789.

4. This view of Paul might seem out of keeping not only with his reputation but also with what he says in his other letters. The problem is partly knowing what Paul actually wrote and partly understanding what he meant. For a brief introduction to the issues involved, see Victor Paul Furnish, *The Moral Teachings of Paul: Selected Issues* (Nashville: Abingdon Press, 1985), 83–114 and bibliography.

5. Cranfield, *Romans,* 790.

6. Ibid, 792–93.

Index of Scripture

APOCRYPHA AND PSEUDEPIGRAPHA

Index of Subjects